JUST SELL THE DAMN THING

The proven, contrarian formula to GROW your business FASTER than ever

(Without complex marketing campaigns... content marketing... social media... blogging... or ANY of the online "grunt work" that rarely, if EVER, results in getting new customers or the actual making of money!)

D O B E R M A N   D A N

Doberman Dan
Visit the Official Doberman Dan Website at:
www.DobermanDan.com

Printed in the United States of America

First Printing: October 2017

Arango Direct LLC

ISBN: 978-1-5136-2567-6

Arango Direct books may be purchased for educational, business or sales promotional use. Special discounts are available on quantity purchases. For more information, please call or write.

Telephone: (800) 290-2817
Email: support@DobermanDan.com

For orders by U.S. trade bookstores and wholesalers, please contact Arango Direct LLC at the phone or email address listed above.

DISCLAIMER

The Publisher has strived to be as accurate and complete as possible in the creation of this book.

This book is not intended for use as a source of legal, business, accounting or financial advice. All readers are advised to seek services of competent professionals in legal, business, accounting, and finance field.

In practical advice books, like anything else in life, there are no guarantees of income made. Readers are cautioned to rely on their own judgment about their individual circumstances to act accordingly.

While all attempts have been made to verify information provided in this publication, the Publisher assumes no responsibility for errors, omissions, or contrary interpretation of the subject matter herein. Any perceived slights of specific persons, peoples, or organizations are unintentional.

Table Of Contents

Testimonials

"JSTDT is a direct response GEM! Loaded with in-the-trenches wisdom the average marketer would ordinarily never get access to. And, in true Doberman Dan fashion, lays-out a potent blueprint for generating sales... so absurdly simple... it could easily be titled, "The Idiot's Guide To Getting Rich With Direct Response.""

Todd Brown
MarketingFunnelAutomation.com

"If you've ever become all excited about the number of clicks you've gotten — only to realize you can't use clicks to pay your employees, or the electric company, or your Visa bill — then you need this book. Doberman Dan drives home the important point all successful entrepreneurs and copywriters know: Nothing really happens until you make the sale. He shows you what to do and how to do it. Besides that—he's very, very funny!"

David Garfinkel
Author, Breakthrough Copywriting

"When I met Dan, I was a young, rookie, hungry copywriter who was so broke I was re-using trash bags. Thanks in no small part to what I've learned from Dan over the years I've made millions online and now live a life that most people dream about. Dan's hard-won advice can change your life. Read this book now."

Caleb Osborne
Entrepreneur & Consultant
CalebOsborneConsulting.com

"Doberman Dan has a unique way of cutting through the weeds and getting straight down to the actionable 'how to make money' stuff. His JSTDT system has made me revaluate my entire marketing funnel…and you will too. Like all the World's great ideas, you'll think it's obvious…once you've seen it!"

Dean Biggs
Veterinary Marketing Strategist and co-author,
Secrets To Growing Your Veterinary Practice In The New Economy

"Thanks to applying the lessons I've learned from Dan I'm able to do the work I love and help others to live healthier and happier lives. So, if you have something of value you want to share with the world, and you're looking for an experienced guide to help you avoid the pitfalls along the way... I highly recommend Dan. Because when it comes to marketing (in all its formats) he's been there, seen it and done it all... So you don't have to. Learn what works, apply it and get the results you want - Buy this book."

Marcus Santer
www.thehapbook.com

"I'm an attorney in a busy private practice and I work in a field where competition for ad words and effective print and web based ads in furious. We are dedicated to a providing a superior client experience and to working for a very specific type of client with very special needs.

Dan's monthly newsletter and especially his advice and training on "Just Sell The Damn Thing" (JSTDT) has made every dollar we spend way more effective AND we're getting better ROI from our time spent on marketing and advertising.

Better yet? We are getting more qualified clients who respect what we do AND more happily pay for our services.

Not using Dan's advice yet? If not, you're leaving money on the table and dealing with too much stress. Go do it and enjoy the results."

Dave Frees - Unruh, Turner, Burke and Frees

www.successtechnologies.com

"Dan has really helped me to focus on what's most important and to remember that 'the main thing is to keep the main thing the main thing.'

When I spend too much time overthinking my ever-so-sophisticated funnels to attorneys and their clients on my website, Closeprobate.com, Dan's insight is helping me to focus on making the sale (aka conversion).

I'm waiting for a JSTDT up-sell program that I'll gladly write the big check for, 'JSTFT' but Dan is too much a gentleman to use the 'F' word (which is also why I need copywriting help).

In gratitude,

Rick Harmon
Closeprobate.com

"Hey, Dan! I just wanted to take a minute to thank you for just how brilliant your thinking is regarding the 'Just Sell The Damn Thing.' I freaking LOVE anything and everything you put out! (Including your newsletter... and I honestly can NOT wait to rip open that envelope and devour every damn word. Your newsletter is freaking awesome.)

And your entire 'Just Sell the Damn Thing' philosophy just makes sense – and the results speak for themselves. I took my little publishing business from me and a kitchen table to a 7-figure per-year, 35-man operation... most of it with a HUGE nod of thanks to your JSTDT common sense.

The deeper and deeper you DIVE INTO the subject, the more and more it makes sense to me. Truth be told, years ago I just couldn't get on board with this 'move the free line.' It just never really made sense to me. And to get a second opinion (from you) on what to do instead made it all come to light much more clearly.

Anyway... keep up the great work. You have a FAN for life here.

Warmly,

Brian Keith Voiles
CEO, Manifest Opulence Publishing, LLC

"Doberman Dan has single handedly revolutionized my idea of back end possibilities. My business was a revolving door of satisfied one-shot customers. Now I find myself constantly thinking of back end possibilities to increase my bottom line. This paired with my new philosophy courtesy of DD, 'movement beats meditation' has really put me in a different place and I am trading in my mantra for moolah."

Douglas O'Connell
Taxgrievancespecialist.com

"Doberman Dan stands out like a boulder sized diamond in a dung heap as one of the few so-called 'experts' in the Internet and Direct Response Marketing arena who doesn't stink to high heaven. He doesn't beat around the bush or butter us up with his supposed amazing 'gooroo' brilliance. Rather, he cuts right to the chase with his no B.S. hard won, battle tested systems and strategies. In my career shift from full-time musician to direct response marketer and entrepreneur, there has hardly been a more helpful virtual mentor. I'm still in the early stages of my new ventures and he is proving to be my Dumbledore in this new magical world amidst all the marketing Muggles."

Dr. Douglas Pew
www.DouglasPew.com

Dedication

To Dan Kennedy, who changed my destiny from one that most assuredly would have been a life of quiet desperation... to the amazing life I now have. You are my original inspiration. The dude who introduced me to direct response marketing and launched me on this wild ride I've been on the last quarter of a century. I'll be eternally grateful that you just sold the damn thing... and *continue* to just sell the damn thing.

To Gary Halbert, who taught me more about direct response marketing, copywriting and how the world *really* works than I could have learned on my own in two lifetimes. And somehow... some way... that I don't yet totally understand... you *continue* to teach me. Your mentorship... the famous "Gary Halbert Seal of Approval" you bestowed upon me... and most importantly your friendship, changed my life. Not a day goes by that I don't miss you.

And most important, to my wife, affectionately known as "The Colombiana." Thank you for always believing me and standing by my side. Even when it looked like I wouldn't amount to much of anything. I love you.

Foreword

by *Dan S. Kennedy*

Why Should You Listen To THIS Guy?

Yeah, I know, you *already* bought the book. But still, it'll be more valuable to you if you are well persuaded to take this guy calling himself Doberman Dan –– like some Saturday morning TV cartoon character – *seriously*. As Halbert would say, *as serious as cancer*, if cancer were a good thing. Or as I once wrote, as serious as the day-old chili with beans, onions and jalapenos in the barely washed bowl at Mama Jean's diner in Amarillo.

Doberman Dan and I do *not* entirely agree on everything. I believe there is a time and a place for complexity. I insist there is even a time and a place for the deliberately delayed sale. This disagreement may reflect that I am a sophisticated fellow and he is a primitive brute. But we agree more than we disagree, because there are many more times and places when you are best advised to just sell the damn thing. And that is a lost or at least disdained art these days.

I have lived long and prospered by figuring out Financial Efficiency in business, which includes getting the new customer acquired and sales made as quickly as possible so as to turn the same $1 of capital invested in marketing over and over and over as many times as possible. My friend Doberman Dan's outstanding book supports that. A great many foolish, faddish approaches to marketing popular with the cool kids do not.

I have prospered by insisting on working with *facts*, **not ideas, opinions; with real money metrics, not misleading new metrics** – mostly popularized by charlatans to bamboozle businesspeople into investing real money but getting only likes and viral views 'n such back in return, and being afraid to question it for fear of looking stupid or sounding like an antiquarian Luddite. Doberman Dan knows no fear. He was once upon a time a street cop in a tough, blue collar rust belt town a few miles from where I grew up. Having Pinterest pointed at him fails to intimidate. His book is fearless and frank.

My own chosen and lived positioning for more than 40 years has been:

Had I not claimed it, it could just as easily be his.

We prize the same elegantly simple thing.

Many entrepreneurs and marketers let themselves be easily distracted by and interested in many, many, many things, to the point they sacrifice all discretion, all focus, and all power. They prize being embraced by all the cool kids. At whatever conference or mastermind group meeting they go to, they prize showing off their clever use of the newest, latest, most hyped technology or tactic. They prize ego gratification, first adopter bragging rights, being ahead of every curve (even those leading off cliffs). They prize being a blogger in the blogosphere. Or having an internet TV show (ie. fake TV show) and being able to invite their impressed peers onto it as guests. They are a new breed of what I've called, since the 1980's, *"Advertising VICTIMS"*. They're being victimized and self-victimized by old fakery in new wrappers and costumes.

Doberman Dan and I have become friends, colleagues, co-petitors (not competitors) because, instead, we prize the same elegantly simple thing:

what works.

His book is tightly focused on that <u>one</u> elegantly simple thing.

It is a mistake to label his book, he or I as "old school". Better to grasp that what he presents here has very deep, sturdy roots, has made marketers into millionaires and even billionaires every year since the turn of the century and right now, this day, and is therefore fact, empirical evidence, and experience based and is therefore *reliable*.

I will swap new and cool for reliable any day, especially when investing money or time, mine or a client's. I call this: profitable pragmatism. It is a non-philosophical philosophy.

I constantly advise clients: do the boring stuff. There's a lot of money made or lost in the boring stuff. Doberman Dan's book is far from boring, yet a lot of it has to do with stuff many consider boring – like identifying and practically managing differential customer value and lifetime customer value.

I'll suggest a goal for you. A life-altering, fortune-making, elegant simplicity liberating goal of goals. As Halbert oft-said, *harken unto me*.....

What you will be best served by lusting for is a reliable *selling* process you can have so much confidence in that you will aggressively invest in buying appropriate customers....that you have so much reasoned confidence in you will twice mortgage your cottage, swipe your kid's college fund and hock your wife's wedding ring (while telling her you took it to the jeweler for cleaning), to pour prospective customers into your *selling* process.

What you should *not* be seduced by is more and more and more work to do and daily disruption to suffer while diluting your efforts over more and more media and needing more and more patience and persistence to finally get to a sale and then ownership of a valuable customer relationship. Doberman Dan's book fully and totally supports the goal I've suggested, and also immunizes against the dangerous seductions.

By the way, *personally*, I've been made a multi, multi millionaire from scratch chiefly by what I call my "Lifers" – customers with me and continuing to support me, reliably responding to offer after offer, over 10, 20, even 30 years, each spending well over $100,000.00 with me. Here is an important fact: virtually all them started with me by directly being sold something by me. *Not* by being gently brought into some polite 'n pleasant place where they could roam around at their own pace, consume endless quantities of 'free', slowly develop trust, and gradually choose to maybe become a customer. Most coming onto Planet Dan that way stay briefly, exit quickly and are worth little. The Lifers came and come by my reaching into their pockets, yanking out their wallets, snatching their credit cards and immediately, directly selling them some damned thing. And that's not old news either. Lifers-in-the-making are being brought onboard that exact same way this very day. There's a secret well presented in this book that a decreasing number of marketers understand: the _right_ customer *wants to* buy *now*.

Finally, let me make a last vital point about Doberman Dan and this important and provocative book…

In the golden age of advertising, when 'advertising' was first becoming a business in and of itself, its streets were stalked by real *characters*. Flamboyant self-promoters like David Ogilvy, who at times appeared at meetings wearing a cape, like a Royal or a super-hero. Feisty, coarse, cigar-chomping tyrants like Leo Burnett. Brilliant and envelope-pushing figures like Albert Lasker. A dozen more. Larger-than-life personalities, each dogmatic about their methods, each sharply intolerant of bullshit, each impatient for results. While visibly and significantly different from each other, all these leaders of this emerging field charitably named a profession had one thing in common:

They all knew how to sell, from actual, street level selling experience.

One way or another, they had all looked prospects in the eye and persuaded them to act against their common behavior and skepticism, to make a purchase – now. They had _lived_ 'just selling the damned thing'. This is lacking in the crowded, chaotic world of today's advertising and marketing agency leaders, copywriters, marketing technologists… most have little or no experience with what actually works in persuading people to act. Few have experience with doing that when success or failure at 3:00 P.M. in the afternoon determines whether you eat supper or go to bed hungry that night.

The guy you get to know and hear from in this book has not only sold nose to nose, toes to toes to eat, he has stared into the barrel of a loaded gun held in a shaky hand and talked the person out of pulling the trigger. _That_ can't be done over months of free content dispensing throughout 23 different media. The guy you get to know and hear from in this book deserves listening to most carefully because he _knows_ how to just sell the damn thing, now, while so many of his and my contemporaries only own theory.

The guy you get to know and hear from in this book is also a character. As he freely confesses, he has had his downs as well as ups, his dark moments in the abyss not just romps in sunshine, and owns a diversified portfolio of personality disorders and dysfunctions. This isn't a textbook. You do get to know the 'Mad Man' by this book, just as you do if you trouble yourself to read Ogilvy, Burnett and the others in their own words. Or read me in mine – which, if somehow you haven't, you are woefully negligent ☹. Anyway, I like this guy and, if you have the soul of a _true_ entrepreneur, you will too. I respect his acumen born of blood, sweat 'n tears, and can recommend his book to you because it is born of real experience and offers reliability in an unreliable world.

Contrary to what you might reasonably assume, that I have contributed this Foreword because Doberman Dan has certain photos or has proffered a phenomenal bribe, I have done so of my own free will, with no quid pro quo. Not that I didn't suggest the latter, but it was refused, and I went ahead and provided these comments anyway. Take the book most seriously.

Dan S. Kennedy

Marketing Strategiest, Direct-Response Copywriter, and Author of the bestselling No B.S. book series including *No B.S. DIRECT Marketing for NON-Direct Marketing Businesses* and *No B.S. Guide to RUTHLESS Management of People and Profits.*
www.NoBSBooks.com www.GKIC.com

How To Get The Biggest Bang For Your Buck From This Book

My very first copywriting mentor was the great Dan Kennedy. In the world of direct response marketing and copywriting, Dan is a living legend.

It was after nine long years of serial entrepreneurial failure that I stumbled onto Dan Kennedy and his *Magnetic Marketing System*. I was almost six figures in credit card debt from my unenviable talent for running businesses into the ground. Actually, it was worse. Running a business into the ground implies that the business had some semblance of success in the first place. During those long, emotionally painful nine years, not one of those businesses ever got off the ground. I didn't make one red cent in profit from any of 'em. At last count it added up to an average of three failed businesses a year. So 27 businesses that didn't make a dime. They only sucked away all my money. Money I didn't even have... while simultaneously sucking the marrow from my bones and the life force from my soul.

But that all changed the day I received my copy of Dan Kennedy's *Magnetic Marketing System*. I implemented what I learned from Dan and started my first mail order business. (This was the early '90s, before the Internet was really a viable media.)

Knowing next to nothing about direct response marketing and copywriting, I studied how Dan sold me paper and ink and cassette tapes for $397 with a simple sales letter. Then I used that as my model for selling a self-published bodybuilding course via two-step magazine ads, followed up by my own somewhat feeble attempt at my first sales letter.

After nine dismal, discouraging and depressing years of serial failure, it was the first successful business I had ever started. In less than twelve months I was making enough money to replace my j-o-b (journey of the broke) income. I stepped out of wage slavery and into the freedom that direct response marketing and copywriting has to offer anybody willing to put in the work. And I haven't looked back since.

For more than two decades I've been using this exact same process as a serial direct response entrepreneur to support my two bad habits: sleeping indoors and eating regularly. (Some would say *too* regularly.)

That's lesson number one (albeit an implied one) about how to get the biggest bang for your buck from this book.

Now for a more overt one.

My second copywriting mentor was a man I heard about from Dan Kennedy's newsletter. He was a colorful and eccentric dude named Gary Halbert. His name, often spoken in hushed reverence, was, and still is, legendary amongst direct response marketers and copywriters.

Halbert's claim to fame was his family coat of arms business. A business launched and driven with a simple one-page "typed on a real typewriter" sales letter. At best estimate, that letter was mailed over 600 million times and put tens of millions of dollars of net profit into Gary's personal pockets. It's still studied today by smart marketers and copywriters.

Based on Dan Kennedy's recommendation, I subscribed to Gary's newsletter, appropriately entitled *The Gary Halbert Letter*.

My soul resonated with him immediately.

Just like Dan Kennedy's newsletter, whenever *The Gary Halbert Letter* arrived in my mailbox, I dropped everything and read it immediately. Those two newsletters were my lifeline. They were all we had back then as far as continuing direct response marketing and copywriting education. I implemented something I learned every month from those two newsletters. (I still reread all the back issues every year.)

Now I already had a moderately successful mail order business at the time. But I believed if I could personally work alongside Gary Halbert, I could get through the learning curve much faster, grow my business faster... and cram copious quantities of cashola into my coffers.

So here's what I did: I used a technique I learned from Halbert's newsletter that showed how to get a big shot's attention. I turned it around and used it on Halbert. And it worked just like he promised. It got lil' ole moi on Halbert's radar.

After that, I meticulously engineered a monthly follow up process – using direct mail with "theater" – to *stay* on Halbert's radar for about a year and a half. Long story short, I wound up working side by side with Halbert for two years. He even became my roommate for four months when I had a home in Costa Rica. (He asked if he could crash at my place "for a weekend." That was one long weekend!)

During that time, I learned a lot of "Halbertisms." Those are witty and/or instructional sayings about what Gary had learned during his four-decade-plus copywriting and entrepreneurial career.

One of the Halbertisms I quote still today is...

Motion Beats Meditation!

And that, dear reader, is your overt lesson about how to get the biggest bang for your buck from this book.

Look, I hope you enjoy the book. Heck, I even hope you're entertained by it at times. (Just for fun, I do try to get a chuckle outta ya here and there.) But much more important, I want you to *profit* from it. And the key to doing *that* is action.

Any action.

This is such an important point, that I've emulated my mentor and come up with a Doberman Dan-ism about that particular life lesson:

I've Seen MILLIONS Made From Even "Wrong" Actions…
But I've Never Seen ANYTHING Good Come From *Inaction!*

You now hold in your hands the key to creating a business that supports any lifestyle you can imagine.

Go forth and prosper.

And just sell the damn thing.

****

How to Get More Information
from the Author

Wanna hear more from me after reading this book? Go to www.DobermanDan.com. You'll find hundreds of articles on entrepreneurship, direct response marketing and copywriting. You'll also be presented the opportunity to enjoy a steady stream of "Doberman Dan-ism" emails. All designed to help you build your business, put more money in your pockets... and make your experience on this planet the best it can possibly be.

Chapter 1

The "What" and "Why" of JSTDT™

The world of Doberman Dan has been shaken up a little bit lately.

If you're marketing online, I'd be willing to bet things have been shaken up for you, too.

You see, a change is afoot, my dear friend.

Not in a good way either.

When I first noticed this, I thought it was a fluke just happening to me.

Ain't so.

Based on my survey of darn near every experienced marketer I know marketing online, it's affecting us all. Some, like me, have recognized the impact of this early. And we're making major changes to avoid losing any more ground.

Others have chosen to cling to hope. Hope that this soon shall pass. And they're making no adjustments in their business model. Foolishly so, based on my 30-plus years as a serial entrepreneur and more than two decades using direct response marketing. (Can you say "Google Slap?" Both Versions 1.0 and 2.0. Most have *never* recovered from that.)

As I've often shared in my newsletter, *The Doberman Dan Letter*, the human brain isn't a window to the truth. It's a delusion generator. So all we can do is let these folks stew in their own juice of delusions until their sales have tanked enough to do something about it.

Or not. I'm not out to save the world. Only a handful of smart people. And hopefully myself in the process, too.

So let's get to me saving you, shall we?

Take a look at these screen captures from my Aweber email account so you can see what I'm ranting about:

	opened	clicked	bounced	complaints
This could topple some business empires... View Stats | Copy to Drafts | Copy to List ▾ Sent to **2,986** subscribers at 06/08/16 05:02 AM	10.5%	0.9%	0.1%	0%
Email open rates PLUNGE Internet wide View Stats | Copy to Drafts | Copy to List ▾ Sent to **2,877** subscribers at 06/07/16 05:02 AM Excludes **1** lists.	15.5%	1.0%	0.1%	0%
$100k with no list, no product, no affiliates... NO PROBLEM! View Stats | Copy to Drafts | Copy to List ▾ Sent to **2,872** subscribers at 06/06/16 05:02 AM Excludes **1** lists.	10.6%	1.9%	0.1%	0%
Confessions of an online biz pioneer - founder of Liquor.com... View Stats | Copy to Drafts | Copy to List ▾ Sent to **3,155** subscribers at 06/04/16 05:02 AM Includes **1 additional lists**.	13.2%	2.6%	0.1%	0%
WARNING: This did NOT make me ANY money... View Stats | Copy to Drafts | Copy to List ▾ Sent to **2,871** subscribers at 06/03/16 05:02 AM Excludes **1** lists.	12.8%	2.9%	0.1%	0%
Breakthrough "DOUBLE your income" system... yours FREE! View Stats | Copy to Drafts | Copy to List ▾ Sent to **2,873** subscribers at 06/02/16 05:01 AM Excludes **1** lists.	11.1%	2.2%	0.2%	0%
How to write FASTER copy and DOUBLE your income! View Stats | Copy to Drafts | Copy to List ▾ Sent to **2,870** subscribers at 06/01/16 05:02 AM Excludes **1** lists.	10.0%	2.4%	0.1%	0%

Yes, I'm talking about the much-ballyhooed topic of...

Email Marketing!

So what the heck is happening with email marketing?

Give me a minute and I'll show you. And you should pay close attention if you want to avoid losing any more cashola than you're currently losing.

By the way, this decline in response isn't just restricted to email marketing. This is happening across *all* media. Due to a lot of different factors. Mostly "attention overwhelm." And also, based on recent research from Microsoft, the fact that goldfish now have a longer attention span than most humans.

The screen capture above is a random sample of my average email open rates from the most recent messages (as of this writing) sent to my opt-in (free) list.

Some would say those results ain't bad for an opt-in list. I disagree. Because just look at what the average open rates and click-through rates (CTR) were just a couple months prior:

	opened	clicked	bounced	complaint
The Colombiana is really getting on my nerves... View Stats | Copy to Drafts | Copy to List ▾ Sent to **3,064** subscribers at 03/26/16 05:02 AM Includes **1 additional lists** .	20.6%	3.3%	‹ 0.1%	0.03%
The "insane" way to make money View Stats | Copy to Drafts | Copy to List ▾ Sent to **2,813** subscribers at 03/25/16 05:02 AM Excludes **1 lists** .	18.3%	2.8%	‹ 0.1%	0%
THIS is the copywriting model of the future... View Stats | Copy to Drafts | Copy to List ▾ Sent to **3,056** subscribers at 03/24/16 05:02 AM Includes **1 additional lists** .	23.0%	6.1%	‹ 0.1%	0%
Is the online gold rush officially over? [Live Training] View Stats | Copy to Drafts | Copy to List ▾ Sent to **3,049** subscribers at 03/23/16 01:25 PM Includes **1 additional lists** .	19.9%	1.4%	0%	0%
Can ya help a brutha out? View Stats | Copy to Drafts | Copy to List ▾ Sent to **3,050** subscribers at 03/23/16 05:02 AM Includes **1 additional lists** .	21.0%	9.6%	0%	0%

This drop in open rates has nothing to do with subject lines. They've been almost cut in half across the board. Even when I employ the cheap parlor trick of offering something "FREE" in the subject line. Even *that* time-tested tactic has tanked.

Who gives a rat's pitooty about open rates anyway? Normally, not moi. Oh sure, I track them. But the only metrics that really matter to me are sales and ROI.

So how are *those* doing?

They've tanked, too. Thanks to this Internet-wide email open rates glitch.

Listen, I have no idea why this is happening. I've got theories (they all involve Google). But no proof. And frankly, it doesn't matter. The only thing that matters is how I react to them. Because that's really the only thing I can control, isn't it?

You retort, "So a drop in open rates. Big deal. Happens all the time." No. Not like this. I've been marketing physical products online to "real" consumer markets (no Internet Marketing/biz-op crapola) since the Wild, Wild West days of 1996. That makes me a frickin' online marketing *pioneer*, for cryin' out loud. And I'm tellin' ya, we're in uncharted territory right now. 'Cuz this is an Internet-wide phenomenon.

Here's where it gets even weirder...

	opened	clicked	bounced	complaints
Big changes View Stats | Copy to Drafts | Copy to List ▾ Sent to **300** subscribers at 06/30/16 09:51 AM EDT	55.7%	0%	1.3%	0%
Darn near MIRACULOUS moneymaking breakthrough [KNIGHTS O... View Stats | Copy to Drafts | Copy to List ▾ Sent to **298** subscribers at 06/28/16 10:51 AM EDT	46.9%	0%	1.3%	0%
Multimillion dollar copy "cheat" from Agora [KNIGHTS ONLY] View Stats | Copy to Drafts | Copy to List ▾ Sent to **289** subscribers at 06/27/16 11:16 AM EDT	52.8%	9.4%	0.3%	0%
I've moved... AGAIN View Stats | Copy to Drafts | Copy to List ▾ Sent to **293** subscribers at 06/26/16 01:48 PM EDT	62.5%	0%	0%	0%

That's a little peek behind the curtain at open rates from the most recent emails sent to a list of people who have whipped it out. (I'm referring to their credit cards, silly.)

In other words, this is a BUYERS list. My BEST buyers.

So what the heck is going on here? There's no drop in open rates to *this* list. How can that be?

No idea. Again, just theories. No evidence.

However, there's an important key word in the description of this list. One that probably explains the inordinately high open rates (and sales), in spite of this Internet-wide "open-rates-cut-in-half-overnight" glitch that sucker punched so many online marketers.

I'm referring to *this* key word:

Buyers!

The difference in monetary value between an opt-in list of freebie-seeking people and a list of buyers is *EXPONENTIAL*. And that unimpeachable and unquestionable utterance is about as close to an absolute as you'll ever get in this life. I've proven it time and time again over the past 22 years. So knowing that – and seeing email open rates, sales and ROI tanking – I had to pull the plug on that old business model. And it was back to the drawing board.

Just so you have a frame of reference, this has been my business model for the past year or so:

1. Facebook ads (and a little "pure dumb luck" organic traffic) driving to my splash page at DobermanDan.com, which offers a free PDF version of *The Doberman Dan Letter*.

2. Daily emails with a CTA (call to action) to sign up for the Marketing Camelot (my membership for entrepreneurs, marketers and copywriters) in every single email. With occasional offers for other products or services.

Pretty simple, huh?

Pretty effective, too. At least it *was.*

However, thanks to this email glitch, the numbers no longer work out versus the investment of time needed for the daily emails. (Relying on Facebook ads is another Internet-wide disaster waiting to happen. But that's a story for another time.)

Seeing the responsiveness of my buyers list and the inordinately high LCV (lifetime customer value) I have, it only makes sense to stop the bleeding of time and money from the freebie seekers and invest them in the *real* people instead. I'm talking about buyers.

When everything finally came out in the wash, here's how this old model worked out:

Almost 99 percent of all the freebie-seeking leads generated from Facebook ads never bought anything over a 12-month period. Based on my experience, that means most of my ad budget was wasted on people who will *never* buy. They just keep hanging around with their hand out expecting, and even feeling entitled to, more and more free stuff. This is the online marketing business model that has been taught for decades. And it *used* to work.

Listen, Facebook, at least in its current format, is a highly *efficient* advertising medium. 'Cuz of all the CIA-like targeting options. However, for my current business model, Facebook is not the most *effective* medium.

So yeah, it kinda worked for my deal for a while. But it's like paying for a big stinkin' pile of cow patties with the mere *hope* of finding a half-carat diamond hidden in there. I'd much rather take the money spent on cow patties and use it to dig in a diamond mine. Heck, I'll invest a *thousand* times more money for that. Yes, the size of my list will be a lot smaller than the "cow patties" method. But infinitely more valuable.

So I've created a business model that's both efficient *and* effective. And one of the most important factors in this efficient and effective funnel is...

Lead Source!

And it may or may not be Facebook. You see, most people are on Facebook to have fake relationships with people they don't know. Or look at pictures of cats in tutus. And look up how fat their exes have gotten. Not exactly the best frame of mind for attracting people to a business proposition, is it? That would explain a lot about the quality of the leads I attracted from Facebook with my old model.

Sure, there can always be a needle in a haystack. But I'd rather just go find a big box full of needles, wouldn't you?

In comparison to the Facebook leads, the last time I checked, my average retention in the Marketing Camelot, my monthly membership for entrepreneurs and marketers, was eighteen months. At $98 a month. Do the math.

And... if we include additional products and services sold... and copywriting/royalty income generated from it...

The Lifetime Customer Value (LCV) Is Insane!

So frickin' high that most people wouldn't believe it. 'Cuz it's such a small list.

That's what finally made me stop, take a look at my results and ask the following question:

Why am I investing the massive amount of skull sweat required to produce interesting and inspiring emails every frickin' day for the 99 percent non-buyers – when I can invest a tiny FRACTION of that time and effort into building and marketing to a buyers list? And make 1,000 times more!

Dumb, dumb, dumb.

Actually dumb, dumb, dumb *squared*. Because I've made this mistake before. (Issue No. 3 of *The Doberman Dan Letter* revealed all the sordid details.)

Just for a sec, let's yak about my "pay money to Facebook to get 'too-much-chlorine-in-their-gene-pool' cheap bastards on my list" business model...

...versus the business model of two of my most successful (and cutest) clients: Allen and Erin Baler. (Well, Erin's cute.)

Here's the Reader's Digest version: Allen and Erin had pretty good corporate gigs. They could have been relatively secure for life and made six figures with a house in the 'burbs and two relatively new Toyotas in the driveway... all that typical sheeple stuff.

But you see, you can't turn a warrior into a slave. One way or another, they'll find a way to attain their freedom. Or die trying. And that's what the Balers did. (Achieve their freedom, that is. NOT die trying.)

When they found me, they had escaped the corporate rat race and had a successful "kitchen table business." At the time, Allen's motto was...

One Man, One Laptop, One Million Dollars!

Which I became enamored with and stole for a book title. With Allen's permission. (But just between us gals, I would've stolen it anyway, with or without. 'Cuz I learned from the best.)

It was at my Gold Mastermind meeting in Orlando, Florida, when they had a major epiphany. And eighteen months later... well, how about I just let them tell their own story:

> "We put into place the things we learned from Dan's mastermind and the result was adding 'rocket fuel' to our growth rate. In fact, in 2013 our little company was named the 304th fastest growing company in America by Inc. Magazine. Our business grew over 1,400 percent, and we credit Dan and our mastermind partners for helping us break through to the next level of growth. Thanks Dan and company!"

What timing! Guess who just called me while you were reading that testimonial?

Allen Baler. He confirmed that they're still using my *Just Sell The Damn Thing*™ (JSTDT™) business model. They've never followed the "build a list of freebie-seeking cheap bastards" opt-in model. They discovered their average order value and lifetime customer value are *significantly* higher with the JSTDT™ model.

Listen, thanks to Al Gore's Interwebz invention, free information – on just about ANY topic – is everywhere. And when there's a proliferation of *anything*, it drives the value lower and lower. Until it arrives at its inevitable destination: ZERO. (Are you deaf, dumb and blind Keynesians listening?)

In many, or maybe even *most* markets, I believe we've arrived at this zero-value point. DEFINITELY in the market I'm targeting for my Marketing Camelot membership. That means if you're following this "give freebies away" business model, you're at a significant disadvantage to any competitors who are following the JSTDT™ model.

There are some interesting psychological reasons for that. Which I'm gonna tell ya all about. Not just to remind you of how brilliant I am, but also to remind you that I'm always right. (And we know that's true because it says so every month in *The Doberman Dan Letter*.)

From a logical standpoint, people should want to receive information for free, right? Especially if it's the same quality as information that costs money. As it turns out, that's not the case. What people *say* they want and what they *actually* want are two totally different animals. **In reality, they don't want the information for free at all.** (The smart ones at least.)

Now they'll *tell* you they want the information for free. But what they do with that free information is vastly different than what they do with information they pay for.

And I'm not the only one who has discovered this dichotomy. In psychologist and Harvard Business School Professor Francesca Gino's book *Sidetracked*, she shares several studies showing why people only trust information with a price tag.

For example: Gino discovered, from a psychological perspective, people attach quality with price. Her research has shown that when people invest money for information and advice, they pay attention to it and use it. They're much more likely to believe it's more valuable because they paid for it. On the other hand, she found that if the exact same information is acquired for free, it's almost always ignored.

The psychological impact of this "price = value" equation gets even more interesting. According to Gino's research...

The More You Pay For It, The More You Listen To It!

Her book demonstrates if someone spends a lot of money for information... and if they also spend a lot of time and effort acquiring it... the information becomes *highly* valuable to them. And the value assigned is proportionate to the amount of money, time and effort invested in acquiring it.

Gino's research was originally inspired by something she observed in her father's medical practice. He invested a lot of time sharing information with his patients about how to eat to improve their health. Some of these sessions were paid and some were free. After a while, he started to notice a consistent trend. When patients paid for the advice, they actually paid attention to it and implemented it. Almost to a fault, the patients who received the advice for free dismissed it.

Listen, because of about a hundred years of conditioning, doctors are perceived as the ultimate authority figures. However, even with all *that* juice behind it, a doctor's advice is ignored if given free. This fascinated Gino. So she decided to study it empirically. In a whole slew of studies. Across all kinds of different fields.

Here's what her research consistently proved:

When people pay for information and/or advice, there's a high predisposition to use it. But... when the exact same information is given away free... the same quality, same quantity, same *everything* as the paid information... its perceived value is darn near ZERO and it's dismissed.

Almost immediately.

Therefore, if people only trust info they pay for... yet your first interaction with a new prospect is giving them free information...

What Does That Say About Your Positioning And Value In The Market Place?

Several things:

1. You're just one of the THOUSANDS of look-alike clones in your market giving stuff away for free.

2. You don't value and believe in your own intellectual property enough to sell it.

3. There's very little urgency to spend money with you... because you set the wrong tone by starting the relationship with bad positioning.

So the psychology is this: when you spend the money, you have to justify the investment to yourself. And the principal way to justify the investment is to actually use the information and/or advice you received. That powerful psychological trigger isn't there when you receive information for free. Because no effort or monetary investment was required to acquire the info. Therefore, there's no investment you need to justify. It's a fascinating psychological bent we all have.

Yes, even yours truly. Case in point:

A few years ago, A-list copywriter extraordinaire Clayton Makepeace was promoting a two-day copywriting seminar for $5,000. I plunked down the

$5k on my credit card and anxiously awaited the event. About a month before, Clayton had to cancel the seminar for personal reasons. He not only refunded my money, he also gave me all the DVDs, audios and workbooks from his copywriting event the previous year. It was a product he had been selling on his website for $5,000.

Even though I knew the information in that product was gonna be awesome, it sat on my shelf for over two years before I even cracked open the cellophane.

Now, about that same time, I bought the legendary Gary Bencivenga's copywriting product. The DVDs and workbook from his "last hurrah one-time-only" *Bencivenga 100* event. Not only did I have to send a "whip it out right frickin' now" $5,000 check, I had to jump through a bunch of hoops to get my greedy little hands on his product.

First, he only accepted a check or money order – no credit cards. And no payment plans. Second, I had to sign a legally binding agreement acknowledging that this information was being *leased* to me. And I was not to share it or sell it. Violation of that agreement would mean Gary could revoke my lease and demand I return the information. Third, the paperwork and check had to be sent Fedex ONLY, not postal mail.

Guess what I did when *that* package arrived? I ripped it open like a kid on Christmas morning receiving his first official Red Ryder, carbine-action, two-hundred shot, range model air rifle with compass in the stock.

Look, Makepeace's product and Bencivenga's product *both* have an inordinately high value to anybody who uses direct response copy to beef up their budding bank balance. But look at how my mind perceived the value of each. Makepeace's information was immediately dismissed. Bencivenga's info was immediately put into action. That very day, in fact.

Now, there are some other subtle psychological shifts going on here. Did you notice them? Smart ole Gary B. not only made me cough up copious quantities of cash to get his costly counsel. He also made me expend a fair amount of time and effort jumping through hoops.

Absolutely. Frickin'. *Genius.*

Here's why: When Joe Marks, the R&D director at Disney Imagineering, was visiting the Disney parks in Tokyo, he observed something interesting. And a bit confusing.

People would line up for hours in front of one particular store to buy a cheap leather bracelet. The bracelets only cost about $10 and Marks just couldn't make sense of it. What was the attraction that had people waiting in line for hours to buy this bracelet?

Marks decided that Disney needed to make it easier and more convenient to buy those bracelets. So he convinced the powers that run Disney (the cryogenically frozen Walt Disney stored underground at the Orlando park) to open several other bracelet stores throughout the Tokyo park. That way they could offer the bracelets in other locations and people wouldn't have to wait in line for hours.

His idea seems perfectly rational, doesn't it? It totally jives with the laws of economics. If you have a lot of demand, your supply should increase so you can meet the demand. Economics 101, right?

But... his idea does *not* jive with the laws of psychology. And it killed bracelet sales.

You see, there was something quite curious about that wait in line for a bracelet. Waiting in line means something very special to the people who are doing the waiting. **What Marks later discovered was this:** it was almost exclusively couples waiting in line to buy the bracelets. And the waiting was a psychological signal showing they cared enough about the relationship to wait for long periods of time to buy the bracelets.

I find this fascinating. Because the bracelets really aren't all that special or unique. But the fact that the couples had to wait in line together to buy the bracelet is what made the bracelets special. It's a psychological message that says, "I care about you and this relationship."

So in this case, it's not the *price* of the product that creates the value. It's the *effort* required to buy the product. **The effort and "jumping through hoops" is what makes the experience of buying and owning the product valuable and memorable.** And it anchors all kinds of feel-good psychological triggers to that product. Which may or may not continue after your wife cheats on you with one of your co-workers, then divorces you, gets your condo and half your police pension. Or maybe I'm just projecting. (Yeah, my experience with the starter wife was a frickin' nightmare. Thanks be to Jeebus, Moises, Booddha and L. Rob Hibbard for wife No. 2, the Colombiana. She's also wife No. 3... but that's a story for another time.)

It's kinda like the hazing rituals fraternities make their initiates go through. Or Army bootcamp. When you make people go through a difficult experience together, it makes them align more with the group.

It reminds me of something I heard from Michael Norton, Professor of Business Administration at the Harvard Business School. He talked about a study of people buying airline tickets online. When people went to a website and searched for plane tickets, half the people saw the search results instantly. The other half saw the results delayed up to a minute. While they were waiting they saw a little icon that said something like, "Just a minute. We're searching for the best flight for you." Even though the results were exactly the same, people actually preferred to wait because they believed they were getting better results.

Hmmmmm... how could a savvy marketer exploit these two observations I so generously and selflessly shared with you to cram copious quantities of cashola in his or her covetous coffers?

Hey, I have an idea. How about...

Charge A Premium Price *And* Make Prospects Jump Through Hoops To Buy Your Product!

That way you're using *both* psychological triggers to attract customers with the highest possible value.

Back in the early '90s when I first heard about Gary Halbert from Dan Kennedy's newsletter, subscribing to Halbert's newsletter was *not* easy. First of all, it was a challenge to even find contact info for his office. After that, I think I waited four or six weeks to get a response. When that envelope from him finally arrived, I immediately wrote a check for $197 for a one-year subscription and sent it Fedex that very day.

And guess what I did every single month when that No. 10 envelope with "The Gary Halbert Letter" in the corner card arrived in the mail. I dropped everything that very *minute* and read it word-for-word. At least twice.

Yeah... this stuff works, my respected reader.

Ya know, over the years I've seen people hawk all kinds of discombobulated and disjointed doo-doo to online marketers. Stuff that's allegedly the "newest cutting edge secret" for making a lot of money online. But I'm just not sure about that. And none of those fads lasted much longer than a year or two. (These days those marketing fads only last months at best.)

Now admittedly, I'm not the most sophisticated and erudite (learned that word when Dan Kennedy wrote about me in a recent newsletter) guy traipsing around this planet. I didn't go to an Ivy League college and study advanced quantum field neurophysics... or whatever it is those people claiming to be smart study. Maybe that's why when I see online marketing funnels like this...

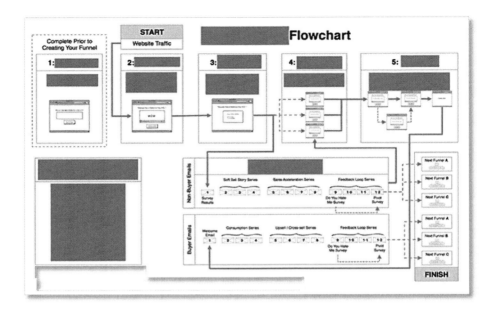

...my eyes glaze over and I retreat into my head, imagining I'm the new guitarist for *Earth Wind & Fire* or *Tower Of Power*. Or, if I really want to dream the *ultimate* guitar fantasy, *Steely Dan*.

And that funnel is actually one of the less confusing ones I've seen promoted by innumerable online marketing wonder kid gurus du jour. Check this one out:

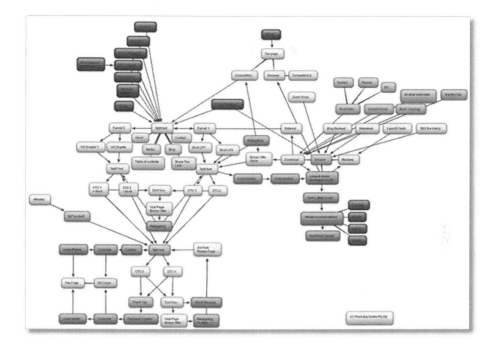

Look, I'm an "ole skool" direct marketing guy. Personally one-on-one trained by one of the most successful ole skool mail order guys in the entire *history* of this business. And I know what it's like to invest my very last cent in an ad, then *have* to make it work RIGHT NOW. Or I won't be able to eat and the sheriff's deputies will be throwing me out of my home in 30 days.

So no, I ain't exactly the most sophisticated guy on this ball of mud. I don't know any of those fancy pants multivariate "Kristie Yamaguchi" formulas that require a PhD in quantum physics to understand. Or those 269-step "ask-a-million-questions-and-give-daily-free-content-for-11-years-before-we-sell-something" funnels.

The funnel I *do* know... and know VERY well... the ONLY one that has served me faithfully for 22 years and counting... and has made me tens of millions of dollars... is the...

Just Sell The Damn Thing™ Funnel!

The best and most reliable marketing intelligence is gained from a JSTDT™ funnel. Because people are voting with their wallets. In my maniacal mind, anything else is just speculation. And that may or may not translate into sales when it comes time to actually ask for money.

Don't believe me? Then how about I lay some very recent proof on ya. From one of the knights in my Marketing Camelot.

Calls	Handled Calls	Handled Conv.	Net Conv.	AOV w/ship	ARPC	Sale	Upsells
8982	6820	66.88%	77.94%	$121.36	$78.67	4561	4287

Or how about this one:

Calls	Handled Calls	Handled Conv.	Net Conv.	AOV w/ship	ARPC	Sale	Upsells
41	26	96.15%	96.15%	$165.10	$156.61	25	17

And this one, too:

| Spring | 21 | 20 | 95.00% | 95.00% | $86.38 | $76.90 | 19 | 18 |

AOV from $10 offer

The last one is showing the average order value (AOV) from an initial $10 offer. Not bad, eh? Actually it's *INSANELY* good. I don't know *anybody* getting a 95 percent conversion with an AOV of 86 bucks and change, do you?

So what's the secret?

It's this:

My knight is using a medium that is both efficient *AND* effective. Which means he's using OFFLINE media. Yeah, he's using online, too. As only one of many channels. And, unlike offline, he's getting single digit conversions online and an AOV about 60 percent less than his offline orders. And piss poor email open rates, CTRs and conversions.

So here's your take-away:

Quit Screwing Around With Fads And Stick To The JSTDT™ Funnel... In Media That's Efficient *AND* Effective!

Do you have any idea how much money you're gonna make because of me? I think the scientifically accurate description is a "metric shit ton."

My thank you gift? How nice of you to offer. But I really haven't thought much abou... *a Ferrari F12 Berlinetta in blue, please.* And make sure you fill the tank.

Chapter 2

What to Do First

During the Christmas season last year I was reminded of something that has baffled me for decades.

I was reminded of this when I saw the kids in line to see Satan.

Yes, I meant to say Satan, not Santa.

You see, I'm 99 percent sure those two dudes are one and the same. And I've believed that for a long time.

Why do I believe that?

1. They both have the same letters in their names. They're just jumbled around a little bit. Almost as if he's playing a game and leaving a few clues... just to see if anybody picks up on it.

Well somebody did. And that somebody is me.

I picked up on *that* global hoax decades ago.

Continuing on...

2. They both wear a red suit and...

3. You *never* see those two guys together.

My theory is this:

Santa works really hard. But only one day of the year.

Sure, for a while he enjoyed his life of leisure, traveling and lounging incognito on beaches throughout the world. But one can only do that for so long. And Santa soon became bored.

Also, he got really tired of having to be a nice guy all the time. I mean, think about it. Kids pee their pants, take a massive dump in their diaper or blow chunks on the guy while they're sitting on his lap. And the only thing he's allowed to do is *ho-ho-ho* and smile. When what he REALLY wants to do is shout to one of his elves, "Get these disgusting little heathen away from me and bring me a Vesper martini, dammit!"

Well, that's what *I* would say if I were in his shoes.

So Santa got bored with his life of leisure. And he was so fed up with being saintly he was about to explode. That's when he created his alter ego, Satan.

Now, when he's not working during the holiday season he runs around as Satan, having fun creating chaos and doing all the things he can't do as Santa.

This isn't the first time a celebrity has done this, ya know. I noticed the same thing with Yasser Arafat and Ringo Starr back in the '70s. I swear to God they are the same guy. I think Ringo Starr got bored with being an über rich rock star and needed a diversion. So he invented the character of Yasser Arafat and became a Palestinian leader.

Here was the dead giveaway:

You *Never* Saw Those Two Together!

Am I right, or am I right? Look, I was a kid at the time but I wasn't an idiot. I can recognize a hoax when I see one.

22

And so it is with Santa and Satan.

So you go ahead and make your list for Santa if you must. Just know that he may be a saint on Christmas Eve... but you do *not* want to know what he was doing just the night before as his alter ego, Satan. And you invite him into your home and let him touch your cookies and milk!

Don't say you haven't been warned.

If Santa were the *only* person perpetrating this fraud it would be bad enough. But this scandal is much more widespread than you know. I could go on and on about all the other celebrities and politicians who have created alter egos. People like...

- Justin Bieber and Miley Cyrus. One and the same.

- Sarah Jessica Parker and Roger Daltrey. The same.

- Penny Marshall and Ozzy Osbourne. (This one's just *obvious*, isn't it?)

- U.S. Representative Barney Frank and Mr. Smee, from Disney's original *Peter Pan*. Same person.

- Presidential candidate and flaming communist Bernie Sanders and the Mad Hatter from Disney's Alice in Wonderland. *The same damn person!*

I could go on and on.

Do you see what I'm doing? I'm telling you various facts to prove my main argument. And the main idea I keep coming back to is this: Santa and Satan are the same person. 'Cuz that's the point I'm trying to get across in the little expository section of this chapter.

In other words, it's my theme.

What's that have to do with your business? How is the ranting of a direct response mad man going to help you make more money?

Haven't you made the connection yet? 'Cuz in my twisted mind it's *glaringly* obvious. I'm talking about...

The Big Idea!

Also known as the theme, the "hook" or the "golden thread" as Michael Masterson calls it. (There's another one for ya: Michael Masterson and Mark Ford. Same dude. And one of my knights in the Marketing Camelot, too. Or should he be considered *two* of my knights? NOTE TO SELF: I need to charge him double.)

The big idea is the lifeblood of your copy. Look at any successful ad, sales letter or marketing campaign. You'll see that the foundation of its success is a unique and compelling big idea. One that captured the market's attention, made them want to find out more and then persuaded them to buy.

Listen, I'll be the first to admit it. Coming up with successful big ideas is *not* easy. But getting that 100 percent right is CRUCIAL. Because if you don't completely nail the perfect big idea, nothing you write will make your copy convert.

Conversely, I've seen even half-assed copy convert like crazy when the copywriter came up with the right big idea at the right time.

Finding the right big idea for your copy is the most challenging and frustrating part of our job as marketers and copywriters. That's why in this chapter I'll be revealing some of my secrets for coming up with big ideas that create big winners.

Here's the ideal way of coming up with your big idea: You dig into all your research like a prospector searching for the Hope Diamond. You cram it all into your noggin as fast as possible. In one fell swoop if you can. (I reveal a highly effective shortcut for doing that in my brand new breakthrough *Intensity Insanity Copywriting* method. It's available FREE to my knights. More details at MarketingCamelot.com.)

Once you do all that, you get as far away from it as possible so you can go...

Goof Off!

And you continue to NOT think about it, involving yourself in other activities to distract your mind. The purpose of this is to let your subconscious work on coming up with the perfect big idea. And it does its best work when your conscious mind is occupied with something else. Usually something relaxing or something you enjoy. Like for me, playing the guitar.

Until, in a flash of brilliance, while you're showering, watching TV or doing the horizontal bop with your significant other (actually, you *could* be doing all three at the same time), the perfect big idea pops into your head.

That's the *ideal* scenario. And it could take days, weeks or even months for that to happen.

But what if you don't have the luxury of weeks or months to allow your cantankerous cranium to work on coming up with your big idea? What if the sheriff's deputy is nailing a foreclosure notice on your front door and you need to make money right frickin' NOW?

Or what if you're a freelancer, your client has already started sending opt-ins to his launch videos, he's telling 50,000 people on his list that the sales page will be up in three days... and you *still* don't have your big idea? What do you do then?

Never fear, dear friend. Sir Dan of Doberman has your back. In this chapter I'm going to show you my "can't fail" system for coming up with the perfect big idea. One that will grab your audience by their ever-wandering eyeballs and make it darn near *impossible* to not engage with your copy.

Hmmmm. What shall I call this system? How about... **"The Customer-Centric Neuro-Linguistic Emotional Equation System!"** *Hmmmm...* that makes no sense. It's just a bunch of nonsensical words that mean nothing. So

I guess that means I just came up with the perfect name for a new Internet Marketing BBSO (bullshit bright shiny object.)

Look, I have no idea what to call this. How about...

"The Doberman Dan System For Big Ideas That Make A Ton Of Cashola!"

Meh. Not great. But I guess it will have to do for now.

Anyhoo, when you come up with a strong big idea you'll know it. First, because you'll be excited about it. Second, because your ad will practically write itself.

David Ogilvy explains how to recognize big ideas of other marketers. I think it's a great way to figure out if your big idea passes the acid test, too. Just ask yourself these five questions:

1. Did it make me gasp when I first saw it?

2. Do I wish I had thought of it myself?

3. Is it unique?

4. Does it fit the strategy to perfection?

5. Could it be used for 30 years?

One sure-fire way of coming up with a big idea that resonates powerfully with your market is through research. You read everything you possibly can about the product you're selling. And when I say "everything," I mean it. Look at just a small part of the research I read for a recent promo.

And this doesn't include all the websites I pored over and the three Kindle books I read. Yeah, I know. It looks like a lot of work. Prepare yourself. Because here's what nobody wants to hear...

It *IS* A Lot Of Work!

When you're writing A-level copy, you can't just phone it in. In fact, you gotta practically sweat blood. I live, breathe, sleep and eat that copy until it's done to the level of my satisfaction. And *my* level of satisfaction is more stringent than anybody's. In fact, my level of satisfaction is impossible to achieve. So I'm always settling for less. (That's the curse of the perfectionist.)

My obsession probably borders on mental illness... and it is *not* healthy. For either your body or your mind. But *that*, my respected reader, is the level of commitment required to create or beat an A-level control.

Look, if you aspire to create copy at this level, I want you to know the truth. However, if you don't aspire to be an A-level copywriter, I'll let you in on a little secret: if you get the big idea right...

You Can Make *MILLIONS* With Even Half-Assed Copy!

So we need to make sure you come up with the perfect big idea for your promo. *But*... what if you've done all your research, you've done all the "research rumination" and you *still* don't have "THE" big idea. Allow me to peel back the curtain and reveal the solution to all that ails you in the "coming up with big ideas" department. And no, we are *not* going to "swipe," aka borrow and adapt existing ideas. You don't come up with breakthrough big ideas that could last 30 years by swiping. Sorry to break it to ya, but you're gonna have to invest some skull sweat.

Let's dive in. The very first thing we're gonna do is...

STEP ONE:
Create Your Customer Avatar

Why can't you just dive in and start writing copy? Because you gotta remember the most important part about this whole direct marketing thang...

It's *ALL* About The Customer!

Here's what we want to do in that maniacal melon of yours. We want to develop a character. One so vivid it will come alive in your imagination. And we want this character to represent the average customer amongst all the prospective customers in your market.

If I just ended this chapter right here you would have already gotten a secret that can make you wealthy. This is one of the most important exercises you can do to create outlandishly successful sales copy.

To really do this right I need you to dig deep into that warped imagination of yours. Because after creating your customer avatar you need to imagine what it would be like to experience life as that person. This is the "walk a mile in their shoes" thang.

You need to discover their emotional "hot buttons"... their deepest desires... their dreams and aspirations. Also their biggest fears, frustrations and the things that wake them up in the middle of the night, dripping in sweat and completely freaking out with worry.

But it's not enough to just discover those things. You have to place yourself inside the prospect's head and FEEL them. That's why I think most health copywriters don't really reach the zenith of their career until they hit at least age 50. Only then can they *truly* identify with their market's pain and fears. (Because, for guys at least, that's the age when your "warranty" starts to expire.)

If you want to experience a wild and whacky way of seeing and feeling your avatar's experiences and emotions, check out Win Wenger's "Borrowed Genius" technique. He also has a book out with that title. No matter what you initially think of it, you're gonna have some intense experiences if you try it.

Let's keep this train moving. We're going to figure out your customer avatar by asking twelve questions:

1. Demographically speaking, what are the things your ideal customers have in common?

2. Are there more men than women? Or vice versa? Or is it equal?

3. How old are they?

4. What kinds of jobs do they have?

5. How much money do they make?

6. Psychographically speaking, what are the things they have in common?

7. What are their fears and frustrations?

8. What are their desires and aspirations?

9. Do they have a shared political view?

10. Do they have a shared experience? (For example, all are Korean War veterans.)

11. Can you sum up your avatar's story? But tell it like *they* would tell it?

12. Can you give your avatar a name that fits with his or her demographic and psychographic profile?

Are you catching on to what I'm trying to do? I'm trying to create an imaginary person in your mind. And I'm trying to get you to experience, and most importantly *feel,* what it's like to live in their reality... if only for a moment.

Here's a cool little trick that should get your mirror neurons lighting up like a Christmas tree. (Appropriate analogy for this chapter considering we started out talking about Santa Claus, aka Satan, huh?) Find a picture of someone who, in your mind, looks like your avatar. Tape it on your monitor while you're doing your research. You'll start to associate all kinds of thoughts and feelings with the person in this picture. And that's exactly what you *should* do if you really want to bond with your market.

If we were working together one-on-one, we could go a lot deeper into this. If I took you through an image streaming or borrowed genius exercise, you would be amazed at the understanding and empathy you'd feel for your avatar. But I'm trying to cover an awful lot of ground in very little time. So I need to move on.

STEP TWO:
Describe Your Avatar's Ideal Outcome

Unless you're a narcissist, sociopath or psychopath, we human beings have a unique little quirk. We can empathize with other human beings. Most badass A-list copywriters have practiced this skill until they're actually sick of feeling what other people feel. (I've gotten so good at this it often makes me *physically* sick.) It's a skill the LMCs (lesser mortal copywriters) and LMMs (lesser mortal marketers) refuse to practice.

So if you don't have much practice, we're gonna activate those neglected mirror neurons of yours. (Those are the neurons responsible for empathy.) Here's what I want you to do:

Write a story, from your avatar's point of view about being in agonizing, scary or frustrating circumstances without knowing what to do. Then describe – again from your avatar's point of view – discovering the solution that YOU offer, taking advantage of it and experiencing all the benefits.

I've found there's a much deeper emotional connection – and a lot more mirror neurons firing – if you handwrite this narrative. But I won't berate you too much if you type it on the computer. The most important thing is that you just do it.

Can you just dictate it and have it transcribed? OK, I'll allow that... if your religious beliefs prohibit you from taking up pen and paper and doing it like a real man or woman. But it doesn't elicit the same strong emotional response and empathy in your nervous system as writing it by hand.

While you're writing this story from your avatar's perspective, focus on his or her feelings and emotions. Especially his fears. Then his pain. Next, focus on the emotions he experienced when he first found your solution. And then the emotions he's feeling after experiencing the benefits of your solution.

Once you've finished your story, here is where the magic starts to happen. I want you to highlight or underline all the parts that are emotional and/or irrational. Review everything you've written, paying special attention to the parts you highlighted or underlined. I want you to see if there's a sentence or paragraph that completely hits the nail on the head as far as summing up your avatar's biggest pain point and/or hot button. If so, you might have just...

Struck Gold!

However, I think if you start to dig deeper you may discover that it's possible to distill it down to even just one single solitary word.

Here's what we're trying to do with this exercise:

We're looking for that one thing that creates rapport or connection. Something that lets our avatar (who by now should be starting to come to life in your manic mind) know that you "get it"... and you're on the same wavelength with him.

By doing this exercise and writing out his ideal outcome, while focusing on experiencing his feelings, you'll have insights that LMCs will *never* have. It often happens unconsciously at first. Then it seems to come alive, as if the heavens have parted and complete empathy with your avatar has flooded into your heart and soul. That's when you have the "A-ha" moment. Then and *only* then is when you can start writing in a way that builds trust and rapport. And writing in a way that will elicit the most desired response in your avatar.

I'm going to let a few guys a lot smarter than me explain why we're going to all this trouble and doing work LMCs and LMMs will never do.

"Before you put pen to paper, before you ring for your stenographer, decide in your own mind what effect you want to produce on your reader – what feeling you must arouse in him."

- Robert Collier

"You will never win fame and fortune unless you invent big ideas. It takes a big idea to attract the attention of consumers and get them to buy your product. Unless your advertising contains a big idea, it will pass like a ship in the night.

"Big ideas come from the unconscious. This is true in art, in science, and in advertising. But your unconscious has to be well informed, or your idea will be irrelevant. Stuff your conscious mind with information, then unhook your rational thought process."

- David Ogilvy

"Tap a single overwhelming desire existing in the hearts of thousands of people who are actively seeking to satisfy it at this very moment."

- Eugene Schwartz

Let's move on to...

STEP THREE:
Explore Your Avatar's Motivators

We're going to start "brainstorming on paper" some ideas for our copy. Start by making a list of your avatar's biggest fears and frustrations. These are the things that cause his most intense anxiety and worries. Ideally, the things that cause him to bolt upright at 3 A.M., drenched in sweat from worry and anxiety.

Several guys with lots of initials after their names, indicating that they're experts in such things, say we humans are driven by fear at least 70 percent of the time. (I think sex accounts for the other 30 percent, but that's just *my* theory.) It dates back to the caveman days when fear kept us alive. Nowadays, it's not only useless but extremely harmful to our personal growth, happiness and prosperity. But it's embedded in our DNA. In fact, a part of our brain named the amygdala, aka the "lizard brain" (with a nod to David Icke) basically exists just to keep us in fear.

The prefrontal cortex is the part of your brain responsible for complex cognitive behavior, personality expression, decision-making and social behavior. It orchestrates thoughts and actions in accordance with your internal goals. In other words, your prefrontal cortex is all about logic and reasoning.

Here's the amazing thing about your prefrontal cortex: It doesn't really have a clear pathway to communicate with the amygdala. That's why you can totally ruffle even a logical and rational Mr. Spock-like intellectual by getting him into "amygdala hijack." That's when their amygdala short-circuits the prefrontal cortex, usually in response to fear or anger.

This little tidbit of knowledge is why, during my cop days, I was often successful talking people out of committing violent attacks. I recognized that they were in amygdala hijack, and nothing I could say or do would have any effect until I could get them to turn off the amygdala and get them operating with their prefrontal cortex. Lots of other officers responded to the situation by going into amygdala hijack themselves. Then I had *two* people to get out of amygdala hijack or face what could have been *all* of our deaths. Here's why this is important:

It Controls Every Decision
Your Avatar Makes!

Actually, every decision we *all* make.

If your offer appeals to your avatar's prefrontal cortex and you think you can motivate his purchasing decision with logic, it will all be negated by doubts and fears from his amygdala. So you have to speak to his amygdala without triggering any kind of "what the heck?" reaction from his prefrontal cortex. That's why we started step three with you making a list of your avatar's biggest fears. 'Cuz you sure can't speak to 'em if ya don't know 'em.

When you're making a list of your avatar's biggest fears and frustrations, live in their nightmares and "feel their pain" like Slick Willy Clinton. (I couldn't resist.) If you connect with your prospect's pain, he'll trust you and will be more likely to buy your solution to his pain. Because pain is a much more powerful motivator than pleasure.

Moving on.

Next, make a list your avatar's biggest desires and aspirations. You probably started to get a pretty clear picture of this when you were doing the ideal outcome exercise.

Now, something super important. Actually, *all* this is super important. But this next secret is one a lot of LMCs and LMMs get wrong.

No matter how much empathy you're feeling as a result of these exercises, don't make the mistake of thinking your avatar is exactly like you... and you can talk to him using *your* language. Talking to your avatar using *his* language is *muy importante*. So don't throw ice on the whole deal by using the language you prefer. (You can figure out the exact language he uses and his particular jargon with your research. But that's a topic for another day.)

Next, we need to start figuring out what your avatar's primary motivations are. We can group these into three categories...

Power, Belonging And Accomplishment

People motivated by power are looking for influence and control. People motivated by a sense of belonging desire love, approval and acceptance from others. People motivated by accomplishment desire a certain result, outcome or progress in a certain area.

We can also add two subcategory motivations to each of the three categories above...

"Toward" And "Away From" Motivation

This means that people are motivated by the thought of moving toward certain things. They're also motivated by the thought of moving away from things. Let's look at an example of using "toward" motivation copy in our three categories.

Power: Imagine how you'll feel when you're the real estate mogul in your area. When you drive down the street and can say, "You see that neighborhood? Almost 60 percent of the residents there are paying me rent."

Belonging: Picture how all your colleagues in the local real estate investing club will look up to you as their mentor. Notice how they all admire you and ask your advice and counsel about their business matters.

Accomplishment: You'll rest well every night knowing you've achieved your goal of financial security and you have more money stashed away than most Americans will earn in an entire *lifetime*.

Now let's look at "away from" motivation.

Away From Power Motivation: You Avatar doesn't want to lose power or become less significant and influential. He especially doesn't want to move down in social status.

Away From Belonging Motivation: He doesn't want to be rejected, excluded, excommunicated... or feel like the group or an authority figure does not approve of him. He moves away from failure. So he'll do anything to not fail or even appear as if he failed.

Away From Accomplishment Motivation: He realizes if he doesn't learn your "three secrets to lifetime wealth," he'll fail.

More than 60 percent of people are "away from" motivated. They'll do almost anything to save face, not lose social status, retain power and avoid disapproval, rejection and failure. That's why an experienced copywriter uses both "toward" and "away from" motivation in his copy.

So in your copy you want to imply stuff like this: *If you discover this information you'll get more power. If you don't discover this information you'll lose power.*

If you discover this stuff you'll get love and approval. If you don't discover this stuff you'll lose approval, get rejected and will be ostracized.

If you discover this stuff you'll get [insert the results your avatar wants]. If you don't learn this stuff you'll fail... and everybody will know you're a failure.

STEP FOUR:
Pair Motivators With Desires

Choose the two most powerful motivators from your "fears and frustrations" list. Then choose the one most powerful motivator from your "desires and aspirations" list.

We're now going to run these three motivators through the three types of human motivation: power, belonging and accomplishment. We'll also use these three motivators in both "toward" and "away from" language:

- Use your avatar's three most powerful motivators in "toward power" copy.

- Use your avatar's three most powerful motivators in "away from loss of power" copy.

- Use your avatar's three most powerful motivators in "belonging" copy.

- Use your avatar's three most powerful motivators in "away from rejection" copy.

- Use your avatar's three most powerful motivators in "toward accomplishment" copy.

- Use your avatar's three most powerful motivators in "away from failure" copy.

It might not be possible to hit on all of these, but here's what I'm thinking during this process:

Can I possibly condense all this stuff to as few words as possible? Or even better, just one word? But one emotionally powerful and symbolic word that, in your avatar's mind, connects to his biggest fear or hot button.

For example, the word "rip-off." If that's a huge fear of our health market avatar, we might have identified a big idea that will grab his attention with a headline like...

The Great Vitamin RIPOFF!

We got into some intense stuff in this chapter, didn't we? Remember, I never claimed this was easy.

Now do ya see why I get paid the big bucks?

Chapter 3

The Best Market To Sell To...
And the Best Way To Reach Them

I am one of the fortunate few people to have been mentored by the late great copywriter Gary Halbert.

In fact, I am one of only five people on earth who have received the "Gary Halbert Seal of Approval." And since the passing of my friend Scott Haines, taken from this world much too soon, I'm now one of only four copywriters alive (as of this writing) to have been anointed with the "Gary Halbert Seal of Approval."

Halbert was a unique dude. Brilliant, but quite eccentric. And I wouldn't trade all the chaotic moments spent with him for all the tea in China. I learned *volumes* from him. And thanks to all the lessons he planted in my cooky cranium, I'm *still* learning from him to this day.

Gary had a list of what he called "Halbertisms," quippy quotes he was famous for. Things like...

- Motion beats meditation.

- Nothing is impossible for a person who refuses to listen to reason.

- You don't have to get it perfect, you just have to get it going.

- A sure-fire way to increase your income is to occasionally give all the money back to some person who has hired you to do a job... and... turns out to be an asshole.

- All young good-looking men with a full head of hair are homosexual.

- Specific claims increase believability.

- Don't worry about offending the dogs when you're selling to the foxes.

- If you are at Point A and you want to get to Point B... before you get to Point B... you are definitely going to make "x" number of mistakes. So my motto is... **let's hurry up and start making them!**

- Scientists have discovered there is one food that very often reduces a woman's sex drive... by as much as 90 percent. *Wedding cake!*

- Use "OPM" (other people's minds) to get good ideas you'd never think of yourself.

- ALWAYS keep in mind that the people of America sort through their mail while standing over a wastebasket.

- "Anything that's worth doing, is worth doing poorly!" - quoting his friend, Joachim DePosada... who was quoting Zig Ziglar, quoting Gilbert Chesterton.

- RUTHLESSLY eliminate all negative human scum from your life.

- 98.6 percent of all statistics are made up on the spot.

- It always looks darkest... just before... everything goes totally black.

- Sell to PWMs (players with money).

Since it ties in with what I want to chat with you about in this chapter, let's talk about that last Halbertism...

Sell To Players With Money!

Halbert had an interesting modus operandi for attracting PWMs, getting them to pay him large fees (multiple times)... AND making them like it.

I closely observed his PWM attraction and money extraction secrets on numerous occasions. Later, when he decided I was ready for it, he schooled me on all the subtle nuances of his process of client attraction and compliance. The down-the-rabbit-hole secrets that go over most freelancers' heads. Which is why most copywriters, consultants and coaches get paid much less than they could... and usually live paycheck to paycheck. But that's a story for another time.

Let's continue kibbitzing about PWMs. Because, as you'll soon see, it will have a significant impact on your financial future. (I hope it's a *positive* impact.)

For now, let's do a comparison of two kinds of clients. "Client A," the typical non-marketing savvy entrepreneur... the kind most copywriters accept and tolerate... and a PWM client.

Client A - The Typical Client

Client A: "My website isn't making any money. I need a new website. One with all those fancy animated doohickeys and some good copy so it will convert better. How much do you charge per hour? And how many hours do you anticipate it will take. More than three?"

Copywriter: "Uh, well, I don't charge by the hour. My fees depend on the project. What exactly is the goal for your website?"

Client A: "My *goal?* I want to make money, dummy!" **[DD's note: Obviously, you're dealing with a tactician, not a strategist.]** "Can you do the job for $50... and have it done by

Friday? There's a guy on eLance who said he'd do it for free. So whaddaya say? Fifty bucks?"

On the other end of the spectrum we have Halbert's interaction with Ed Dale, one of Gary Halbert's former clients. Ed Dale was a PWM. I've lost contact with him but I'm assuming he still is. Unless, like me, he developed a penchant for expensive vices... boutique guitar gear.

How Halbert attracted, hooked and reeled in a "whale" like Ed Dale is worthy of your study. I could do an entire seminar on that process and STILL not cover all the subtleties.

When he contacted Halbert, Ed was still quite ignorant (in comparison to Halbert) about direct response, online marketing and copywriting. I was seated right next to Halbert and heard the conversation with Ed first hand. It went something like this:

> **Halbert:** "Ed, this is a lot of work to tackle. Doberman Dan and I can't handle it all by ourselves. I'll need a couple more copywriters. I have two guys in mind I'd like to bring on board.
>
> Ed, one thing I've learned is this: when someone is worried about money, their creativity is stifled. To create world-class copy, I need these guys' minds free from worry and working at 100 percent. I can't afford to have them worried about making ends meet. So to get started I'm gonna need a check for $40,000."
>
> [DD's note: Thanks to the currency creators destroying this once great republic, that's equal to more than $80,000 in today's fiat dollars.]
>
> **Ed Dale:** "Mwaw, mwaw, mwaw, mwaw, mwawwww." [Like the teacher's voice on all the *Peanuts* cartoons.]

I was too far from the phone receiver to understand Ed's actual words. All I know is $40k was wire transferred to the account the very next day. Halbert requested nearly equal amounts of money two more times. Both times the money arrived the very next day.

What was the biggest reason Halbert was able to get immediate compliance and high fees? Because he was working with a...

Player With Money!

Selling to PWMs was a good idea two decades ago when I first heard the term from Halbert... and... it's an even *better* idea now. In fact, in just a couple more years, it'll not only be a good idea... it could be the biggest contributing factor that determines your level of prosperity. Or, depending on what happens at the grand finale of this failed experiment in Keynesian economics... **it might even mean the difference between paying your mortgage and putting food on the table... or freezing your ass off standing in a soup line.**

How can selling to PWMs go from just a good idea to a matter of basic survival?

Rapidly Changing Demographics!

Right now Baby Boomers and seniors make up more than 50 percent of the U.S. population. More important to us marketers, they control 70 percent of all disposable income in the country. Even now, according to Nielsen.com and Boomagers.com, Boomers account for 49 percent of all packaged goods sales.

This is a significant socioeconomic change that is going to directly affect your way of life. *How* it affects it, good or bad, is entirely up to you. My concern is this: I see a lot of entrepreneurs who don't know this is coming. And if they continue with their current business practices, they're gonna be in for a world of hurt.

You see, most young online marketers (anybody under 40 is young to me) are clueless about this trend. They're ignorant about the REAL demographics and psychographics of the 20 percent, the people responsible for 80 percent of their income. They mistakenly believe their customers and prospects skew to the younger demographic like them. Therefore, they believe their customers prefer to be marketed to the same way (and via the same media) as they themselves prefer.

They couldn't be more mistaken.

What worries me most is this: if these entrepreneurs don't wake up soon... VERY soon... these rapidly changing trends are gonna blindside them, sucker punch them with the power of a Howitzer cannon... and... most likely...

Put Them Out Of Business!

You see, if Boomers and seniors control most of the wealth, have the highest incomes and are responsible for 70 percent of the money being spent... which pond do you want to be fishing in? The 70 percent pond... or the 30 percent pond?

Not sure? Well, let me enlighten you about what kind of fish will soon make up the 30 percent pond and you tell *me* if you want to sell to that crowd.

The proper name for this demographic is "The "Millennials" (the 80 million Americans born between 1980 and 2000)... but I prefer to call them...

Generation Eff'd!

The Boomers have money and the ability (and desire) to spend it. Within this group is where you'll find PWMs of varying degrees of wealth. From the mass affluent to the super duper stinkin' honkin' "own-a-yacht-and-light-cigars-with-$100-bills" rich. This market is a proven one.

The Millennials? Not so easy to define.

They shift their buying habits just as rapidly as the socioeconomic world shifts around them. Many marketers with super deep pockets (like GM and Ford) have tried time and time again to discover the master key to turning these young'uns into constant calculable, conspicuous and consistent consumers.

(Don't-cha just love alliteration?) In spite of the tens of millions invested, they continue to fail to get any significant money out of these young-uns.

Not just GM and Ford either. In spite of hundreds of millions invested, the advertising industry's attempts to win over the Millennials are falling flat on their face. For those of us in the know, it doesn't surprise us one bit. We knew the Big Boys' efforts were doomed to fail from the start.

Why?

The Millennials Ain't Got No Money... And Most Never Will!

Most are broke and in debt. If they went to college, they're deeper in debt than any other generation before them. And what will they get in return for all that debt accumulated studying to "guarantee their future?" A piece of paper that MIGHT (if they're lucky enough to even *find* a j-o-b) lead to an employment opportunity complete with paper hat, name tag and requisite repeating several times a day of...

"You want fries with that?"

The Pew Center calls Millennials the "boomerang generation" because almost 40 percent of all Americans between the ages of 18 and 34 still live at home with their parents. We haven't seen numbers this high in more than 70 years. And the boomerang trend is expected to worsen. *The National Bureau of Economic Research* reports that those who graduate during a recession will earn 10 percent less over a decade of work. Research shows that 70 percent of overall wage growth occurs in the first 10 years of a person's career. Yeah... *70 percent!* Generation Eff'd isn't just a droll designation... these kids are eff'd... seriously!

But those who *do* manage to find jobs are also struggling. Young people with high school degrees have seen their wages decline by 11.1 percent. College graduates (straddled with debt that will burden them for DECADES) have seen a smaller, yet significant decline of 5.4 percent, according to the *Economic Policy Institute*. As a result, Millennials aren't taking on more debt and making economy-boosting purchases. They aren't buying houses or cars and they're delaying marriage and children. It's not a matter of not *wanting* to do all that stuff. It's simply not even a possibility for them.

According to *The Pew Center*, home ownership amongst young people has fallen from 40 percent in 2007 to only 34 percent in 2011. And 73 percent of young households owned or leased a car in 2007 compared with only 66 percent in 2011.

Sadly, the future isn't looking too bright for Generation Eff'd.

Knowing all this, is *that* a market you want to target?

Apparently, the answer is "yes" judging by what I see many online marketers doing.

Look, rookie... if you learn only one thing from this chapter I hope it's this:

You Are Not Your Customer!

Just because you're a 20-something or 30-something entrepreneur constantly connected to the Internet with your iPhone and all your other social media time-sucks... that doesn't mean your ideal customer is, too. It is definitely not how a majority of PWMs prefer to stay connected and do business.

According to the newest data from the U.S. Census and the Mendelsohn Affluent Survey (ipsosna.com) eight out of 10 PWMs still prefer to get their news and information from newspapers and magazines... with the ultra-affluents the heaviest readers of such media.

Yup... PWMs still prefer that "dying" (or already dead, depending on who you talk to) media. When surveyed, a majority point to newspapers and magazines as the media they trust the most. Blogs and online media? *Meh.*

Very low on the trust factor index with this demographic. A majority never even *consider* reading them.

Hmmm... maybe print isn't dying as fast as many have predicted. *And...* maybe... just maybe... since so many ignorant marketers believe it to be no longer viable and choose not to even test it... YOU could get some killer deals at CPMs (cost per thousand) lower than any other time in history.

And maybe... just *maybe...* since this is a media PWMs prefer and trust... you might also discover you get a much higher quality customer...

With A *Significantly* Higher Lifetime Customer Value!

Hmmm... maybe targeting PWMs via the media they prefer would be a good idea. Instead of trying to force a square peg into a round hole just because it's convenient for you. Just sayin'.

Check out what Greg Renker, co-founder of Guthy Renker (HUGE in DRTV), the 800 lb. gorilla direct marketer of health and skin care products, said in a recent *Success Magazine* article:

> "Our company is shifting its target demographic toward the 45 and older market. These people will have the same TV watching patterns over their lifetimes while most college kids don't even have TVs in their dorm rooms."

Now Guthy Renker has sales of more than $1.8 billion (with a capital "B") per year and has experienced an average annual growth rate of 25 percent over the last 10 years. Do you think these guys know a thing or two about marketing? Interestingly, a large portion of that $1.8 billion each year is attributed to sales of an acne product... for teenagers. If *they* are changing their focus to Boomers and seniors, don't you think there's a very good reason for it?

Listen up, rookie. If you're smart enough to sell to PWMs... *and* sell to them the way they prefer to be sold... you'll probably see a transformation in your business over the next few years that will blow your mind. (That'd be a small explosion, wouldn't it? ☺)

So wise up, harken unto me, and do what I'm telling you to do, for cryin' out loud! (I have a new baseball cap for my *Gold Mastermind* meetings that says "OBEY ME.") Start restructuring your business NOW to sell to...

Players With Money!

But that's *still* not good enough. We need an effective strategy for keeping these PWMs around and continuing to spend money with us.

How do you propose we do that? Well... let's ask *them*, shall we?

I'll repeat a CRUCIAL fact I discovered from numerous "deep dive" customer database analyses. The most affluent PWMs – the customers who make the biggest purchases and most frequent purchases – opt out of emails almost *immediately* after making their initial purchase. Darn near 50 percent have opted out after getting the email receipt. The rest have usually gone bye-bye after follow-up email No. 1 or No. 2, at the latest. Many just use a throw-away email or, like me, an email monitored by an assistant, who immediately opts out and deletes the message. The PWM never even *sees* your email.

What the heck?! We spent months (or years) and large amounts of money testing to figure out how to convert these PWMs... but most of them don't want to get our emails? How the heck are we supposed to keep in touch with them?

Again, let's ask them.

- A key finding from the *International Communications Research Study* is that despite today's digital world and plethora of electronic media, Boomers clearly prefer mail to all other communication vehicles, notably including e-mail. Especially for receiving product and service offers.

- Seventy-three percent prefer mail for receiving new product and service announcements, promotions, offers and other information from companies they do business with versus only 18 percent who prefer receiving the same content by e-mail.

- For confidential information such as invoices, statements, bank statements and financial reports, the preference is 86 percent mail, only 10 percent e-mail. (The other 4 percent were too busy spending money to take part in the survey.)

- Seventy percent prefer mail for receiving information from companies they are NOT currently doing business with. This makes new customer acquisition by all other means pretty darn tough. And expensive.

- Less than 10 percent prefer e-mail for receiving information from companies they are NOT currently doing business with.

- Only 31 percent of Boomers say they frequently discard mail unopened identified as commercial in nature, but 53.2 percent say they frequently delete such e-mail unopened.

Interesting, huh? Would you like to know their reasons for preferring an "outdated" media like direct mail as opposed to email or other online media? Consider these stats:

- 45.3 percent say it's less intrusive and doesn't interrupt other activities.

- 40.2 percent say it's more convenient and can easily be saved and considered at a more convenient time.

- 30.2 percent say it's less high-pressured and lets them arrive at a decision intelligently.

- 22.7 percent say it's more descriptive and provides better and more complete information.

Hmmm??? Could the reason for that last one be that direct mailers spend a lot of time and money on market and list research *and* hire the best copywriters in the world? Compared to many online marketers who hire "discount" copywriters, throw a bunch of mud against the wall to see what sticks... and basically do a half-assed job on everything because email marketing is "free?"

Hypothetical question but one worth pondering... and maybe worth some self-evaluation.

More than two decades of direct marketing experience, and the wisdom and know-how gained from working and mentoring with the best of the best direct marketers in the world, has unequivocally proven to me that information sent in hard copy is:

- Valued and appreciated exponentially more than the same information delivered via any other possible digital format...

- Has more than a 90 percent chance of actually getting opened and read... as opposed to being just *another* unread email or PDF taking up space on a hard drive.

- Proven in numerous double-blind studies as easier and faster to read than the same information presented on a computer monitor...

- Comprehension and retention is significantly enhanced when read in hard copy as opposed to a computer monitor, tablet or smart phone...

- MRI brain scans have shown that our brains process paper-based and digital marketing in different ways. Interestingly, the MRIs showed paper ads caused more emotional processing.

According to a recent study, physical media left a "deeper footprint" in the brain and increased what is called sensory processing. Printed material generated more activity within the area of the brain associated with the integration of visual and spatial information (the left and right parietal).

Tangible materials involved more emotional processing in the subjects, which is extremely important for accurate recall. It also proved that more processing is taking place in the right retrosplenial cortex. This is the part of the brain involved in the processing of emotionally powerful stimuli and memory. So basically, hard copy materials generate more emotionally vivid memories.

The MRIs also showed that hard copy materials generate increased activity in the cerebellum, which is associated with spatial and emotional processing as well as motor activity. That's even *further* evidence of the enhanced emotional processing.

[From Millward Brown Case Study - *Using Neuroscience
to Understand the Role of Direct Mail*]

This confirms something us "ole skool" marketing dudes have known for decades: Physical material is more "real" to the brain. It's also better connected to memory because it engages the brain's spatial memory networks.

So now you know *who* to sell to... and *how* to sell them.

By the way, you don't have to look very far to find some PWMs to sell to. They're already on your customer list. PWMs of varying affluence levels... from the mass affluent to dudes with Rolls Royces, offshore bank accounts, using "Benjamins" to light their *Altadis' Behike* cigars (a mere $19,000 for a box of 40) while sailing around the world on their yacht. Yeah, you probably already have customers like this on your list. *IF* they haven't jumped ship to a competitor who *does* understand how to identify them and market to them like they prefer.

Problem is, you don't know how to find them. And even if you did, you probably wouldn't know how to sell 'em. *But...* when you figure all that out... they'll reward you with an explosion in sales that will astound you.

Even better... this bountiful boost in business will continue if you understand and implement what I've revealed to you in this chapter.

Ya know, it amazes me the amount of time I invest researching, writing and persuading you to do things you already know you should be doing. But I guess that's what dads do, huh?

I never lose hope that one of these days you'll finally get it. Or you'll simply wise up and hire someone with a proven track record to do it for you.

Somebody like... oh, I don't know... maybe... *ME!*

Chapter 4

Putting Together
Your Irresistible Offer

A door-to-door vacuum cleaner salesman manages to finagle his way into a woman's home in rural Alabama.

"This machine is the best ever," he exclaims, while pouring a bag of dirt all over the living room floor.

The woman expresses her concern that the vacuum cleaner might not be able to clean up all the dirt.

So the salesman makes what he believes to be an irresistible offer...

"If this machine doesn't completely remove all the dust and dirt, I'll lick it off myself."

To which the woman replies...

"Do you want ketchup on it? We're not connected for electricity yet."

<Rimshot>

You better be darn sure you're making the right offer. 'Cuz it could come back to bite you if you're not.

Speaking of offers...

About once every three months I offer a "deep dive" discovery day with one lucky and meticulously vetted client. By the way, it looks like that opportunity will be ending sometime this year. Because demand for me has now *significantly* exceeded supply. And the older I get, the more appealing the J.D. Salinger plan starts to look. (Go to http://dobermandan.com/clients for more details about a discovery day with me.)

In some sort of twisted masochistic way, I like watching people squirm at these meetings. And I can make that happen with just one simple question:

What's Your Offer?
And Explain It To Me
In 15 Seconds Or Less...

It's fun to watch the expression on their face change. Nobody has ever asked this question. Therefore, few have invested the time to figure it out. Nor have they invested the skull sweat necessary to craft a simple, easily understandable and concise presentation of that offer.

Look, if you can't tell me your offer in 15 seconds or less in a way a sixth grader can understand, no amount of "copywriting pyrotechnics" is gonna be able to do it either. Which is just plain dumb. 'Cuz my two-plus decades using direct marketing to start and build my own businesses... backed by my own money and driven by my own copy... has shown me this:

Your Offer Is One Of The Most Crucial Elements To Your Success!

In fact, I'd have to say it's No. 2 in order of importance. With No. 1 being your market/list like we spoke about in depth in Chapter 2.

So let's have a heart-to-heart about offers. More specifically, the best way to create *irresistible* offers. *My* way. The JSTDT™ way. It's my thang... my "superpower." It's also my positioning... my platform... my branding. (And yes, I really *have* applied for trademark protection of both the acronym and phrase.)

Why JSTDT™? Because I'm sick and tired of seeing good people lose their shirts chasing a bunch of BBSOs (Bullshit Bright Shiny Objects. *Hmmmm...* maybe I should trademark that one, too.)

So let's have a jibber-jabber session about developing great offers. We'll start with the most important stuff.

To be a super-salesperson – whether in person or in copy – you have to believe in whatever you're selling. The stronger your belief, the more powerful the impact your message will make in your prospect's heart and mind.

Listen, you can get all anal retentive and study the sales process, analyze it, "template" it, break it down into steps, study which words and phrases to use, which not to use... yadda yadda yadda. But if we want to break it down to its core essence...

Selling Is Transference Of Emotion!

That's why you must be sold yourself before you can successfully sell others.

Ya know, I used to roll my eyes when I'd hear stuff like this. *Cut the rah–rah bullshit, Zig. Just give me the magic words to say that will close sales. And back off on the religious stuff, too.*

How wrong I was. The "rah-rah stuff" *was* the magic I was looking for. And this secret works in copy exactly like it works belly-to-belly. Read the chapter about enthusiasm in Frank Bettger's book, *How I Raised Myself from Failure to Success in Selling*. You'll see the miraculous transformation he experienced when he did everything wrong in his sales presentations except this one secret.

And yes, somehow... some way... cultivated through complex and curious components of the cosmos... your prospect can sense your emotion and enthusiasm in your copy. The *exact* enthusiasm and emotion (or lack of) you had the moment you wrote it. Google the "Weizmann Institute Israel double slit experiment" if you want to explore the scientific explanation as to how your thoughts, emotions and enthusiasm affect your prospect's thoughts, emotions and enthusiasm via your copy. Even when you're separated by distance or time. The amount of distance, whether six inches or 10,000 miles, is irrelevant. The amount of time transpired from when you wrote the copy, also irrelevant. (Word of warning: this could take ya down the proverbial rabbit hole. Make sure you're ready for it.)

Enthusiasm (n.) c. 1600, from Middle French enthousiasme (16c.) and directly from Late Latin enthusiasmus, from Greek enthousiasmos "divine inspiration, enthusiasm (produced by certain kinds of music, etc.)," from enthousiazein "be inspired or possessed by a god, be rapt, be in ecstasy," from entheos "divinely inspired, possessed by a god," from en "in" (see en- (2)) + theos "god" (see theo-). Acquired a derogatory sense of "excessive religious emotion through the conceit of special revelation from God" (1650s) under the Puritans; generalized meaning "fervor, zeal" (the main modern sense) is first recorded 1716.

My point? If you want others to get excited and buy into your offer, *you* need to be excited about it and sold on it. When you're truly, *genuinely* consumed by enthusiasm, people will gather around to watch you burn. Even when it's "enthusiasm in copy," separated by time and distance.

So here are a couple suggestions:

1. Get enthusiastic about the value you're bringing to this world... then...

2. Create the most compelling, kick ass, astonishing, breathtaking, rousing, titillating (I really like that word for some reason), hair-raising, mind-blowing, irresistible offer possible.

So let's talk about some effective ways I've discovered to do No. 2. (The No. 2 above. Not the bathroom No. 2. I've got a warped mind, don't I?) Listen, you can have a "starving crowd" list (a nod to my mentor), hard-hitting JSTDT™ copy written by an A-list copywriter...

You can have Jeebus, Moises, *Moooo*-homud (the cow prophet), Booda, Shirley MacLaine and the ghost of L. Rob Hibbard pray over it and anoint it...

But if your offer sucks, ain't nobody gonna respond.

Soooo... since offers are so important, let's talk about what makes a good offer. Just like everything else, the answer comes from the market. You have to know the market so well – their desires, their pain, their fears – and craft your offer so it appears to be the most immediate solution to those desires, pain and fears. Even better, if your copy does a good job of discrediting all other solutions, it will appear to be the *only* solution for their desires, pain and fears.

Now, before we get into the nitty gritty "how to" stuff, here's a million dollar tip:

Stop Selling Products And Services And Start Selling Offers!

Since my goal with this book is to not just give you theory... let's roll up our sleeves, put on our writer's hat (mine's "the Heisenberg" by Goorin Bros.) and get started creating a kick ass JSTDT™ offer.

Listen, to do this right – and you *should* do it right because even just *one* good offer can make you rich – it requires you to drum up a little creativity from inside that kooky cranium of yours. Now don't freak out when I say "creativity." Some people don't think they're creative. Great! You don't have to be creative. Because really, you don't have to "create" anything. All you have to do is "synthesize." That means find elements from different sources, then combine, rearrange or modify... and out pops something new. The best ideas – the ones that make stockpiles of shekels – are always an expansion and combination of previous ideas that worked.

Creativity is simply finding new ways to solve problems. It's like putting a jigsaw puzzle together. You take all kinds of different pieces and see how you can fit them together in a new way.

So the first step is to start "synthesizing" an offer. It probably won't be your best possible offer, but it's a start. And that's all you need. Because I can guarantee that if you do what I'm about to tell you, your offer is gonna get better and better. And you'll eventually wind up with an offer so compelling... so tantalizing... so *titillating* (I can't seem to stop saying that word)... it'll be irresistible to the ideal prospects you want to attract.

Here's a secret:

For reasons I don't totally understand... if your intention is improvement...

Whatever You Measure Improves!

Every good business idea must grow and expand and develop. Because it's a living thing that feeds off the desires of another living, breathing entity: the marketplace. So let your offer grow, expand, and develop as you work on it. As long as you're measuring results... and making adaptations and changes based on those results... your offer will get better and better.

Ya know, I've often gotten into trouble by assuming things. For example, so far in this chapter I've been blabbing away about offers and how important they are. But I haven't taken the time to make sure you understand what an offer is. So let me back up and define what an offer is... so it's crystal clear in your kooky but comely cranium.

An offer is made up of all the irresistible, value-packed stuff your customer is going to get in exchange for giving you their money.

Simple, huh? Your job is simple, too. Find out what's irresistible to your prospects and then let them have it. And I'm about to let you in on a little secret to help you do that. A 19th century philosopher figured it out a long time ago...

"For every man there exists a bait which he cannot resist swallowing."

- Friedrich Nietzsche

We just gotta find the right bait. Because the bait you throw out there determines the type of customer you'll catch. And lucky for you, after decades of enthusiastic practice, I'm a *master* baiter. (Ya know, darn near every chapter in this book proves one thing: I've never mentally matured past age 14.)

Listen, to be successful in this direct marketing thang, we have to give our market the things they most want. But let's drill down on that for a minute. Because if you totally... completely... "DEEP-in-your-neural-network" internalize what I'm about to share with you... all your LMM (lesser mortal marketer) competitors won't have a snowball's chance in hell of *ever* catching up to you.

So this is important. Let's define exactly what a "want" is. In *my* manic marketing mind it's an...

Unfulfilled *Emotional* Desire!

Emphasis on "emotional." Because you can never forget this one thing: no matter how normal they might appear, you're selling to illogical and irrational people in a constant state of cognitive dissonance. And just like a pig being led around with a nose ring, they are controlled, albeit unknowingly in most cases, by their emotions. Hence the reason I said *emotional* desire, not just desire.

What I just shared... that one thing alone... *if* you really grasp it... can allow you to...

Stockpile More Gold Than Midas Himself!

And that's sayin' a lot. 'Cuz *everything* that dude touched turned to gold! (I bet that made going to the bathroom a *major* problem.) So, as marketers, our job is to fill those unfulfilled emotional desires. And we'll start by asking some questions:

What do they want? I mean what do they anxiously... frantically... *desperately* want? And how can we give it to them better than anyone else? The answers will be different for each market. Although, regardless of the market, since we're always selling to human beings, there are some constants.

You see, we humans aren't the superior creatures we believe ourselves to be. In truth, what we really are is prey. Don't believe me, you big shot, conquer-the-world entrepreneur? OK, I'll prove it to you. Let's strip you down buck nekkid, take away all the guns and ammo you've stockpiled, leave you penniless, and drop you in the jungle for a month. With nothing to survive on but your wits. Now, to damn near every animal in that jungle you look like prey. A nice, fleshy pink meal. And for good reason. You *are* prey. They're almost all physically superior to you. And you stand very little chance of getting outta there without becoming lunch for some hungry animal.

You see, for many years (some experts say millions of years) that was the lot for us poor, weak, defenseless humans. That's why we have the fight-or-flight programming hardwired into the limbic system of our brains. And it's a darn good thing we do. Or we wouldn't have lasted a New York minute around most of the creatures we were surrounded by. That programming performed well in response to all the daily dangers we faced. But we're not being chased by saber tooth tigers these days, are we? Instead, the "dangers" we face are things like getting cut off in traffic. Or, stepping outside your comfort zone to try something new... like launch a new business. None of these things are even remotely life-threatening. Yet the survival programming hardwired into your limbic system causes the same reactions in your mind and body just as if you were about to be eaten by a saber tooth tiger.

This is one of those constants. Not logical, no. But it's permanently hardwired programming. That's why self-interest is the ruling force of our lives. It's our survival instinct. We'll do everything possible to survive. And more important, thrive. It's part of our nature. This explains why the desire for power and superiority are paramount. Survival of the fittest is just as real for us "human beans" as it is for animals in the jungle. Our survival mechanism is a powerful, all-consuming drive. One that overrides all rational thought. And that, my revered reader, explains why...

Greed Hypnotizes!

A strong appeal to our prospect's greed goes straight to the heart of this desire for power and superiority. We respond like Pavlov's dog to any carefully crafted message that promises to give us a fast and easy way to more power. A strong appeal to your prospect's greed hits him hard, like a two-ton boulder dropped on his crusty cranium. His survival programming in the limbic system takes over and overrides all rational thought. His eyes glaze over. His desires become inflamed. He becomes *intoxicated*.

A powerful and believable message of greed has the same seductive power a smokin' hot woman has over a horny guy. (If you've ever seen how guys act around attractive women, you know *exactly* what I'm talking about. They *immediately* turn into stupid, mouth-breathing animals.)

Based on what you now know about the human survival mechanism, greed and the promise of power should be in every offer. These can come in different forms. More money, security, sex appeal, love, one-upmanship, entitlement, you can now be in the "cool kids" club, etc.

Here's why I've focused exclusively on this copywriting/persuasion/psychology stuff the last 22 years instead of chasing BBSOs:

Media changes. Technology changes. Tactics and strategies change. But human nature *never* changes. We all want the same things. Love, sex, power, money, recognition, respect, security. We all want to feel important. To feel loved and protected. To feel safe. To feel good about ourselves.

Whether they're conscious of it or not, people look for the fulfillment of these desires in the products and services they buy. In fact, they're almost never consciously aware of it. That's why I said that this whole creating offers thang has to start with discovering your prospect's unfulfilled emotional desires. And that, my treasured troubadour, is what you're *really* selling. If you're not, it's what you *should* be selling. That is, if you want the best possible results from your copy and all your marketing efforts.

You see, a true master of selling doesn't sell products or services. He sells concepts. He sells solutions. He sells fulfillment of desires. He sells images, dreams, blue sky, hope for the future. He sells all things great and imagined our prospect is longing for. He sells to people's greed for more... their lust... all their deepest (and usually unstated) desires.

Now we're starting to hit pay dirt, my courageous caballero. Craft your offers with this in mind and the advantage you'll have over all your poor LMM competitors is almost unfair. (Aren't-cha glad you have lil' ole me in your corner?)

Does all this street cop psychology sound complicated? (It's not.) Does it sound like a lot of work? (It is.) However, there *is* a shortcut. It may not get you all the way to the finish line but it'll get you closer to the finish line.

Here's my shortcut to finding out the answer to the question "What do my customers want?"

MORE Of What They Bought And/Or Are Currently Buying!

You can't truly know and understand what a person values until you know what he's buying with his disposable income. Find that out and you'll know without a doubt what's most important to him.

It is where a man spends his money that shows where his heart lies.

- Cleric Edwin Keigwin

That's why I put very little value on surveys. Unless it's surveys of buyers. But even that has limited value in terms of down and dirty, rubber-meets-the-road, "I-need-to-make-money-right-frickin'-NOW" market research. Instead, you need to discover and verify – with actual data – what people in your market are buying right now. (I've shown how to do this several times in past issues of *The Doberman Dan Letter*. Most recently in the May 2016 issue. More info at www.MarketingCamelot.com.)

That means if someone has bought a gasoline-powered turtleneck sweater, there's a pretty good likelihood they'll buy another one. Maybe in a different color. Or maybe a diesel-powered turtleneck sweater.

If they bought that gasoline-powered turtleneck sweater *recently*, there's a very high likelihood they'll buy another one soon.

If they bought multiple gasoline-powered turtleneck sweaters, there's an even higher likelihood they'll buy another one.

If they bought multiple gasoline-powered turtleneck sweaters... and they bought them recently... there's an even higher likelihood they'll buy another one.

So, if we discover this information during our market research, take a guess at what our offer should be.

Duh, right? That's why I want to sell porno to dirty old men. I want to sell crystal meth to addicts. I want to sell water to dehydrated people in the desert. Not literally, of course. But you get the idea.

Listen, I don't want a challenge. I have enough challenges. Learning jazz improvisation is enough of a challenge and frustration to last the rest of my life. In business, I just want to get to the money as fast as possible. I don't need any more challenges. And the way to "get to the money as fast as possible" is to simply...

Find Out What People Want And Offer It To Them!

And yes, it *is* that simple. You just might have to get a little creative and find new ways to repackage what you're offering.

Now, once you've put together an offer that addresses all the things we've been talking about, here's a million dollar tip that'll put things on steroids...

"P. T. Barnumize" Your Offer!

Ever heard of Phineas Taylor Barnum? Founder of the Barnum & Bailey circus? What's not normally known is that he was also an author, publisher, businessman, philanthropist and, for a time, politician.

But here's how he described himself:

"I Am A Showman By Profession... And All The Gilding Shall Make Nothing Else Of Me."

And a showman he was. One of the best who ever lived. So why not use P.T. Barnum's success secret and add a little showmanship to pump up your profits?

- ✓ Wow 'em!

- ✓ Make it BIG!

- ✓ Blow it up!

- ✓ Make it BOLD!

- ✓ Make it explosive!

- ✓ Make it "history making!"

- ✓ Make it whiz-bang!

- ✓ Hype it up! (Ethically and within reason, of course. Don't say anything that's untrue... or even *appears* untrue.)

- ✓ Jazz it up!

- ✓ Make it ROCK!

Alrighty then. We've been talking about the most important part of creating offers. The mindset and big picture stuff. Let's start to get a little more micro and talk about some pragmatic, rubber-meets-the-road stuff.

I recently recorded a video module about offers. It's part of a brand new copywriting course called *The 60 Minute Copywriting Cure* coming out soon. (If you just want "show me the money" from your copy as fast as possible... without the painfully long learning curve most of us have to go through... you're gonna get *really* excited about this. It's about as close to done-for-you, fill-in-the-blanks sales copy as you'll ever get. All the details are at http://60MinuteCopyCure.com.)

Anyhoo, in that video, I shared eight components and questions to help you create a winning offer:

1. **Hook:** How is this different?

2. **Premiums:** What else do they get?

3. **Value:** Is it worth 10 times more than the price?

4. **Terms:** How do they pay?

5. **Delivery:** How do they get it?

6. **Guarantee:** Remove the risk.

7. **Reason Why:** Why are you offering such a great deal?

8. **Scarcity:** Why act now?

Cover all these – along with everything else we talked about in this issue – and you've got yourself a winning offer.

Let's look at one of my most recent offers. One you may or may not have seen yet. As of this writing I'm still waiting on my geek to finish up all the membership site technology stuff. This is a new dealybop I call *How To Make BIG Money From Small Lists*. It's not available to the world. It's only available to my DobermanDan.com readers. Let's take a look at how I put this offer together. We'll start with No. 1 above so you can see how I addressed that.

Last year I tested a system of marketing and selling coaching and consulting that worked better than anything I've ever done.

Like I said, even though I made a bunch of mistakes, it brought in an extra $205,000 with just a handful of emails sent to a list of only 130 people.

Since then, I've learned from my mistakes and have tested and tweaked to get it working even better.

And now, it's working so darn well, I'll never go back to the old way of doing things.

That explains why – unlike most info marketers – I rarely come out with any new products anymore. I'm so busy with this new and improved way of making money... and it's so darn profitable.... this new model has replaced almost EVERYTHING.

And I'm confident it will work just as well for you, too.

In fact, I'm pretty sure you'll do even better than I have.

Although the only way we can know that for sure is if you get the chance to learn it from me firsthand.

So the hook to this offer is that I've figured out how to create a really high income with a super small list. The copy goes into more detail about this. But due to space limitations in this book I'm only showing you a little segment. This program consists of eight video modules, although there's no time to go into the details. So let's move on to No. 2 on our list, premiums:

But that's not all you're going to get. I'm also including something I've NEVER revealed before...

EXTRA SPECIAL BONUS
Video Module 7:
Behind The Scenes Secrets Of Successful Newsletter Publishing!

I've said it before and I'm sure I'll say it again...

Yadda yadda yadda...

But that's not all. You'll also get...

EXTRA SPECIAL BONUS
Video Module 8:
"Superhero Writing Secrets!"

I've written a lot of stuff over the years about copywriting... and all the editorial/content writing secrets I've learned over the past two decades.

But this is something new. Something I've NEVER revealed before.

Yadda yadda yadda.

But we're not done yet. Not by a long shot.

You're also going to get...

✓ **All my copy templates needed to make this system work for YOU.** (Emails, website copy, my CRAZY high-converting phone script... EVERYTHING! All the stuff written, tested and used by me to make an extra six figures a year... working only part-time. You'll get it all! Simply make a few tweaks, adapt the copy for your offer... and you'll be ready to launch in no time at all.)

✓ **My personal guidance** - I'll lead you through the entire system, A-to-Z, showing you how to customize everything for your business... and get it making money for you as soon as possible!

Onward to No. 3 on our list, value:

This is a PROVEN system. One I've invested lots of time and money into figuring out.

And since it has such an extremely high value... because you can use it to make as much money as you desire... and create the kind of lifestyle you've always dreamed about...

It Ain't Cheap!

But hey, I'm sharing skills that have paid me almost a quarter of a MILLION dollars over the past 12 months! Simply from doing some fun, part-time work.

Heck, even if I charged you $100,000... you second-mortgaged your home, sold all your earthly possessions... and sold so much of your blood plasma that you stumbled around like a hollow-eyed heroin addict... it would still be a screaming bargain.

In fact, if you don't make back at least $100k in the next 12 months, you're just slacking off.

But don't worry. It ain't gonna cost $100k. (Although it should.)

The fee is actually $497.

Yes, I know that's not exactly pocket change for some folks.

However, if you do what I say, **your return on investment could be 1,000 times that. The first year ALONE.**

THAT'S how effective this is.

How do I deal with No. 4 on our list – terms? As of now the terms are pay in full. However, in the future I might test offer a two- or maybe three-payment option.

On to No. 5 – how is it delivered? All the content is delivered on a password-protected private membership site. And although I do have *this* copy...

> As soon as you click the button above you'll get INSTANT ACCESS to *How To Make Big Money From Small Lists.*

...now that I take a second look at it, I need to do a better job of explaining that. I think I'll add some copy like this:

> Immediately after submitting your order, you'll be taken to a private password-protected membership page. Once there, you'll register with your email and select a password. As soon as you do that, you're in! And you can start using all this material right away to create your very own *Make Big Money From Small Lists* "money machine."

Or something along those lines. That's a "first take." I'll probably come up with something better. Or maybe that's GE (good enough) copy and I should just get over my damn perfectionism that I've allowed to make me miserable for decades. (*Another* example of fear-based thinking, which makes *everything* suck.)

Let's move on to No. 6, the guarantee:

> You'll FEEL GREAT about your decision to join me in *How To Make BIG Money From Small Lists...* because you can...

Try It RISK FREE For 60 Days!

> You can take your time and go through the entire program at your leisure.
>
> Access all the training modules...
>
> Download all the handouts...
>
> Download and swipe all the sales copy templates...

There's no rush. You can take your time and have a full 60 days to go through everything.

See it all for yourself... put it into action... heck, go ahead and start making money with it.

THEN you can decide if it's right for you.

If you don't feel that *How To Make BIG Money From Small Lists* is everything I've promised in this letter... simply send an email to Jackie or Briana in Customer Support within 60 days and...

I'll Refund Every Single Penny You Invested!

No hassles, no run-around... and we'll still part as friends.

I can't make it any more risk free than this. That's why you can feel 100 percent confident about investing in this program.

Onward to No. 7, reason why you're offering such a great deal:

I recently added up the income I brought in from my list over the last 12 months. When I shared my results with a few veteran marketers, they were completely blown away. (I'll explain why in just a minute.)

They INSISTED I share my secrets for making more money than most doctors... while only working part-time.

My "reason why" is kinda peppered in here and there throughout the copy. Why did I do this? No idea. Most times, I'm a "second brain" writer. A gut intuition writer. And *that* brain is *way* smarter than my head brain alone. (Another quantum physics lesson we don't have time for.) Anyhoo, here's more "reason why" copy.

Since then, I've learned from my mistakes and have tested and tweaked to get it working even better.

And now, it's working so darn well, I'll never go back to the old way of doing things.

That explains why – unlike most info marketers – I rarely come out with any new products anymore. I'm so busy with this new and improved way of making money... and it's so darn profitable.... this new model has replaced almost EVERYTHING.

And I'm confident it will work just as well for you, too.

In fact, I'm pretty sure you'll do even better than I have.

Although the only way we can know that for sure is if you get the chance to learn it from me firsthand.

That's why I'm willing to walk you through the entire system... step-by-step... from start to finish... with my new program called...

How To Make BIG Money From Small Lists!

Am I totally happy with that? I'm *never* happy with *anything* I release. That's the power of a deadline. Either self-imposed or imposed by others. If I didn't set a deadline, I'd never release anything. (Damn perfectionism.)

Let's take a look at No. 8, my scarcity/why-do-it-now copy. The biggest scarcity reason is this:

21 : 12 : 55 : 52
DAYS   HOURS   MINUTES   SECONDS
For the first time ever... my PROVEN system reveals...

The countdown timer is right at the top of the page. 'Cuz I'm releasing this product with a Doberman Dan style launch. And it's one of the most powerful "get 'em off the fence" techniques you can use. So there's that. However, I'm using another reason for investing in this now:

I MIGHT offer it again in the future. But I have no idea when.

If ever.

So if you miss out now, you could be missing out for good.

And that would mean losing out on MILLIONS in income... literally.

Besides, I've learned something about the people who are successful.

Successful people take action NOW.

ANY action.

As a matter of fact...

I've Seen MILLIONS Made From Even "Wrong" Actions... But I've Never Seen ANYTHING Good Come From *Inaction!*

You see, the people who make this world go 'round...

The ones who make their dreams come true...

The ones who are free... financially, mentally and spiritually...

...are the decision makers.

The people who live lives of quiet desperation...

The people who are always broke...

The ones who die with the music still inside them...

...are the people who have to "think about it."

And really, "I need to think about it" is just a way of letting your fears stop you from doing something that could totally transform your current life into the lifestyle of your DREAMS.

And possibly make you RICH!

So right now... you have a decision to make:

You need to decide what kind of person you are.

If you're not prepared to do what it takes to be successful, I'll wish you God's speed on your travels.

However, if you ARE ready to be successful... and you want to create the life you've always dreamed about... then I invite you to do THIS:

Click here now and take part in this breakthrough training with me before this offer expires.

Get it? I'm explaining another reason for acting now. All the money you could miss out on. With a little guilt/it's-time-to-man-up copy sprinkled in.

How did this offer and copy work? Spectacularly well. And they continue to perform spectacularly well. (I took a cue from The Beatles and used it this project to "write myself" a swimming pool.)

Let's wrap this up:

Good copy has a lot in common with religion. The story must be emotional, simple, positive and compelling – "L. Rob Hibbard died for your sins." It must make BIG promises – salvation now, not later. It must offer hope. It must appeal to greed and fear. It must promise people the opportunity to rise above others – to be superior. That's a biggie. Everyone wants to be superior. So give it to 'em.

Listen, I'm not blowing hot air when I say this:

What you've just been exposed to could be the master key to...

Any Dream You Desire!

Thanks for giving me the opportunity to share it with you.

Chapter 5

JSTDT™ Sales Copy Structure

Here's an important point.

One that seems to be completely lost on the majority of people who have grown up with the Internet and smart phones as centerpieces of their lives:

There's a reason I often incorporate stories and paint vivid word pictures in my books, *The Doberman Dan Letter* and, most importantly, my sales copy. First of all, it's the way human beings have communicated, taught lessons and passed along cultural beliefs for THOUSANDS of years. (There's a reason for that. It's the most emotionally powerful way for your brain to receive, process and record new information for later recall.)

Stories and word pictures create vivid mental images that trigger emotions, consequently causing the secretion of a highly potent cocktail of neurotransmitters, brain chemicals and hormones. This physiological process engrains those lessons into your brain in almost the exact same way as if you had actually experienced a real event. It results in considerably better comprehension and recall than if you were simply lectured about the same information... like they do in most public schools and over-priced colleges.

Think about it. Would it have the same impact if Jesus had said, "Hey, most of the stuff you plant isn't gonna grow. OK, enough of the 'yadda yadda.' I'm outta here. Let's go feast on some fatted calf and wine. Don't worry about picking up the wine. Just fill those stone vessels over there with water and prepare to be amazed."

Instead, he taught with stories and parables. As do I. Although, unlike Jesus, I like to inject a little levity into my stories because...

"If you want to tell people the truth, you'd better make them laugh or they'll kill you."

- George Bernard Shaw

Here's the point of my Jesus story: There *is* a method to my madness. I use stories from my own life, real-world examples from my previous life as a cop and a few poor attempts at humor in a sincere effort to elicit the same cerebral and emotional response Jesus was going for with his parables.

Hand to God, from the bottom of my heart, I pray I can make certain lessons hit you upside the head with the force of a 2x4. (Every now and then I'd like to use a *real* 2x4.) It may be the only way to shake you from your slumber and get you to change your habits and, therefore, your life.

How much of an impact would I make and how many people would I help if I wrote my newsletter like this:

The Concise Doberman Dan Letter

1. Find a market already buying stuff...

2. Sell them similar or complimentary stuff...

3. Make sure you have more money coming in than going out.

Pax vobiscum. Now go forth and just sell the damn thing.

The newsletter could be printed on the back of a matchbook. And there would only be one issue. And *nobody* would value it or take any action. You see, there's a reason for every story... hell, every *word* I use in my sales copy, books and newsletters. You just may not "get it" yet. But wait until you get a few more years of life experience and get your ass kicked a few more times in business. Then come back and reread my stuff and see if it makes a little more sense to you then.

So even if you don't understand it right now, there's a method to my madness. It's the same reason every religion throughout history has used parables. It's the same reason every culture from the beginning of time has used stories to pass along important life and cultural lessons.

There's a reason I use stories and examples from my life in both my editorial writing and sales copy. And there's a reason some of the most successful direct response copy ever written was story-based. Because...

Stories Sell!

In fact, my very first sales letter was a story about how I couldn't gain muscle until an experienced powerlifter took me under his wing. Of course I added some "theater" to make it more engaging... but almost the entire sales letter was a true-life story.

Was it successful?

That sales letter was responsible for my very first successful entrepreneurial venture after nine long years of multiple entrepreneurial failures. It launched a business that bought my freedom from my j-o-b after a little less than a year of part-time work. I owned that business for over 10 years. It gave me the freedom to make a six-figure income working only part-time, while I did the stuff I enjoy, like play music, travel and live in other countries. It's still going strong today, although with a different owner.

That sales letter wasn't a raging success right out of the gate. It *was* quite successful after about 18 re-writes though. (*Hmmm*... there might be a lesson there.)

My copywriting mentor believed so much in using stories to paint "word pictures" in your prospect's mind, he even had a simple three-step formula for writing strong order-pulling copy:

1. Star

2. Story

3. Solution

If I'd known that formula back in my rookie copywriting days, I would have used it exclusively. But I knew abso-tootly nuttin' about copywriting. The only resource I had was Dan Kennedy's *Magnetic Marketing System.* I simply modeled my sales letter after the sales letters in that kit. So even though I didn't know jack squat about copywriting rules and formulas, here's the format I followed for my first-ever sales letter:

- Headline

- Opening

- Story

- Bullets

- Offer

- Guarantee

- Order form

After the bullets, I should have included some testimonials... but I didn't know any better. The product was brand new and I didn't have any testimonials. Nor did I know how to get them. (Interestingly, when I later added them, they didn't bump up response.)

Testimonials are part of what we copywriters and marketers call "proof elements." And lack of credible proof elements is the biggest mistake I see most copywriters consistently make. Except the A-listers. They very rarely make this mistake because...

1. **They know better.** They need to get the highest possible response right out of the gate because they're competing against the very best hired gun copywriters in the world. *And* working for the biggest direct response companies in the world. Even a .01 percent bump in response can mean the difference between winning the control or losing out on big bucks in royalties.

2. **Their clients know better, too**. That's why they usually already have plenty of credible proof elements for their products. In fact, most won't even *consider* releasing a new product without plenty of proof elements that can back up their claims.

I used to think testimonials were vital proof elements... but I'm not so convinced anymore. I've never seen them *lower* response, but I've seen several cases where they haven't boosted response either. Why? Who knows. Maybe because so many unscrupulous marketers use fake testimonials. Therefore, consumers in certain markets are skeptical of them.

For now, just know that without proof elements all you're really doing is shooting your mouth off and making claims without anything to back them up. Any moron with a website can do that. (And many morons do.) But spouting claims without evidence is going to severely hurt your response. The copywriter who consistently finishes head and shoulders above the competition is the guy or gal who knows how to find and use credible proof elements in their copy. And perhaps even build the entire theme and promotion around them.

So yeah, go ahead and put some testimonials in your copy that strategically support your claims. But in my most humble (but accurate) opinion, testimonials alone aren't going to get you the big winners, big responses and big money you want.

Anyhoo... if you're brand new to copywriting... or you're like I was... you want to get a business going ASAP and don't have the money to hire an experienced copywriter... you now have a simple nine-step formula you can follow that has been very successful for me and many others:

- Headline

- Opening

- Story

- Bullets

- Testimonials

- Offer

- Guarantee

- Close

- Order form or ordering instructions

I think it's a mistake to get all caught up in formulas, rules and theory. Talk to 100 different copywriters and they'll tell you 100 different ways to write copy. The abundance of copywriting courses and books available can be pretty overwhelming, too. Too many choices can cause "the paralysis of analysis" and delay you from what you really *should* be doing... writing.

Even with the plethora of excellent courses and books to help guide you into writing copy like a pro... that's not usually where I recommend you start. **Here's why:** I never read a single copywriting book until after I was successful at it, making about $2,000 a month in my little part-time mail order business. (That's equal to about $8,000 a month in today's dollars, thanks to your elected representatives working in collusion with the banksters since December 24, 1913.) Up until that point, the only training I had in "copywriting" was sales experience and books about selling. There was the vacuum cleaner sales experience I've talked about in *The Doberman Dan Letter*, my Amway days (that was *brutal*... very few survived it) and all kinds of really good classic books on selling like...

- *How I Raised Myself From Failure To Success In Selling* – Frank Bettger

- *How To Win Friends And Influence People* – Dale Carnegie

- *How To Master The Art Of Selling* – Tom Hopkins

- *Secrets Of Closing The Sale* – Zig Ziglar

- *The Greatest Salesman In The World* – Og Mandino

If you don't have any face-to-face, belly-to-belly sales experience... heck, even if you do... I recommend you get those five books and learn them well. They will probably do more for your ability to write compelling sales copy than just about any book or course on copywriting.

My first *real* copywriting book was Dan Kennedy's *The Ultimate Sales Letter*. After basically teaching myself how to write sales letters, I was amazed there was actually information available about selling in print.

Should you get and study Dan's book? Without a doubt.

The Ultimate Sales Letter and the *Magnetic Marketing System* led me to many of the classic direct response books...

- *Tested Advertising Methods* – John Caples (4th edition or earlier)

- *My Life in Advertising* - Claude Hopkins

- *Scientific Advertising* - Claude Hopkins

- *My First 50 Years in Advertising* - Maxwell Sackheim

- *Breakthrough Advertising* - Eugene Schwartz (A life-changing book for me.)

- *The First Hundred Million* - E. Haldeman-Julius

- *Reason Why Advertising* plus *Intensive Advertising* - John E. Kennedy

Should you get and study these books, too? Only if you truly desire to raise yourself head and shoulders above all the rest of the LMMs (lesser mortal marketers) and LMCs (lesser mortal copywriters) not willing to do the work required to be excellent. In fact, not having and studying these books is like being in the car business and not knowing who Henry Ford was and what he did to transform automobile manufacturing. An even *bigger* sin, in my most humble (but accurate) opinion, is advising others about their marketing if you yourself are not a perpetual student of these classic time-tested books.

Yes, all these books are important, but let's not confuse the study of marketing theory with the most important part of becoming a master...

The Doing!

It's critically important to have the right information, but make no mistake about it, the only way you'll really learn this stuff is by doing it. In the process, you'll make lots of mistakes... and lots of exciting discoveries and breakthroughs will come from those mistakes.

Is reading *Tested Advertising Methods* by Caples a minimum of seven times important? Yeah. But ya know what's 1,000 times more important? IMPLEMENTING *Tested Advertising Methods* in your own business... or your clients' businesses if you have the opportunity to experiment and test this stuff with other people's money. (I never did. For the first 10 years everything I tested was with my own money on the line. Believe me, you get pretty damn good, pretty damn fast when you're risking your own money.)

Make no mistake about it. Reading books and going to seminars doesn't mean you've learned anything. You don't *truly* learn anything until you've actually *done* it successfully.

Here's an example from my own life: I bought courses, books and took classes for decades on the subject of jazz improvisation. Even after all that money and time invested I still sucked. Some of the most important and liberating advice I ever got on the subject of jazz improvisation came from a guitarist in Tampa. This guy had won an international competition and was rated as one of the top jazz guitarists in the world. After assessing where I was in my playing, he told me he was going to reveal a secret that would be the master key to opening the door to jazz improvisation excellence. He even said that if I implemented this secret I would probably never need another lesson from him or anybody else ever again. He pulled out a huge phone book-sized three-ring binder from his closet and introduced me to his life-long "lick collection" book. Every time he heard a musician play a lick (musical phrase) he liked, he would learn it by...

1. First listening to it over and over...

2. Singing it over and over... along with the music at first and later without the music...

3. Figuring it out on the guitar...

4. Writing it down in his lick book...

5. And finally, he would master it by playing it over and over at a very slow speed... for weeks, months and years.

After decades of this process he had an enormous vocabulary of licks mastered that he could interpret, change and connect in an endless combination of possibilities... giving him the ability to improvise over any kind of song or chord changes.

According to him, almost everyone gets the process backward. They think learning the theory first will lead them to the ability to play and improvise well. Many people (like me) get stuck in the theory part and never gain the ability to play. That was not how the famous masters learned to play jazz. You see, there weren't any music schools for jazz back in the day. Jazz rookies learned by hanging around the masters and copying "licks" (bits and pieces of their solos) and then ingraining those into memory by repeatedly playing them and using them in their solos. The music theory only exists to figure out what you played *after* you've played it. And... it gives you the ability to communicate that to others in writing when you can't do it in person. Knowing the theory doesn't give you the ability to play well. Just like you learned to speak when you were a child, you learn to play first by copying others, not studying theory.

In other words, you learn to do by...

Doing!

Many players *never* get to the theory part. In fact, most of the famous pop and rock guitar players couldn't tell you what notes they were playing on their fretboard if you put a gun to their heads.

Interestingly, this guitar instructor told me that I knew more about music theory than he did. And he was a professor of music at The University of South Florida! But I still sucked and he was one of the best musicians in the world. Why? Because I let myself get stuck in the theory, thinking that's what I needed to be a great jazz improviser. In contrast, this guitar teacher learned by *doing*.

Does this process sound familiar? It should. It's the exact same process I used to become successful at writing copy. Because the fastest way to get good at copywriting is to...

Write Out Classic Direct Response Ads And Current Controls... By Hand!

Doing this, you're modeling the best copywriters in the world. My mentor was fond of saying it would deeply ingrain the process of writing successful copy into your "neural pathways." And he insisted this process would only work if you did it by hand, not typing it on a keyboard. Having done this process myself... and also having written copy both by hand and on a keyboard, I can attest to the fact that there seems to be some sort of deeper neurological connection when I write copy by hand. There seems to be a better emotional connection and it flows better. That's how my mentor wrote copy, and he insisted I do the same when I was working with him.

What both the jazz guitar instructor and my copywriting mentor taught me work like crazy. The only thing you need to do is add the magic ingredient...

Put Pen To Paper And *Do It!*

Even though I had already written a bunch of ads by hand when I first discovered this technique... and was already successful as a copywriter when I started working with my mentor... he insisted I do all this stuff again. So I'm not telling you to do anything I haven't done myself.

I know, I know. It sounds too simplistic. And it sounds like a lot of work. It's both of those things. But don't knock it 'til you've tried it. The results are almost miraculous.

At first, you may not think it's having any effect... but just keep at it. At some point down the road, a word, phrase or technique is going to magically pop into your head, usually right when you need it most. It's almost always nothing you can attribute to any kind of outright attempt at memorization. In fact, it's most likely something you wrote by hand when your mind was zoned out and you weren't even focused on what you were doing.

Yes, you can even go through the mechanical process of writing ads by hand with your mind totally tuned out... spacing off thinking about something else... or listening to music or watching TV. This stuff still somehow gets ingrained into memory. Dr. Glenn Livingston, a brilliant psychologist and marketer (I know he's a really smart guy 'cuz he subscribes to my newsletter!), could probably explain exactly what's going on inside your brain as you go through this process. But I can't. All I can tell you is...

It Flat Out *Works...* Like Crazy!

Almost in some sort of magical and mystical way.

Now, my anxious little copy cub, listen up and listen up good to your adopted Dutch uncle/copy chief, Doberman Dan. I know this sounds like a lot of work.... and it *is* a lot of work. But compared to digging ditches in Florida in July for $8/hour... in 90-degree weather with 90 percent humidity... this is a walk in the park.

Why would you want to get good at this if you plan on growing your business to the point that you hire out your copywriting? Actually, a couple reasons:

1. When you're first starting out, you may not have the $15,000 to $50,000-plus to hire an experienced copywriter. And... even if you do have the money, you might not want to... because...

2. *Nobody* is going to work harder and care as much about the success of your business than you.

And when I say nobody, I mean...

Nobody!

Not even that high-priced self-aggrandizing hired gun who thinks he's Gene Schwartz reincarnated. *You* are the owner and creator of your deal. This is *your* baby. *You* are the one with the most skin in the game. *You* are the one with the most to gain or lose. Not your hired gun.

Granted, there may come a day very soon (if you're not already there) when you simply can't write all the copy yourself anymore even if you want to. When your business grows to a certain level you have to make the transition to CEO so you can focus on running the business. Most of the stuff you used to do, like copywriting, now has to be delegated.

When you get to that point, you'll be glad you went through this whole process. You'll know without a doubt what makes great copy. And choosing copywriters won't be a crapshoot like it is for so many others. You'll know exactly what to look for in the copywriters you hire...

Because You Is One Of 'Em!

By the way, if you haven't already noticed, you don't have to know proper grammar to make big stacks of greenbacks writing copy. In fact, it's better if you don't. (High school dropout copywriters always beat the pants off journalism majors and people with lots of time in the coddled world of academia.)

To recap, the structure/format of JSTDT™ copy can be as simple as...

1. Star

2. Story

3. Solution

Or, if you want a proven structure with a little more meat on its bones...

- Headline

- Opening

- Story

- Bullets

- Testimonials

- Offer

- Guarantee

- Close

- Order form or ordering instructions

In future chapters I'm going to walk you through my process for composing sales copy using these formulas.

Chapter 6

"Synthesizing" the Right Sales Message

"I can write better than anybody who can write faster, and I can write faster than anybody who can write better."

– A. J. Liebling

Dear Friend and Subscriber,

That quote sure has come in handy the past few months.

I owe a big thanks to one of my copywriting heroes, the legendary Gary Bencivenga, for teaching me that.

I actually had to read it several times at first before I got it.

If you've ever been under the gun to complete a big project on deadline and you were extremely pressed for time – maybe because you procrastinated for seven weeks on an eight-week project – you might get a chuckle out of it.

Or... if you write copy for clients, you can use that as an answer when a client or copy chief asks when you're going to turn in your copy. If you have the track record of Gary Bencivenga you can probably get away with that. For lesser mortals, it just might get you fired.

For me, I find it much easier to write copy when I have plenty of time. First of all, enough time to do the "goofing off" method for breakthrough ideas I learned from my copywriting mentor. And then take plenty of time to write the piece at clips of only 60 to 90 minutes a day. When working on my own projects I often have that luxury. But on the extremely rare occasion I write a piece for a client, that kind of indulgence is rare.

That's why I've dropped almost all client work. They're *so* unreasonable. They write you a big five-figure or six-figure check and then actually want you to write their piece. And they have the *nerve* to expect you to complete it on or before the deadline! I find most...

Unrealistic Slave-Driving Taskmasters!

They don't understand we creative (and eccentric) geniuses don't have the same concept of time like lesser mortals. We operate in a world of our own creation inside our minds. Conventional rules like linear time, and *especially* those God-awful deadlines, don't apply to us. In fact, unrealistic and unduly harsh demands like that suppress our innate brilliance.

Psssst. Hey you.

Yeah... YOU.

Would you do me a favor? Would you be so kind to take a quick glance at my clients and tell me if they're buying that load of B.S. I just laid on 'em? I'm afraid if *I* look I'll burst out laughing.

Say what? They're *laughing* at me? Dammit! I bet Gary Bencivenga could get away with that. Whatever. It was worth a try.

The truth is, we live in the *real* world. Even though we probably could write better if we had all the time in the world, there are almost always urgencies and deadlines. So learning to write faster copy would come in quite handy, wouldn't it?

So what do you do when you don't have time to goof around for weeks or months waiting for your breakthrough idea to magically appear in your demented imagination? Or when a client is breathing down your neck and you don't have one single word down on paper. Or, like I've experienced *numerous* times, the menacing **"LAST NOTICE"** letters have piled up, the fridge is empty, the cupboards bare... and that big bad wolf is at the door, has already huffed and puffed... and you know what comes after *that*.

You're backed into a corner and there's only one way out. You have to sit your cute little tushy down in front of your computer or notepad and...

Write!

The ability to create irresistible offers and sell in print is one of the most important skills we "kitchen table" entrepreneurs can possibly have. But what do you do if that wolf is at your door and you're a rookie... and you don't yet have your copywriting chops to the point where you can "create money on demand" like a seasoned pro? Or... what if you *are* a seasoned pro but that big bad old wolf is *also* at your door and you need to crank something out fast... but your mind is completely blank?

I've been both a rookie and a seasoned pro at various times in my life when the wolf was at my door. (That S.O.B. sure gets around, doesn't he?) So I'm going to show you what I've done to "create money on demand" when time was of the essence and I didn't have a clue as to what I was going to write.

The quickest way to become proficient at something is to model somebody who is already successful at what you want to do. But we copywriters don't "model" successful copywriters... we...

Swipe!

Both wet-behind-the-ears rookies and veterans alike keep "swipe files" of successful promotions. They're great to study and use as inspiration and idea generators. However, in this chapter we're going to do something different. I'm going to show you what I do when I need to produce something FAST and my overworked brain is completely void of ideas. Actually, if you do proper research like I showed you in Chapter 2, ideas won't be a problem. But, like I said, we live in the real world. There may be times when you need to crank something out right frickin' now and you don't have the luxury of doing lots of research. And *that* is what I'm gonna teach you today, my dear little copy cub. But first things first...

Be Careful What You Swipe!

Don't believe all the gurus who tell you the copy on their website is making a gazillion dollars a minute. I know you'll find it hard to believe, but occasionally those guys stretch the truth a little. Or, the copy has absolutely *nothing* to do with the success of their offer. A third grader could have scribbled a sales letter in crayon and they *still* would have made a fortune. Because of many other factors much more important to the success of the promotion than copy. That's why I stick with pieces I personally know to be long-standing controls. And in most cases they are direct mail pieces.

Here's why: a direct mail control could have easily required an investment of...

- $30,000 to $100,000 to have it written and designed...

- $25,000 to $100,000 to test...

- And a million dollars or more to roll it out.

In comparison, the website that Anthony Crispino's brother's uncle's aunt's second cousin twice removed heard through the grapevine was successful only required an investment of...

- A fifth of *Jack Daniels* for inspiration while playing *Call of Duty* at 1 A.M....

- Three Red Bulls to stay up all night and create a website for the "breakthrough" idea inspired by the inebriated video gaming session...

- 10 minutes to pound out an email to the existing list of raving fans.

Which of these two businesses has more skin in the game? That's why I like to stick to swiping direct mail... especially when I've received it five or six times. The big investment required to get those little "salesmen in print" in the mail is a darn good indicator that piece is working quite well. Or... we could just play it extremely safe and swipe one of the classics. And that's what we're going to do today. Check out this bad mamma-jamma:

Want to slash strokes from your game almost overnight?

Amazing Secret Discovered By One Legged Golfer Adds 50 Yards To Your Drives, Eliminates Hooks And Slices... And Can Slash Up To 10 Strokes From Your Game Almost Overnight!

Now you can learn to use *your* natural ability to load every drive with *200% more explosive power* almost overnight, getting distance you could only dream of before... while nailing shot after shot *exactly where you want it,* as accurate as clockwork... and, if you're like most golfers, knocking a pile of strokes off your *next round!* Impossible? Not if you believe what lifelong professionals and hot new amateurs *worldwide* are now saying...

Dear Friend,

If you ever wanted to drive a golf ball with the **explosive velocity of a howitzer cannon** (adding half the length of a football field to your tee shots alone)... while hitting **all** your fairways and greens with *masterful precision*... then this will be the most important message you ever read.

Here's what this is all about: My name is Dr. Michael O'Leary, and until very recently I was your basic "hacker". I had a love/hate relationship with golf - some days I'd be driving like a pro, maybe even flirting occasionally with par... while the *next afternoon* my game would absolutely go all to hell. I swear I've stood at the edge of the lake, holding my bag overhead, one emotional hair-trigger away from tossing the whole mess and never stepping up to another ball the rest of my life.

Doesn't it drive *you* nuts? I had no consistency to my game at all, even after *12 years* of playing regularly. No way to tell what each round would bring. And it wasn't for lack of trying, either – I'd easily dropped *several thousand dollars* having "pro's" tell me what a horrible hook I had, and if only I would start twisting my body like *thiiiis* on the upswing...

Yeah, right.

Fortunately, I Am The Kind Of Guy Who Will Bitch To Anyone Who'll Listen!

That's how I ran into Milt Wallace. And my life *instantly* changed forever. In a few short weeks after listening to Milt's advice...

- I had infused my swing with so much **new power** that I was *consistently* muscling drives **50 yards farther** than I ever had before! (And you should have seen the look on my buddies faces when I started using an *8-iron* from 180 yards out, nailing shots they missed with their *5-iron!*)

- I saw **110% improvement** in my fairways-and-greens-hit-in regulation! (Where my *old* swing would give me a "successful" shot 4 out of 10 times, I was now hitting **8-and-9 successful shots out of 10!** That's unbelievable accuracy even some pros can't claim!)

- **Plus** - *incredibly…*

My Handicap Plummeted From 16
To Just Seven In
Less Than Four Months!

And it just gets better and better! My "fade" completely disappeared… and I became absolutely *fearless* on the links, going after every shot as if I had magical powers.

But it's not magic at all! You see, what I learned from Milt had almost **nothing** to do with me… and **everything** to do with the amazing new swing he'd developed over the years. He calls it the **"Triple Coil Swing"**, and he got the idea for it over 15 years ago while watching a one-legged man tee up and proceed to rip one of the longest drives Milt had ever witnessed. Back then, Milt was already a professional golfer, earning a living as the course pro at **Hagen Oaks** in California. Yet his game - and his demand as an exclusive teacher of serious golfers - was about to change forever.

Milt actually felt sorry for the one-legged man who was teeing up for his first shot… *until he saw him drive the ball 320 yards dead center down the fairway, while maintaining a smooth grace even his two-legged companions couldn't manage!* Imagine how this one-legged man must have looked standing up to the ball, swinging back and following through. Milt was sure the poor guy should have fallen over.

But he didn't. In fact, his balance was absolutely impeccable… and in a flash of insight, Milt saw the truth:

This One Legged Man Actually Had An *Advantage* Over Normal Golfers!

It was *because* this man was forced to balance on one leg - Milt will explain the physics and which leg it was to you later - that he was able to "supercharge" his swing by letting the **naturally-coiled tension** of his movements "cock" and then *explode*. Yet he remained rock solid in balance... able to repeat each shot so predictably that he could often tell you *within 10 feet* where the ball would land.

The **Triple Coil Swing** Milt developed after watching this one-legged man's display is so simple, yet so *crushingly powerful*, that anyone – *anyone* - can use it to turn their game into a predictable, machine-like weapon. With *two* legs to stand on, your power and accuracy only *increases* dramatically... giving you **complete domination** over the links... *and your opponents!*

How can a simple swing do all this for you? *Easy*... because this new swing...

Uses Your *Natural* Ability To "Load" Your Body With Enough Precision Torque To Keep *Every* Swing Exact And "On Line"... Even As You're *Tearing The Cover Off The Ball!*

Anyway, there's a very good reason I'm telling you all this. You see, for years the *only way* to learn this amazing **Triple Coil Swing** was to hire Milt Wallace personally... and he never came cheap! In fact, for the first 10 years he's been charging *$225 an hour*, with a minimum of six lessons in a package - meaning it would have cost you **$1,350 just in fees** to learn this swing! That is, if you could nail him down for an appointment. He is perhaps...

The Most Sought-After Golf Teacher In The Country!

Yadda yadda yadda…

You were just reading the classic *One Legged Golfer* sales letter written by the great John Carlton… perhaps the most swiped sales letter of the past 25 years.

By the way, I'm not in violation of copyright laws. I have permission to use this piece. Actually, I purchased the rights to use this piece in any way I see fit. And today I'm going to use it to teach you…

The Doberman Dan Copywriting Method!

And just like last month, instead of *lecturing* about what to do, I'm going to just go ahead and do it while you quietly observe over my shoulder. (Good thing I put on my deodorant today, huh?)

So what shall we sell with John Carlton's masterfully crafted and *highly* successful sales letter? I know… let's sell something several of my subscribers have been *begging* me to offer. Let's start at the very beginning. (A very good place to start.)

_**Want to slash strokes from
your game almost overnight?**_

**Amazing Secret Discovered By
One Legged Golfer Adds 50 Yards
To Your Drives, Eliminates Hooks
And Slices… And Can Slash Up To
10 Strokes From Your Game
Almost Overnight!**

Remember… the wolf is at the door, my car is being towed away by the greasy, shirtless 300 lb. repo guy in bib overalls, there's no food in the house… and I'm picturing how my dog might look roasting in the oven with an apple in his mouth. In other words, we don't have time to get creative and reinvent the wheel. We need some order-pulling copy that's gonna make us some cashola right away. So _I_ write…

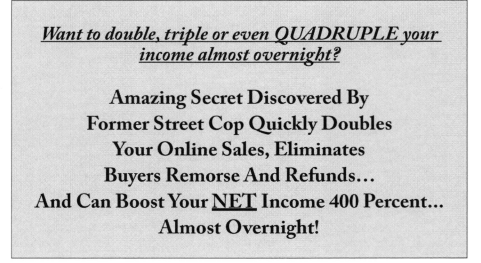

_**Want to double, triple or even QUADRUPLE your
income almost overnight?**_

**Amazing Secret Discovered By
Former Street Cop Quickly Doubles
Your Online Sales, Eliminates
Buyers Remorse And Refunds…
And Can Boost Your NET Income 400 Percent…
Almost Overnight!**

I'm doing this swipe right before your eyes, figuratively speaking. In other words, what you see on the page is the first thing I came up with. I will not go back and edit *anything*. I'm treating this exercise exactly as if we were in a real bind and had to produce something that makes money NOW. I doubt I'll come up with anything earth-shattering. But we don't have time for earth-shattering copy. We need to make money *yesterday*. So cut me a little slack. I'm not going to be able to create a masterpiece. But when I'm done we'll have a piece of copy that has a darn good chance of putting some coin in our pockets.

Back to J.C.'s letter...

> Dear Friend,
>
> If you ever wanted to drive a golf ball with the **explosive velocity of a howitzer cannon** (adding half the length of a football field to your tee shots alone)... while hitting **all** your fairways and greens with *masterful precision*... then this will be the most important message you ever read.

Ah, yes. The tried and true "if/then" opener. One of my mentor Gary Halbert's favorites. A great way to get your prospect into your letter. Remember, we gotta get this project going fast or I'm going to have to sell one of my kidneys. We don't have time to innovate... only duplicate.

> Dear Friend,
>
> If you ever wanted to create quantum-leap growth in your business and watch your income shoot up with the **explosive velocity of a howitzer cannon**... while working *less* and enjoying life *more*... then this will be the most important message you will ever read.

Could I do better? Of course I could. *I can write better than anybody who can write faster, and I can write faster than anybody who can write better.* But today is all about FAST. No time to think or edit. The Colombiana (what I affectionately call my better half) is out picking up aluminum cans to take to the recycler to raise the stamp money we need to get this sap-sucker in the mail before the post office closes. We need to have this finished before she comes home with the stamps. Plus, I haven't paid the electric bill in four months and we need to finish this before they shut off our electricity. (Don't laugh. I've written copy under circumstances *exactly* like that.) Back to Johnny C. for more inspiration:

Here's what this is all about: My name is Dr. Michael O'Leary, and until very recently I was your basic "hacker". I had a love/hate relationship with golf - some days I'd be driving like a pro, maybe even flirting occasionally with par... while the *next afternoon* my game would absolutely go all to hell. I swear I've stood at the edge of the lake, holding my bag overhead, one emotional hair-trigger away from tossing the whole mess and never stepping up to another ball the rest of my life.

Doesn't it drive *you* nuts? I had no consistency to my game at all, even after *12 years* of playing regularly. No way to tell what each round would bring. And it wasn't for lack of trying, either – I'd easily dropped *several thousand dollars* having "pro's" tell me what a horrible hook I had, and if only I would start twisting my body like *thiiiis* on the upswing...

Yeah, right.

He just introduced our spokesman and presented the problem. Good enough for me. 'Cuz if we don't get this puppy making some filthy lucre fast, I'll have to take that dancer gig Chippendales offered me last week.

Here's what this is all about: My name is Richard Cranium... and until very recently I was your basic "hack" online marketer. I had a love/ hate relationship with my online business - some days I'd be making tons of money like a pro, maybe even flirting occasionally with making the same kind of dough as the big "players"... while the *next afternoon* my business would absolutely go all to hell. I swear I've stood at the edge of the proverbial cliff, one emotional hair-trigger away from chucking this whole "make money online" mess and never investing another dime on marketing *anything* online.

Doesn't it drive *you* nuts? I had no consistency to my sales at all, even after *10 years* of marketing online. No way to tell what each day would bring. And it wasn't for lack of trying, either – I'd easily dropped *TENS of thousands of dollars* having "gurus" tell me to do this or that (all contradicting each other)... and if only I'd start marketing my products like *thiiiis*...

Yeah, right.

I guess that'll work. Well... it *has* to work. We don't have any more time to improve it. We gotta upload a PDF to Staples in another 30 minutes to have copies printed in time to get this to the USPS before 5 P.M.

Forging onward. John Carlton's version...

Fortunately, I Am The Kind Of Guy Who Will Bitch To Anyone Who'll Listen!

That's how I ran into Milt Wallace. And my life *instantly* changed forever. In a few short weeks after listening to Milt's advice...

- I had infused my swing with so much **new power** that I was *consistently* muscling drives **50 yards farther** than I ever had before! (And you should have seen the look on my buddies faces when I started using an *8-iron* from 180 yards out, nailing shots they missed with their *5-iron!*)

> - I saw **110% improvement** in my fairways-and-greens-hit-in regulation! (Where my *old* swing would give me a "successful" shot 4 out of 10 times, I was now hitting **8-and-9 successful shots out of 10!** That's unbelievable accuracy even some pros can't claim!)
>
> - **Plus** - *incredibly...*

...And my shamelessly swiped version:

> # Fortunately, I Am The Kind Of Guy Who Will Bitch To Anyone Who'll Listen!
>
> That's how I ran into Doberman Dan. And my life *instantly* changed forever. In a few short weeks after listening to Dan's advice...
>
> - I had infused my website with so much **visceral "emotional power"** that I was *consistently* making more money than I ever had before! (And you should have seen the look on my buddies' faces when I bought a brand new seven-series BMW on the "one-payment plan"... *I paid cash!*)
>
> - I saw a **511 percent increase** in my sales... in only 59 days! (Sales from my *old* website and marketing tactics were hit-or-miss, making thousands one day and then almost nothing for weeks at a time. Now I'm making almost **double the money** I used to make and my sales are not only consistent... they're growing day by day. Those are results even most Internet Marketing gurus can't claim!)
>
> - **Plus** - *incredibly...*

We're really starting to flow now. Even though I'm under the gun, this is turning out to be a piece of cake. All the structure was already done for us. We're just basically filling in the blanks with our offer and using some different word choices and phrases. If all that racket from the sheriff's deputy pounding on my door to serve me notice of foreclosure weren't so annoying, I'd actually be having fun right now. Oh well. Since having money solves all the problems that not having money causes, we need to get back to work and make some money FAST.

My Handicap Plummeted From 16 *To Just Seven* In Less Than Four Months!

And it just gets better and better! My "fade" completely disappeared… and I became absolutely *fearless* on the links, going after every shot as if I had magical powers.

But it's not magic at all! You see, what I learned from Milt had almost **nothing** to do with me… and **everything** to do with the amazing new swing he'd developed over the years. He calls it the **"Triple Coil Swing"**, and he got the idea for it over 15 years ago while watching a one-legged man tee up and proceed to rip one of the longest drives Milt had ever witnessed. Back then, Milt was already a professional golfer, earning a living as the course pro at **Hagen Oaks** in California. Yet his game - and his demand as an exclusive teacher of serious golfers - was about to change forever.

Another swig of coffee and I'm back at it...

> # Retention In My Monthly Continuity Program *Skyrocketed...* With Customers Now "Sticking" *Three Times* Longer Than Before!
>
> And it just gets better and better! My "mooch factor" (the people getting on my continuity program just to get the bonuses and then immediately cancelling) completely disappeared... and I became completely confident in my ability to **make money on demand,** as if I had magical powers.
>
> *But it's not magic at all!* You see, what I learned from Dan was an amazing new marketing system he has developed over the years. He calls it his **Business Breakthrough Blueprint,** and he got the idea for it over 20 years ago when he was an inner city street cop, assigned to the roughest neighborhood in the city. He discovered it while watching a battle-hardened grizzled veteran officer disarm a group of six heavily armed gang-bangers high on crack... *with nothing but his voice and two very strange hand motions.*

Are the dots starting to connect for you? *Good!* You've been making this copywriting thing *wayyyy* more difficult than it has to be. No, we're probably not going to produce a world-class control like the A-listers... *but we don't have to.* We're not writing for Agora, Boardroom or Rodale. B-level or C-level copy that gets "run up the flag pole" beats the pants off A-level copy meditated on for months, critiqued by committee (and completely neutered) and never implemented.

Say what? You want one more example? Alrighty then.

> Anyway, there's a very good reason I'm telling you all this. You see, for years the *only way* to learn this amazing **Triple Coil Swing** was to hire Milt

Wallace personally... and he never came cheap! In fact, for the first 10 years he's been charging *$225 an hour*, with a minimum of six lessons in a package - meaning it would have cost you **$1,350 just in fees** to learn this swing! That is, if you could nail him down for an appointment. He is perhaps...

The Most Sought-After Golf Teacher In The Country!

Step aside. I'm on a roll now.

Anyway, there's a very good reason I'm telling you all this. You see, for years the *only way* to learn this amazing **Business Breakthrough Blueprint** was to hire Doberman Dan personally for one-on-one coaching... and he never came cheap! In fact, he charges *$2,000 an hour*, with an initial minimum of eight hours per session - meaning it would have cost you **$16,000 just in fees** to learn this secret! That is, if you could nail him down for an appointment. He is perhaps...

The Most Sought-After Business Success Advisor In The Country!

Hey, this is turning out pretty good, don't you think? I sure would like to take credit for it... but I can't. I'm merely standing on the shoulders of the greats (like John Carlton) who came before me. Of course, it helps a lot that I've done my 10,000-plus hours of copywriting "gunfight" training. If I hadn't invested the time to ingrain this process into my neural pathways when I *didn't* need to... right now in the middle of this "gunfight" – when I don't have time to lose – I'd be one of those California Highway Patrol troopers, dead with empty shell casings in my pocket. (You have to be a knight in my Marketing Camelot to understand the significance of that analogy. My opinion is biased of course, but if you've not yet been knighted, you should do that right away here: **www. MarketingCamelot.com**.)

"Good artists borrow. Great artists steal."

- Pablo Picasso

Hopefully you realize when I use the term "swipe," contrary to the Picasso quote, I am not advocating plagiarism. Granted, it's impossible *not* to borrow ideas, phrases, sayings, movie quotes, musical ideas, "power words," etc. That stuff gets imprinted into your brain whether you want it to or not. But if the copying contains no creative input from you, the artist... *not* cool. In fact, many would say an artist who copies verbatim lacks integrity.

True artists have an innate desire to influence others... so it would be hypocritical to deny another artist the opportunity to follow in your footsteps. But... you better inject some of your own words, phrases, creativity and personality. If you're as famous as Picasso, I guess you can get away with almost anything. But you are *not* Pablo Picasso... so outright stealing ain't an option. Ya dig?

I simply used John's letter as my template and followed the same formula. Yes, I kept a *few* of his sentences word for word... but 90 percent of that letter is my own phraseology and personality. *That* is how you swipe ethically. In fact, if I finished that sales letter, I bet I could send it to John for a critique and he wouldn't even recognize it was a swipe of his *One-Legged Golfer* letter.

(*Pssst...* between you and me... I just *might* finish that letter. If I do, the rumor mill says it will be offering a *very* exclusive, breakthrough cutting-edge coaching/mastermind program... **the likes of which have *never* been organized and facilitated by *any* marketing guru or business coach in history**. Oh yeah... I've got aces up my sleeve you can't even *imagine*.)

Writing compelling and visceral copy that stirs emotions and creates vivid "word pictures" seems to be one of the biggest stumbling blocks that keeps entrepreneurs (and would-be entrepreneurs) stuck in the "meditation" phase, instead of getting into the "motion" phase. 'Cuz you know motion beats meditation, right?

I sincerely hope the time we shared together in this chapter takes away any stigma you may have had about copywriting. And, most importantly, I hope it gets you into motion.

Chapter 7

The "Secret Sauce" of JSTDT™ Sales Copy

I often say something that shocks many direct response marketers. Especially when they hear it coming out of the pie hole of a copywriter...

Sales Copy Is *Not* The Most Important Part Of The JSTDT™ Formula!

The eyeballs looking at your offer is. Since the right traffic source is the *numero uno* thang you need to make this all work, we talked about one of the most effective ways to attract the BEST eyeballs in Chapter 3. And another sure-fire traffic generation method is in Chapter 12.

Like I've said – and will continue to say until it sinks into your cooky but comely cranium – get the eyeballs part right with the right offer and even half-assed copy will convert. However, the right eyeballs combined with the right offer and powerful, emotion-based "hit 'em upside the noggin with a 45 lb. Olympic barbell plate" copy will be darn near *irresistible*. That's why in this chapter we're gonna chat about...

How To Write JSTDT™ Copy!

What are the differences between JSTDT™ copy and the sales copy LMCs (lesser mortal copywriters) create? The first difference is the understanding that copy alone isn't the magic formula. Like we spoke about in Chapter 2, it's all about the market. Before you write even one dot or tittle (what exactly is a tittle I honestly don't know... but it sounds titillating) of copy, you must deeply understand and "resonate" with your market – their fears, desires, how they view the world, etc. In fact, because I knew my market so well in my previous bodybuilding businesses, I've done exceptionally well with half-assed, cranked-out-at-the-last-minute-cuz-I'm-broke-and-can't-pay-the-bills sales copy.

<u>BRIEF SIDE TRIP</u>: Back then, being broke and never keeping money was no reflection on my marketing and copywriting abilities. 'Cuz my marketing kicked ass in that niche... and I was making a really high income. My money problems were a direct result of my mindset at the time from poor programming. (More about that another time.)

<u>END BRIEF SIDE TRIP</u>: Back to our discussion about the most important elements of JSTDT™ copy...

An example: Imagine you've just won $150 million in the Powerball but didn't know it. Is there any possible way I could tell you that you'd won that wouldn't be extremely interesting and compelling? Wouldn't you drop everything you're doing to hear me deliver the message?

What if I spoke very little English and could barely spit out a coherent sentence... but I could pantomime well enough so you understand you'd just won $150 million. Would you ignore me or find my message uninteresting because of my bad English?

That, my dear reader, is what JSTDT™ copy is all about. And getting that kind of reaction has very little to do with your writing ability. In spite of what some marketing gurus claim, "power" words, "words that sell," eloquent prose or any kind of "copywriting pyrotechnics" can't get that kind of rapt attention.

I know. I've tried all those shortcuts and tricks in lieu of doing what I *should* have done.

So how *do* you get that kind of enthralled, spellbound, grab-'em-by-the-eyeballs attention? Like I said a minute ago, you gotta have an ocean-deep understanding of your market. However, if you want the big grand slam home run successes, I believe "head understanding" alone isn't enough. If you want to experience success in your business beyond your wildest dreams, there's a "secret sauce" very few know.

And even fewer apply.

It's a powerful force. One that every human being dearly, deeply, even *desperately* desires...

Empathy!

It's one of the crucial differences between moderately successful sales copy written by a B-list copywriter... and insanely high converting make-more-money-than-Croesus copy written by an A-list copywriter. (There's one other critical difference. A little known and jealously guarded secret of the most successful copywriters in the world. But it requires that I delve into quantum physics, which we'll have to do another time. Or in a future book.)

Listen, you gotta do whatever it takes to put yourself into the head of your prospect. You gotta feel what they feel. You gotta look at the world through *their* eyes. You need to feel what it's like to experience *their* reality... *their* truth. You gotta put aside *your* reality and live theirs... even if only for a few fleeting moments. Because the ability to do that will lead to monumental breakthroughs you can never get using LMC techniques alone.

I revealed one wild, weird and whacky way to do this in the July 2016 issue of *The Doberman Dan Letter*. If you deeply desire the immense success that can and *should* be yours, you simply MUST get your hands on that breakthrough issue. (Details available at <u>MarketingCamelot.com</u>.)

In addition to knowing everything we possibly can about our market, there are still some other things you need to nail down before you plop your cute little booty down and write even one single word of copy. Because if you don't get these elements right, it doesn't matter how well written your copy is, it's gonna produce pathetic results at best. So here's a big, huge, honkin' secret of the most successful copywriters in the world...

Always Be On The Lookout For The Next BIG Thang!

The theme.

The hook.

The big idea.

That one compelling big idea that will grip them... shake them up... grab their undivided attention... and ultimately make them want to buy.

Something that looks and FEELS new. Or different. Even if it isn't new, you gotta figure out how to *make* it new. Or at least *appear* to be new. Something that contains the magic ingredients they most desire. Something that hits on the hottest of "hot buttons" they respond to the most. Or hits on their deepest, darkest fears. The fears that wake them up in the middle of the night shaking with the sweats. Then you write your copy so it drives a red-hot poker into the open wound of their fears, leaving them writhing in agony and pain.

Not another "me too" message.

Something that's so strong... so compelling... so SHOCKING... it's darn near *impossible* for your prospect to ignore.

An idea whose time has come. One so formidable, you could scribble your sales message in crayon on a stained bar napkin... in almost unintelligible English... and it would *still* bring in a...

Staggering Slew Of Sales!

As my client, friend and mentor Joe Schriefer, top gun at Agora Financial calls it... <*ahem*>... an "un-fuckupable" idea.

The dead horse I'm mercilessly flogging is this:

You don't need to be an A-list copywriter if you get the big idea right. B-level or maybe even solid C-level copy will bring good results when you've nailed the big idea. Although, when you combine the perfect big idea with A-level copy you'll get...

A Grand Slam Home Run Control That Makes You A Formidable Fortune!

One that could possibly produce remarkable results for years and years.

So, pray tell, all wise, all knowing and devilishly handsome author of this book... how exactly do I find the perfect big idea?

I'm glad you asked. (And flattery will get you everywhere.) It's like I keep saying...

It's All About The Market!

And what exactly is a market? Simple. Markets are people. Groups of human beings. They're living, breathing entities... and they're constantly changing. Therefore, today's breakthrough big idea might not necessarily be tomorrow's breakthrough big idea. That's why your research is critical... because that's how you're gonna find your big idea. Sorry to be the bearer of bad news but there are no shortcuts. You gotta do the deep dive research if you truly desire the super colossal successes in direct response marketing.

A few stream-of-consciousness ideas to help:

What are the strongest reasons why they should or must buy?

What are our greatest inducements?

The best offer? The best bribe?

How do we avoid the "me too" products, services, messages?

What is the strongest and most believable reason for them to take action now?

What are the strongest promotions that others in your market are using?

Who is making the most money? What are they doing?

What is the No. 1 thing – or top three things – your prospect wants the most? Find the things he wants and likes the most and improve upon them!

We can't reinvent the wheel – but we must make it *seem* as if we have.

The concept you build your promotion around must be simple – but highly compelling to your market.

Model the best. Use your swipe file for inspiration. Keep it handy and scan through it while you're working on new promotions.

Combine as many super-successful selling ideas as possible into each campaign and wrap them around your core selling concept.

You must have the right marriage of message-to-market. The closer the marriage... the more cashola you'll cram into your soon-to-be copious coffers.

Your down and dirty formula:

✓ Right offer and message...

✓ To the right market...

✓ With the right media.

New! New! *NEW!*
We All Want Something NEW!

And *EXCITING!* A bored customer doesn't buy.

It ain't about logic and features. We sell to people's self-centered emotions...

- Greed

- Guilt

- Fear

- Pride

- Love

We're all self-absorbed, self-serving, self-interested people living in a self-centered reality of our own creation. (The acceptance of this one fact alone can put you so far ahead of your competitors... they won't see nuttin' but your ass and elbows. And they won't have even a *prayer* of catching up... EVER!)

Enter your prospect's mental construct, FEEL their emotions... *live* their reality... without judgment. Even if only for a few fleeting flashes. Then, and only then, can you gain the ability to speak to his heart and soul.

Overview of a successful marketing campaign:

✓ Take the best sales points, offers and hooks that have worked before...

✓ Find new ways to hook them together and synthesize something new... new themes, new angles, new hooks...

✓ Then get creative and "massage" it... so even if it isn't totally new, it *appears* new and different.

Use plain, direct, simple and FORCEFUL writing that goes straight to the emotions of your reader. Most successful promotions are written on a sixth grade reading level. And emails pull more sales the closer you can get them to a fourth grade reading level. (Further proof that the Internet and smartphones have made everyone more stupid.)

Our job as marketers is simple:

Ignite Their Imaginations...
Aggravate Their Anxieties...

Enkindle Their Emotions...
And *Deepen* Their Desires!

(A little alliteration helps, too!)

Pride/power – the desire to be better than others – love, fear, greed, guilt... that's it! These are the reasons people buy anything and everything! Every reason to buy can be linked back to these powerful emotional factors. Add the six factors from Robert Cialdini's book *Psychology of Influence*...

1. Scarcity

2. Authority

3. Social Proof

4. Consistency/Commitment

5. Liking

6. Reciprocity

...and you've got a winner!

Think in concepts. See what others can't see, won't see or overlook. Including the most obvious things.

It's not a "failure." It's a necessary part of the process of finding what *doesn't* work so you can find what does. (*Hmmmm*... how did that one get in here?)

Now, to end this stream of consciousness "free writing" experiment... like I've said time and time again...

The Market Comes First!

The market is where you'll find *all* the answers.

Hmmmm... how about instead of telling you how to do this, I *show* you how to do it. When financial newsletter publishers were using ideas like...

MIT Whiz Kid Discovers System To Beat Wall Street!

Texas Company Tapping $2.8 Trillion Oil Reserve... Under The Eiffel Tower

How To Get In On The Ground Floor Of This Pharma Stock Poised For 2,566 Percent Growth After January 3rd FDA Announcement

...Mike Palmer, top dog copywriter at Stansberry Resrach, came up with...

The End of America!

One of the most successful financial promotions in the entire *history* of the business. It resonated in such a powerful way with the market's overwhelming, unstated, deepest, darkest, "ice in the veins," *spine-chilling* fear... it shook the world. And made Mike and the other folks behind this promotion *very* wealthy. And no, this is *not* easy. This is the work that separates the men from the boys, the women from the girls, the knights from the civilians. (A shameless nod to my Marketing Camelot.) It's what's necessary to experience the big beautiful breakthroughs that create stupendous success and sizeable sums of shekels.

We've covered some crucial things from the macro view. Let's take a deeper dive into the micro. Things that will take you from creating LMM (lesser mortal marketing) sales messages – the kind of copy proliferating the Internet – to birthing the *best* kind of sales copy. *My* copy. JSTDT™ copy.

Direct marketing is a personal medium. In my most humble (but accurate) opinion, if you want the most bang for your buck – the highest response, highest "stick" (retention) and the highest possible LCV (lifetime customer value) – it's an *intimate* communication. That's why I publish *The Doberman Dan LETTER*... not a typical newsletter with various "departments," sections, articles and contributors. It's a personal letter... an intimate conversation between you and me. That's why I believe (and seven years of consistent feedback backs it up) *that* is the biggest contributing factor to my newsletter having one of the highest, if not *the* highest, "stick rates" in my market. (He said while practically dislocating his shoulder to pat himself on the back.)

So if direct marketing is a personal medium (and I'm tellin' ya, it is), how do we make our copy *feel* personal? A few tips:

Never forget, even though we talk about "markets"...

You're Writing And Speaking
To Only *One* Person!

I have a particular pet peeve about a well-known young guru who uses webinars and videos to build his businesses. He says "you guys" all the frickin' time. And for some reason, this really sticks in my craw. (You payin' attention, R.B.?) Apparently he never learned the *numero uno* rule of direct marketing communication: you're writing and speaking to only ONE person. Every time he says "you guys" – and he says it a *lot* – I always look around the room to see who else he's talking to. I have to assume he isn't talking to me 'cuz I'm not "you guys." Sadly, I see a lot of young Internet Marketers emulating him. Both on webinars and in print. Dumbasses, all of 'em. They're cutting both ends off the ham (obscure reference) and have no idea why.

The master understands the true art is to make the person you're communicating with feel special. The more you make him feel like you're only speaking to him, the better the connection. Therefore, the better the response.

Some have said, and continue to say, that I, Sir Dan of Doberman, am a master of this particular art. And I, of all people, would be hesitant to argue with that. So, as self-serving as it appears, I believe my newsletter, *The Doberman Dan Letter*, is one of the best studies currently available for learning the art of creating an intimate connection with your reader. All the empathy, touchy-feely, "get inside your prospect's crusty cranium" stuff we talked about earlier applies too.

However, there *is* a shortcut. One that many writers, including yours truly, find helpful. I call it...

The Jealously Guarded "Instant Empathy" Secret Of The Most Successful "A-List" Copywriters In The World!

The first time I discovered this ingenious little trick was back when I was broke (again!) and still digging my way out of my fun little "living in my car" period late 2005/early 2006. I needed "now money" and took a gig with one of Agora's health affiliates. One that's out of business now. (I promise you, my copy had nothing to do with that.)

As part of my research packet, they included the most comprehensive market research information I've ever been provided. They included a customer profile of their top three customer avatars, including demographic info, psychographic info and – here's where the magic started to happen for me – a photo representation of each avatar. Sure, it included stuff like "The 'empty nester Boomer' customer is a Caucasian woman, age 55, living in the Midwest." Typical demographic stuff. But the mental picture in my nutty noodle really started to get clear when they included stuff like this:

Her name is Theresa and since her oldest daughter had her first child this year, she enjoys taking care of her new granddaughter three times a week. When she's not doing that, one of her biggest pleasures is working in her garden. She has developed quite a green thumb for raising roses. Although some days when she's working in the garden, she worries about her husband's recent heart problems... and often worries how she would take care of herself should her husband, Bill, get too sick to work or have a heart attack.

I'm tellin' ya, they really went deep describing the lives of these customers, including all the emotions they experience. I don't know if they hired a marketing firm to do this or had it done in house. Either way, it was brilliant. Because it prompted me to start imagining this person's life in my kooky cranium, as if she were a real, living, breathing human being. And that, my dear reader, is when your copy can start to come alive. Because now, you're vibrating at a different frequency. A *higher* frequency. (528 Hz is *my* goal.) And when you reach that state, your copy is imbued with a different energy. A "heightened" energy. In terms of connecting with your prospect on an emotional level, this "enhanced copy" is so far superior to the "swipe," crank-it-out, phone-it-in copy LMCs produce...

It's Like Comparing A Model T Ford To A Brand Spankin' New Magnum Red Ferrari!

When you create copy like that, the response increases exponentially. Conversions, average unit of sale, stick rate in continuity, lifetime customer value... EVERYTHING gets better. And gets better in a *monumental* way.

The woo-woo rantings of a marketing madman? Most LMMs and many "B-list and below" copywriters probably think so. However, if you ever get the opportunity to work with a top-level A-list copywriter... a true master... after a few Vesper martinis, he'll reveal that this one thang is *THE* secret. It's a quantum physics/energy thang. One the LMMs and LMCs don't understand.

When you invest the sweat equity to do this... the emotional energy... when you pour your very heart and *soul* into it... and you've nailed the right big idea... THIS is how you produce blockbuster breakthroughs that can bring you avarice beyond your wildest dreams. Even better than the money, you'll be given a glimpse into pure possibility... your true potential.

When you do whatever it takes to gain this ability, no longer is there any competition. You are "da man!" Or for the ladies, "da *whoa* man!" Because damn near NOBODY will risk it all and invest themselves with that level of intensity. You will be one among very, *very* few.

When you've mastered this skill... at this level... you now hold the keys to the kingdom. You have an ability that can make you financially free for life. And, should you choose, you'll have the power to make *others* financially free for life, too.

And that's better than a poke in the eye with a sharp stick, isn't it?

Chapter 8

How To Get More New Customers In The Next 33 Days Than You've Gotten In The Past YEAR!

Did that chapter title grab your attention?

I hope so. Because that's exactly what you're about to discover. And it gets even better. I'm going to show you how to do that in the most efficient, effective and *enlightened* way.

My way.

The JSTDT™ way.

How is JSTDT™ different than what LMMs (lesser mortal marketers) are doing online? First and foremost, a JSTDT™ marketer is a smart steward of his or her limited time on this planet. Because they've made the decision to stop wasting their time and money with the LEGION of freebie-seeking, cheap bastard, entitlement-attitude losers trolling the Internet.

In fact, with JSTDT™ we're gonna go out of our way to *repel* those people. That way we can skim the crème de la crème off the top immediately by only focusing on...

The Buyers!

Because that's the most efficient and effective way. Almost all the marketers who used to brag about their big opt-in lists are all broke. And many are even out of business. Even many well-known gurus with opt-in lists of 100,000 or more. One I personally know had 1.4 MILLION people on his opt-in list. He can't even pay his bills now. I wish I could tell you this was the exception... but there are more Internet marketers in this position than you think. Including many I *still* see bragging (lying) about how well they're doing.

That's why the few remaining smart online marketers have abandoned that old model. Because really, when you boil it all down, it's all about sales, isn't it? Sales will cure all that ails ya. You can yap all you want about how great your business plan is... how high your conversion is to your freebie giveaways... and how big your opt-in list is. You can fool yourself by making up your own opinions about the value of all that stuff. But you can't make up your own facts. And the most important fact I wanna know is this:

Is what you're currently doing producing sales in the most efficient and effective way possible? And does it produce those results consistently, predictably and reliably?

Because JSTDT™ does.

Now, if possible, I'd like you to take this JSTDT™ "only target buyers" formula and put it on steroids. I'd prefer you focus only on *affluent* buyers. Because thanks to John Maynard Keynes and your globalist leaders, if things continue as they currently are, the affluent market might be the only market you have left. (The middle class is going the way of the dinosaur. But that's a topic for another time.)

If you've been following the old model – the "piss away your time and money building an opt-in list of freebie seekers, 99 percent of which will probably never spend any money with you" model – then JSTDT™ is gonna require a shift.

First, a mindset shift. (*There he goes with that mindset stuff again.*)

Second, a media shift. Because it's likely the media you're currently using to generate opt-ins... or have used in the past... isn't gonna get your offer in front of the right eyeballs.

You see, JSTDT™ isn't just a sales copy thang. Yes, you need strong JSTDT™ copy. But it doesn't matter how great your copy is if it's not in front of the right eyeballs. So to reiterate ('cuz I used to work at The Department of Redundancy Department), step one is mindset shift. And step two is a...

Media Shift!

Right off the bat, that probably eliminates almost every online marketer's pet media, Google Adwords and Facebook pay per click (PPC) advertising. I say "almost" because there *is* a work-around that can allow you to use them with JSTDT™. (Which I'll have to cover another day.) But, for a plethora of reasons, that's not where we're going to start your JSTDT™ funnel.

<u>IMPORTANT AND RELEVANT SIDETRACK</u>: Google isn't run by dummies. They know which side their bread is buttered. That's why they've made it supremely difficult, if not almost impossible, for their platform to work for "bootstrap" direct marketers. They want to repel those advertisers in favor of the big brand advertisers. Because there's exponentially more advertising money there for Google. Even better, the big brand advertisers don't track results. They're the perfect sugar daddy clients. And you, the kitchen table entrepreneur with a bootstrap budget? You're just an annoying little gnat buzzing around and sucking up valuable resources. Their sole goal is to whack you DRT (dead right there) with a fly swatter.

Zuckerberg and crew aren't exactly dummies either. They're following Google's lead. Heck, as it stands now, you'll get the rug pulled out from under you almost *daily* with Facebook ads. You can spend weeks or months testing your ad until the numbers are working perfectly for you. Then almost to the day, your ad will be shut down for some new compliance rule they came up with that very morning. Or worse, your entire account will be shut down forever.

If your business is entirely dependent on Facebook advertising, mark my words, you'll soon be out of business. And don't even get me *STARTED* on the Facebook prospect quality issue. When you're targeting people whose sole reason for being there is to look at pictures of cats and see how fat their exes have gotten, well, that's not the ideal JSTDT™ prospect.

Onward.

So for new customer acquisition, we're going to do something different. Something much more efficient and effective. We're going to repel the legion of freebie-seeking cheap bastards who proliferate the Internet and attract our best beloved buyers with...

Online Media Buys!

Why are the smartest marketers I know (including yours truly) investing their time and money in online media buys? There are three reasons:

1. **It's "slap proof."** Those who lived through Google Slap 1.0 and 2.0 can totally appreciate this. And God knows how many more iterations of "Facebook Slap" we'll soon see.

2. **Compared to pay per click (PPC) there's a HUGE inventory available.** There's probably at least 20 times more inventory available through display ads than PPC. That means once you get something working, there's a ton of inventory available to scale your business SUPER fast.

3. **Higher barrier to entry.** It lowers your competition by discouraging and deterring the dreamers, dummies and dunces. Because it takes more strategic thinking, planning and marketing savvy than most LMMs are willing to invest.

One quickie thang: My eternal gratitude and a big ole Doberman Dan hug go out to two knights in my *Marketing Camelot* for helping me navigate the minefield of this media buying stuff... Sir Allen of Baler and Sir Steve of Gray. Both of them have used and continue to use the secrets I'm sharing in this chapter to transform "bootstrap" businesses into eight-figure monsters. Both of these knights now have businesses that are the 800 lb. gorillas in their respective markets. (The *Marketing Camelot* is a community of renegade entrepreneurs, marketers and copywriters who get access to my brilliant but slightly batty brain on a regular basis. Each month they receive my knights-only newsletter, *The Doberman Dan Letter...* ongoing access to video and audio content from yours truly on a secret membership site... and "live" access to me on a monthly webinar. Many of my knights are experiencing exponential income increases as a result. All the details are available at MarketingCamelot. com.)

Since one of the tenets of JSTDT™ is putting your offer in front of the right eyeballs, it's crucial to look at the traffic source first, rather than starting with your product or offer. Because when it comes to media buying, what matters most is knowing what kind of people are visiting the site where your banners are going to run. So the key question to ask yourself isn't "How can I sell my product?" The key question to making this genius JSTDT™ thang work for you is...

"Where Are The People Who Buy Products Like Mine?"

Most people will be looking at buying media for an existing product or business. But here's something to keep in mind. This goes back to the "ole skool" days of what I used to do with the SRDS (Standard Rate and Data Service) when I wanted to find a hot new product or business idea.

If you find a great traffic source and the demographics and psychographics match a certain buying behavior different from your product... there's nothing to prevent you from creating that product. Or having it created for you. Just like us ole skool direct mail entrepreneurs used to do back in the day with the SRDS. (The smart ones, of which there are few, *still* do it.)

That, my treasured troubadour, has been the formula for *all* of the businesses I've birthed:

1. Find the market...

2. Find out what they're buying...

3. **Find out *how* they're buying...**

4. *Then* **develop the product based on points one through three.**

If you want to create the grand slam home run winners that make the big bucks, it's *all* about the market.

Most LMMs take the exact opposite approach. They have a product and then they look to find people who will buy it. Not too smart. However, I'm assuming since you're one of *my* brilliant, brainy and beguiling believers, YOU have already done the research. And you've confirmed that there *is* a market for what you have to sell. Now we're simply looking for the crème de la crème buyers of similar products – and I emphasize BUYERS – and where they congregate.

Onward.

Another important reason for learning media buying is this: you can easily, expeditiously and effortlessly...

"Reverse Engineer" Your Competition!

You'll discover all the smart things they're doing and the not-so-smart things. Then you can "borrow" the smart things for your advertising and improve, or eliminate, the not-so-smart things.

There are a couple of tools for doing this. I learned about them from Sir Allen of Baler, a master media buyer. The first is a free web browser plug-in called Ghostery at **www.ghostery.com**. Here's what it does: when you're on a website, it shows you the advertising pixels (code) and the networks running advertising on that site.

Here's why that's useful and potentially profitable:

Let's say you've researched a website and you're interested in testing a display ad there. You *could* contact them directly to work out a deal. (More about that in a minute.) But it might be faster and easier to start with a self-serve network like Sitescout.com. You can open an account, put up the grand total of 50 to 100 bucks and start buying traffic from that site darn near immediately.

Pretty cool, huh?

The second tool is one called *What Runs Where*, which you can find at **WhatRunsWhere.com**. It ain't exactly cheap. It's over $2000 a year. But it gives you such a competitive advantage, it's more than worth it.

Here's what it does:

WhatRunsWhere.com shows you everywhere your competition is advertising online. It shows you their banners and it shows how long their banners have been running. That's important because if a certain banner has been running for a long time, that's a darn good clue that it's successful.

And why is that important? Because you can use this information as inspiration. Then you can design a banner that's similar. Or better.

But that's not all. Since you'll know exactly where those successful banners are running, you can place your ads on all your competitors' best performing sites.

In addition to searching on WhatRunsWhere.com by product or company, you can also search by publisher (website). It will show you all the different advertisers and banner ads running on that particular site. This can be helpful when you've found a site you want to advertise on, and you need to get a sense of the offers and banner ads that work well with their audience.

Listen, this thang is so damn good, I often wonder if the commies (your gummint) will soon make it illegal. Like they have with everything else. We'll soon see.

So that's <u>WhatRunsWhere.com</u>. Not cheap... but they have a three-day trial. So if you want it check it out, you can do that for free.

Once you've done your competitive research, the next step is...

Formulate Your Creative Strategy!

That means you need some banner ads.

Eye grabbing, attention arresting, impossible-to-ignore banner ads are super important. Because unlike Google FraudWords and Flakebook PPC, you're buying media on a flat rate CPM (cost per thousand) basis. If your banner ads suck, you'll get thousands of views and little to no clicks. And that means you'll burn through all your advertising dollars with nothing to show for it. (Except the experience of finding out what doesn't work. Which is HIGHLY valuable, by the way.)

But... if you can create ads that produce high click-throughs, you're gonna be happier than a pig wallowing in a big ole steaming pile o' doody.

Listen, a complete rundown of how to create banner ads that produce lots of clicks would take an entire frickin' seminar. So let me just summarize the steps:

1. **Focus on just one size initially.** Media buying rock stars like Allen Baler and Steve Gray usually start with 300x250... so follow their lead.

2. **Develop at least five radically different concepts.** At this point, don't screw around with "Gee, I wonder if this shade of chartreuse is better." Test things that scream, not whisper.

3. **Run traffic to find the concept winner.**

4. **Create at least five different "incremental improvement" versions of the concept winner.**

5. **Run traffic to find the incremental improvement winner.**

6. **Create all banner size versions of your incremental improvement winner.**

7. **Roll out and scale up.**

8. **Translate to foreign languages and expand to non-English speaking countries.** (Well, actually, only the ones where the people are spending money on stuff like yours.)

Wow! You're getting some good stuff in this chapter, huh? Way more than you deserve. But that's just the kind of guy I am. Now I gotta move on and show you...

How To "Pay To Play" Like The Big Boys!

I'm talking about ad placements. And it's pretty straightforward. Simply start with the sites and networks you found during your competitive research stage with WhatRunsWhere and Ghostery. Then use tools like Quantcast, Alexa.com and Google Display Planner to get an idea about each site's demographics. And also which sites are their referring sites. (That's called "clickstream.")

Here's a brief list of traffic sources you can start with. Again, my thanks to Allen Baler and Steve Gray for these:

- AdMarketplace.com

- AdBlade.com

- Sitescout.com

- Advertising.com

- Newsmax.com

- Arcamax.om

Sounds simple enough, right? Good. Now let me share my favorite traffic source. It's the one I recommend you start with because it's what Allen Baler suggested I start with...

Direct Site Buys!

This is the "bootstrap" method of getting into media buying. And it could turn into a cash cow for ya. Because you just might find that these are the buys that give you the highest return on investment.

Here's how it works:

Instead of going through a network to place your banner ad, you negotiate directly with the Webmaster or website owner. Another thing I like is you can get maximum control about where your ad runs, how long it runs or anything else you can negotiate. Plus you can do these ad buys on a shoestring budget. That's not always the case with the networks.

Here's a quick tip that will allow you to place a lot of ads: If possible, make the initial contact with a FedEx or snail mail letter. And do it with a little "theater" like I've so graciously showed my knights many times in *The Doberman Dan Letter*. Then follow up by phone. Email should be your last resort. 'Cuz if you only use email you're only gonna close a single digit fraction of the deals you *could* be closing. Yeah, it's grunt work. But it could be highly profitable grunt work.

Yes, eventually you could train someone to do this for you. But in the beginning you'll probably have to do it yourself. However, I know people who have negotiated direct buys like this that have turned out to be as "set it and forget it" as can be. The CPA (cost per acquisition) stayed so crazy low, they were able to run their ads for months. In some cases, even years.

Here's a template letter you can use:

Dear Firstname,

You don't know me from Adam. However, I think you're going to be THRILLED you met me. Because... **I want to give you money for doing NOTHING!**

And the crisp new dollar bill I've attached to this letter is just the beginning. I want to give you a LOT more money. (How many times in your life have complete strangers contacted you out of nowhere offering THAT?)

Here's what it's all about: I'm the publisher of a product for men called *How To Get Your Wife To Pork You Again... Without Her Putting a Bag Over Your Head!*

So far, I've sold over one thousand copies. And the feedback from our customers has been 99 percent fantastic. (Only one guy named Dan Kennedy posted a negative review. Apparently there was nothing he could do to get it to work. But that's really about him, not our product.)

Our product has sold well from ads we've placed on Newsmax. com, DrudgeReport.com and FoxNews.com. (It appears that there are a lot of grouchy old conservative guys having trouble getting their wives to pork them.)

Anyhoo, based on what I know about your butt-ugly audience, I think it will do well on your site, too. Would you please send me advertising info and rates for your site, including traffic stats? Our best performing banner ad unit has been a 350x250 banner.

I'll touch base by phone in a few days to see if you have any questions.

Sincerely,

Richard Cranium

Direct site buys sound good, right? But there are a couple downsides. Obviously, it requires your time to do it. And there can be a lot of back and forth and missed connections when reaching out to these site owners. So it's not necessarily a very scalable traffic source in some cases. Or who knows. If there are enough smaller sites that cater to your market... and you train someone to do the grunt work for you... this could be a great ongoing strategy.

Look, I know all the online media buying stuff I shared might look a little overwhelming. I've tried to cram decades of online media buying knowledge into only one chapter. So let me keep it simple. When it's all said and done...

It's All About The Math!

It's a hit and miss process to accomplish one thang: find placements, creatives and offers that maximize your EPC (earnings per click) and CPA (cost per acquisition). It probably ain't gonna be an overnight success. However, once you get this doohickey dialed in and working like a finely tuned Swiss watch, it could bring in enough customers to make you so frickin' rich, you buy a new yacht every time the old one gets wet.

Chapter 9

How To Create Rivers of Revenue

Plant your booty in a comfy chair, grab your favorite beverage and let your Uncle DD tell you a titillating tale. (My tale will be *much* more titillating if your choice of beverage is an adult libation.)

Ahem...

Once upon a time, there was a man named King Gillette.

(Notice how I used a drop cap and old-timey font just like in a real storybook? Just having a little fun. You should see the bizarre and crude stuff I write to amuse myself that never gets published.)

Gillette was known as an eccentric fellow... but by all accounts, there was nothing really special about him.

Nobody expected much more from him than they expected from the millions of other human beings inhabiting the earth at that time. They would be born, consume, produce a new generation of little do-nothing consumers and die. Without ever improving this world one teeny-tiny iota. Most were expected to live their entire lives without leaving even the most *minuscule* mark upon humanity. Sadly, the exact same as we expect from most people today.

But... none of that prevented King Gillette from becoming a HUGE success... albeit rather late in life.

A bit of back-story on our protagonist:

Gillette was a traveling salesman for the Crown Cork & Seal Company, which marketed the first major disposable product in America...

Bottle Caps!

Yeah, these handlebar mustache-wearing old timey dudes were making a frickin' *fortune* on mundane ole disposable bottle caps.

But I digest. (And I temporarily broke the Alistair Cooke-type character I was trying to emulate while waggishly weaving this whopper of an anecdote.)

[PREGNANT PAUSE]

Unlike the rest of his colleagues at Crown Cork & Seal, Gillette had a dream. (It all starts with a dream, doesn't it?) He wanted to be much more than just a traveling salesman. Day in and day out, he vividly visualized himself a victoriously wealthy man with his own business empire.

But unlike most people who dream of a better life, Gillette actually *did* something about it. He saw the success his employer was enjoying selling disposable bottle caps and he wondered how he could model their success in a business of his own. But he was clueless about exactly how to do that to build a successful business for himself and his posterity.

After racking his brain for weeks without success, Gillette decided to use his own version of what I shared with you in Chapter 6. Instead of rooting through a massive swipe file, he painstakingly pored over the dictionary, word by word, looking for an idea... *any* idea. A spark of inspiration for something he could invent, make or publish... and sell over and over again to his customers. Just like Crown Cork & Seal was doing with their disposable bottle caps.

Gillette had not gotten very far with his "synthesizing" search when an idea hit him on the chin... literally. He was shaving one morning with one of those straight razors all the barbershops of the time used. The blade had become dull, so he had to go out and get it sharpened. That's when his breakthrough came...

A New And Safer Way To Shave!

In his own words...

I saw it all in a moment... the way the blade could be held in a holder. Then came the idea of sharpening the two opposite edges of a thin piece of steel, thus doubling its service, and then came the clamping plates for the blades, with a handle centered between the edges. I stood there in a trance of joy.

Gillette went to work developing a safety razor with disposable blades. That way he would only have to get a customer once. Then he could continue to sell them replacement blades over and over... for years and years.

What he didn't anticipate were the challenges that followed. You see, ideas are a dime a dozen. A great idea and $500 will buy you a small cup of coffee at Starbucks. The REAL value is in the *implementation* of a great idea.

The implementation part is where Gillette ran into his first roadblock. He knew practically nothing about creating a mechanical product. And even less about working with steel. With materials and tools bought in a Boston hardware store he cobbled together a crude model.

Was Gillette heralded as a brilliant inventor and future business mogul who would establish an empire that would prosper for the next 118-plus years?

Ummm... not quite.

He was criticized, ridiculed and laughed at. Even by the people you would most likely expect to support him, his "friends" and family. (If you've ever attempted to stick your head above the crowd, this probably sounds familiar.)

King Gillette

"The razor was looked upon as a joke by all my friends."

King Gillette - Founder of The Gillette Company

Who's laughing now?

From 1895 to 1900, Gillette couldn't get any technical advice from experienced craftsmen to improve his invention. Instead, they preferred to criticize and dismiss him as a weirdo. And instead of financial assistance from the potential investors he approached, all he ever got was discouragement and criticism.

For five long years the only "help" Gillette had was his own persistence and unwavering faith. Five l-o-n-g years of continuous ridicule and rejection. And I imagine what appeared to him as darn near zero progress.

But he persisted in spite of everything.

Then, as often happens when one has a single-minded stubborn determination to succeed no matter the obstacles, Gillette finally got a break. Two businessmen introduced him to William E. Nickerson, a graduate of the Massachusetts Institute of Technology. Nickerson saw the potential of this new-fangled safety razor and perfected the device for Gillette. A company was formed the next year and stock was issued to raise money.

Investors were skeptical at first, but a PWM (player with money) caught the vision and gave Gillette the seed capital he needed. Finally, after eight painfully long years of rejection and disappointment, in 1903 the company started production in a tiny, dingy, dark room in Boston. American men soon began to respond to the safety, time-saving and money-saving themes in Gillette's early ads.

An interesting little sidetrack: Have you ever noticed that many of the old-timey ads used direct response style copy? Like this one:

And this one:

Back to our titillating tale: (I really like saying "titillating.")

In 1904, Gillette sales totaled 90,844 razors and 123,648 blades. The following year, four times as many razors were sold and 10 times as many blades. By 1917 the company was selling more than one million razors a year and 120 million blades. Not bad for an eccentric guy with an idea laughed at by all the business "experts" of the day, huh?

A true entrepreneur, King C. Gillette was always looking for innovative marketing ideas to get his safety razor into the hands of more and more customers. The advent of World War II and the huge influx of new army recruits turned out to be one of Gillette's biggest marketing breakthroughs. He came up with the idea of "gifting" one of his safety razors to every man entering the armed forces. You see, Gillette knew he could take a loss on the razor because he would make it all back (and more) with the ongoing sales of the blades. His marketing team improved on this idea and instead of *giving away* the razors and taking a loss on the front end, they sold the government 4.8 million razors at cost and let Uncle Sam present them to the new military recruits. Imagine the continuity income guaranteed to Gillette from acquiring...

5 Million New Customers... Practically Overnight!

The best part? Gillette's blades were the only ones that fit his proprietary safety razor, guaranteeing *years* of ongoing income.

After the war, the millions of soldiers introduced to the new habit of self-shaving continued this practice after returning to civilian life, providing King Gillette with tens of millions in continuity income.

In the process of building his business empire, Gillette had become a master of marketing. While most businessmen only focused on one-shot sales – much like business people of today – Gillette was one of the few businessmen who understood lifetime customer value. He understood the back-end is where the money is *really* made.

In fact, just before the patents on his safety razor were about to expire in 1921, Gillette thwarted a flood of imitations by lowering the minimum price of his razor from $5 to $1. You see, Gillette's experience proved it wasn't important to make a profit on the razors. He could even afford to "go negative." He knew almost all of his income came from the sale of the blades.

Today the Gillette Company manufactures 10 million razors a year. And God knows how many replacement blades they sell every year. The back-end potential simply boggles the mind, doesn't it?

Have you picked up on the point I'm trying to drive home with my titillating tale? (I can't seem to stop saying that word.) You don't make money *getting* a customer...

You Make Most – Or In Many Cases 100 Percent – Of Your Profits Selling To An *Existing* Customer!

So if you focus most of your time and money on just getting new customers, you're stepping over dollars to pick up pennies. And you're missing out on a literal *fortune*. Amazingly, every business I've been hired to work with hasn't been working their back-end enough to make maximum income from their customer base. Not a single one.

We'll talk about how to correct that problem in just a minute. But before we get into that (and it could make you *obscenely* wealthy), let's talk about another HUGE mistake I see most business owners making. And it's preventing them from getting rich.

Mistake No. 1

Believing Good Marketing Can Overcome Bad Math

A *fatal* mistake I see a lot of business owners making. Even people who should know better.

Can we talk like rational adults for a minute? The 1 percent (or less) who can think logically and ignore that annoying "bullshit fairy" who, since you were born, has been filling your cranium with lies like...

- Santa Claus, the Easter Bunny and the Tooth Fairy are real living entities...

- There really *is* such a thing as a free lunch...

- You can think yourself rich... while sitting on your ass in front of the idiot box drinking beer and eating pizza. (If only!)

- The world really *does* owe you a living... *and...*

- That charismatic and likable sociopath with perfect teeth, Armani suit and teleprompter is going to make sure you get everything the world owes you.

Are you one of the precious few who have decided to pull back the curtain and face the truth, no matter how painful it may be? Even if it means turning your back on a lifetime of conditioning? Great! Then you're one of the infinitesimal number of human beings intelligent enough to evaluate FACTS (not beliefs backed by zero evidence) and realize the following unequivocal truth:

No matter how much you're in love with your product...

No matter how "good" of a human being you think you are...

No matter how much favor you think you've gained with your supreme being of choice because of your faith or works...

No matter how much you think the world desperately "needs" what you have to offer...

And *especially* no matter how much of a rock star marketer or copywriter you believe you are...

2 + 2 Will Never... Ever... EVER... Equal 5!

Amazing I have to explain this to adults, isn't it?

You'd probably be surprised at how *often* I have to explain it. You'd be even *more* surprised if you knew the famous people (well, famous in *our* little world) I've had to explain this to. Recently, that includes a *literal* household name who, in the past, had built a $100 MILLION business. For some reason, he seemed to believe his past success could overcome bad math in the new venture he's trying (unsuccessfully) to get off the ground.

What am I ranting about?

You Can't Build A Business Based On Bad Economics!

For a direct response business (online businesses are direct response businesses - duh!), you need a *minimum* five-to-one mark-up. In other words, your selling price should be at *least* five times your product fulfillment cost. For our purposes, "fulfillment cost" is your product manufacturing expense plus whatever other costs are involved in getting your product into the hands of your customer.

Five-to-one is the absolute minimum. Eight-to-one is *my* preferable minimum. Ideally, if you want to grow your business as quickly as possible... and as big as possible... you should have a 10-to-one mark-up. Or even more.

These aren't just random numbers I dreamed up in my demented cranium. There's a very important reason for all this. You see, anything less than five-to-one and you're going to have a tough row to hoe. In fact, you may not even have a *real* business. Instead, you'll have a revolving cash machine. What's a "revolving cash machine?" It's when you see the cash come in... then watch as it all (and possibly more) goes out just as fast (or faster) than it came in.

Want to siphon off a little bit for yourself? Good luck with *that*. You'll have to decide which expense you'll cut to generate a teeny-weeny slice of profit. While this allows you to take a few bucks out of your revolving cash machine for yourself, inevitably it contributes to a downward trend that lowers your incoming cash flow. Which makes it even harder to keep your "ruse" of a business going.

Anything less than the minimum mark-ups we've been talking about is going to severely limit what you can afford to pay to acquire customers, therefore significantly suppressing business growth. Or... it will slowly and painfully kill your entire business over time.

An example? Alrighty. Let's say you sell your "thang" for $100... whatever that thang may be. (For all the anal-retentive spelling nazis, I *meant* to spell it that way.) That means your fulfillment costs can't be a penny more than $20. Ideally, your fulfillment costs on a $100 product should be $10 or less. That's one of the many reasons I like info products and services. A 10-times mark-up is chump change; 100 times, 1,000 times... or even a 10,000-times mark-up is quite common.

Ignore my advice at your own peril. Many a brilliant marketer with a huge marketing budget – and even multiple millions in venture capital – has gone bust arrogantly believing they could be the first person in the history of the world to overcome faulty arithmetic.

Mistake No. 2

Failing To Create "Rivers Of Revenue" From Your Customer Base

This is the entire point of the tale I just shared. (Which I *hope* you found titillating.) This is what you want to set up with some (or all) of your products and services... endless "rivers of revenue" (ROR).

King Gillette created one of history's greatest marketing models because he set up endless rivers of revenue. Mobile phone companies use the same strategy. They sell you a cell phone at or below their cost. In some cases, they can afford to *give* it to you because they make money on every phone call. Many times for years and years. Believe you me, they know almost to the *day* how long they keep a customer on average. And based on that information, they know exactly how much they can afford to spend to...

"Buy" A Customer!

That's really all you're doing with your advertising and marketing, isn't it? The better your mark-ups, and the better you know your back-end numbers, the more customers you can afford to buy. And the guy or gal who can afford to buy a lot of customers – as quickly as possible – is the person who will dominate their market. Everybody else is left to fend for the scraps.

Speaking of great back-ends... (no, not Kim Kardashian you pervert)... how about the Apple iPod? Sure, it's a great piece of technology... but its *real* "raison d'être" is to sell you songs for 99 cents apiece through the iTunes music store. *That* is how they really make money. They've already sold over 15 BILLION songs at 99 cents a pop!

Another "King" of marketing, Bob King, formerly the rainmaker marketing guy at Phillips Publishing (a wildly successful newsletter publisher), used to tell all his hired gun copywriters...

"We're not in the newsletter business... we're in the *renewal* business!"

Very sharp guy, Bob King. He understood that when you build long-term relationships with your customers instead of "wham, bam, thank you ma'am" one-night stands, you don't have to reinvent your marketing wheel every year. You can begin each year secure in the knowledge that a big portion of your income is already locked in for the year. Because the lion's share of your customers keep coming back to buy more.

Another big benefit of my rivers of revenue (ROR) strategy? Your cost of acquiring a customer gets amortized over many years worth of purchases, driving your average cost per sale way, way down.

My beat-a-dead-horse point is this:

Don't think in terms of just one-shot opportunities to make money. A one-shot sale or just one successful front-end promotion is *not* a business. It's a moneymaking opportunity. And there's a *BIG* difference between business builders and opportunity seekers. Business builders make money long term. Opportunity seekers are always running in circles, jumping from one fad to the next. (Remember all the poor suckers who jumped on the Google AdSense bandwagon?)

A better way to think is this:

How can I leverage a one-time transaction into a permanent and self-renewing river of revenue (ROR) from each and every customer? This kind of thinking will make an enormous difference in the wealth you acquire over the life of your business. *And...* it just may establish...

An Uber-Successful Empire That Lasts Your Entire Lifetime, Your Childrens' Lifetimes... And... Your Children's Childrens' Lifetimes!

Just like King Gillette.

Alrighty, I've talked about *why* you should create RORs. Now let's talk about *how*.

In January of 2012, one of my *Gold Mastermind* members started a biz on his kitchen table with nothing but his brain and a laptop. And his wife's *superior* brain. He's now getting more than 500 new customers a day at a $65 average unit of sale. He has ZERO fulfillment costs if a customer chooses the digital delivery option. If they choose the hard copy version, he only has a few bucks in fulfillment costs. Multiply 500 new customers a day bringing in $65 each on the front-end by 30 days. You do the math. It may have *started* as a kitchen table business but it ain't no small "pertaters" now.

With my help we've started to work on improving his back-end income. With a front end like *that*, he's going to make *CRAZY* quantities of cashola once we start maximizing his back-end. One of the options we've been exploring is developing an ROR like I've been rambling about in this chapter. Let's explore a worst-case scenario and see how that might affect his bottom line:

500 new customers per day x 30 days per month =

15,000 New Customers A Month!

Now let's say the conversion into his ROR (continuity program) is absolutely horrid. We only get 2 percent of those new customers each month to sign up for continuity.

15,000 x 2 percent = 300 customers per month in continuity.

Actually, with the strategy I have in mind, I expect we'll convert anywhere from 25 percent to 30 percent. He'd probably get more than 2 percent conversion into continuity even if all he did was put a one-line upsell on his check-out page. But we're playing with a worst-case scenario in this example, so we'll keep the conversion percentage ridiculously low.

Let's assume an average $30/month price point. I actually think we can get closer to $49... but we're being conservative in this example, remember?

**300 customers per month in continuity x $30 = $9,000
"river of revenue" business added each month.**

Don't be a marketing Pollyanna like I used to be and assume most of your customers will stay in your continuity program for years and years. Some will. Others will stay on for several months. And others will leave almost as fast as they came in.

So in this example, let's figure an average "stick rate" (retention) of three months. (Actually, with *my* stick program in place, I expect his retention will average at the very *least* five months.)

Let's play with these numbers and see what the next year could look like when this ROR starts to build exponentially:

Continuity Drop-Off Rate Calculator

Customers per Day	10	2% of 500
Customers per Month	300	"Worst-case" low price
Price per Month - 1	$30.00	
Price per Month - 2	$49.00	Possible higher price
Price 1 Drop-Off Rate	33.33%	
Price 2 Drop-Off Rate	33.33%	

This spreadsheet allows us to see the difference in potential income with two different price points, $30 and $49 in this example. I'm showing a 33.33 percent drop-off each month to arrive at our average retention of three months.

Check this out:

PRICE 1	Month 1	Month 2	Month 3	Month 4
New Customers	300	300	300	300
Total Customers	300	500	633	722
Monthly Revenue	$9,000.00	$15,000.30	$19,000.70	$21,667.77

This shows the cumulative total of customers in continuity and additional income for the first four months. Keep in mind, if my client bumps up his front-end acquisition numbers, he'll have a bump in continuity customers, too... even at this crappy 2 percent conversion.

Total Yearly Revenue	PRICE 1
3,600	NEW CUSTOMERS
893	YEAR END CUSTOMERS
$270,435.45	YEAR END REVENUES
9,015	TOTAL BILLING CYCLES
3	AVG BILLING

An extra $270k with a horrible conversion to continuity and a so-so stick rate. Since these are back-end sales, making most of this net profit, wouldn't it be worth doing to put an extra quarter million or so into your pocket? I'd say so.

Here's the first four months at the $49 price:

PRICE 2	Month 1	Month 2	Month 3	Month 4
New Customers	300	300	300	300
Total Customers	300	500	633	722
Monthly Revenue	$14,700.00	$24,500.49	$31,034.48	$35,390.69

And total yearly revenue at $49:

PRICE 2	
3,600	NEW CUSTOMERS
893	YEAR END CUSTOMERS
$441,711.24	YEAR END REVENUES PRICE 2
9,015	TOTAL BILLING CYCLES
3	AVG BILLING

Things are starting to heat up a bit, aren't they? Now let's leave the price points and stick rate the same but bump up the conversion to the low end of what I think we can *really* get... 25 percent:

PRICE 1	Month 1	Month 2	Month 3	Month 4
New Customers	3750	3750	3750	3750
Total Customers	3750	6250	7917	9028
Monthly Revenue	$112,500.00	$187,503.75	$237,508.75	$270,847.08

Let's look at the end of year one with a 25 percent conversion:

Total Yearly Revenue	PRICE 1
45,000	NEW CUSTOMERS
11,164	YEAR END CUSTOMERS
$3,380,443.15	YEAR END REVENUES
112,681	TOTAL BILLING CYCLES
3	AVG BILLING

	PRICE 2
45,000	NEW CUSTOMERS
11,164	YEAR END CUSTOMERS
$5,521,390.47	YEAR END REVENUES PRICE 2
112,681	TOTAL BILLING CYCLES
3	AVG BILLING

Now let's keep everything the same as the previous example but bump the stick rate one additional month:

With 4-month average stick rate	
Total Yearly Revenue	PRICE 1
45,000	BIG difference! NEW CUSTOMERS
14,525	YEAR END CUSTOMERS
$4,092,763.08	YEAR END REVENUES
136,425	TOTAL BILLING CYCLES
3	AVG BILLING

4-month average stick rate		
	PRICE 2	
45,000	Looky here!	**NEW CUSTOMERS**
14,525		**YEAR END CUSTOMERS**
$6,684,846.36		**YEAR END REVENUES PRICE 2**
136,425		**TOTAL BILLING CYCLES**
3		**AVG BILLING**

If you'd make an extra seven figures when your continuity customers stick one additional month, what would you do? Would you send a couple direct mail pieces and maybe have somebody give 'em a quick phone call? Maybe bribe them with a free gift? You'd be stupid not to, wouldn't-cha?

What are we going to sell these folks every month? That's the easy part. Here's a short list: Monthly newsletter, CD, DVD, software, USB thumb drive with videos and audios, teleseminar, webinar, consulting, done-for-you services, a membership or membership website, nutritional supplements... heck, *anything* that eventually goes down the drain or toilet.

Listen, after more than two decades in direct response marketing, both online and offline, I've never seen it more difficult or more expensive to acquire a new customer. It's CRUCIAL you use ALL possible methods to maximize your profits from your back-end. Or soon, you may not even *be* in business.

That's why in the next chapter I'm going to give you some more "maximum money" secrets to boost your back-end. Use them and prosper. Ignore them and you're toast.

Now... one more for the road: *Titillating.* ☺

Chapter 10

Four Secrets
To Keep Customers for Life

The most reliable way for the little guy to get rich isn't the stock market or the lottery. It's developing a business with a customer base that keeps buying from you over and over again. While sifting and sorting for the 4 percent of your customer list who keep buying from you over and over again, at higher and higher prices.

The quickest way to go broke? Build a "revolving door" business where your customers go out just as fast as they come in.

Acquiring a customer and building a business these days is about as difficult and expensive as I've ever seen it. I truly believe those that don't get this concept... and continue to invest most of their time and marketing budget always chasing new customers... well, they probably won't last very long in this current economic climate.

But not you. Why? Because you've got *me* in your corner.

So let's *platicar* about how you can get your customers to stick around a lot longer... and spend more money with you, more frequently.

One important tip for doing that is simply adapt Robert Collier's admonition to copywriters. (If you haven't read *The Robert Collier Letter Book* you need to put that on your to-do list immediately.) Remember his oft-quoted advice? It was originally intended as a technique to write better sales copy. But you can also use it to keep customers for life, make maximum money from your customer base and build a rock-solid business that endures for decades...

"Enter The Conversation Already Taking Place In Your Customer's Mind!"

Here's what I mean. If you truly want to enter the conversation in your customer's cranium, you have to look at things from *his* point of view. Why in the world should he continue to do business with you? What reason have you given him to be loyal to you?

An email every week or so? Get real. *Everybody* does that. (So much so that it probably just annoys him.)

Low price? You can bet your sweet booty that isn't gonna keep him loyal. Amazon or Walmart will kick your butt in *that* department. Or the hungry (and stupid) start-up will under-cut you in a heartbeat. Scratch that one off your list, too.

So what *will* keep your customer loyal to you?

REVERSE Customer Loyalty!

What's that? you ask befuddled. I'm not talking about your customers being loyal to you. I'm talking about *you* being loyal to your customers. Combine loyalty with REAL heart-felt appreciation and sincerely trying to see the world through their eyes and you've got one powerful combination.

Sadly, I almost never see this in *any* business. The prevailing attitude seems to be "churn 'em and burn 'em." And believe me, Hoss, your customers can feel it.

And the problem is epidemic.

Think about it. Isn't every Internet marketing guru war story you've ever heard all about their "million dollar day?" Some variation of "look how I make money in my underwear by only pushing the send button." They never talk about what they did for these new customers *after* the sale... or how long the customers stuck around, do they? Nope. The stories only focus on what a clever marketing genius the guru is. They never shine the spotlight on the *true* star of the show... the customer.

Hey, everybody likes a good success story. It's instructional to hear how a crafty copywriter or marketer discovered a unique hook that tripled sales. But nobody ever shares the most important part of the story. How did the *customer* win?

That brings us back to my "see the world through your customer's eyes" admonition. If you really want to do that, treat him like *you* would want to be treated. Simple, right? Well, since you're smart and have decided to use this powerful "reverse customer loyalty" secret, my question to you is...

What Happens *After* The Sale?

Sadly, with most businesses, not much. Sure, entering them into an auto-responder series is better than nothing... but it sure ain't what it used to be. In fact, several of my clients this year have hired me to run a special crystal ball-like semi-clairvoyant analysis on their customer lists. What we discovered was quite shocking. (To the clients, not me.) **And you can make a FORTUNE if you understand this important discovery:** in every single analysis, we found that the most affluent customers... the ones who make the biggest purchases... and most *frequent* purchases... are also the biggest email opter-outers. In fact...

At Least 50 Percent Opt Out IMMEDIATELY After Getting The Email Receipt!

The remaining ones are usually long gone by follow-up email No. 1 or No. 2. (I fall into this "immediate opter-outer" category. As do most other affluent people I know.)

At last, for the love of all things good and holy, do you *FINALLY* understand why I keep brow beating you about incorporating offline methods to communicate with your customers? Geez, you can be thickheaded sometimes. I'm not just saying this stuff to listen to the sound of my own voice.

So knowing all this, my question again is, what happens after the sale? Or a better question, what *should* happen after the sale? Well, what would *you* like to happen if you just made your first purchase with a company you had never done business with before? Is getting a thank you email something unique and unexpected? Would you feel the business owner went the extra mile to make you feel special? Not likely. It's expected. And everybody does it. It has darn near zero impact.

Would you feel kinda special if you got an email from the owner a couple days after the sale, sincerely expressing his gratitude? Maybe giving you some advice on how to use, profit from or enjoy the product you recently purchased? Yeah, that's kinda unique... actual customer follow-up to make sure you're happy with your purchase. I don't see a lot of that going on. We could count that as a somewhat positive "touch." It gets us some brownie points in our new "romance." Well, at least with the customers who haven't opted out, deleted the email unread, or never even received it due to a plethora of possible email delivery problems.

We're headed in the right direction... but it's *still* not enough. You put your heart and soul into creating the sales copy... you invested money you *could* have put into your pocket... and you probably haven't even made a dime yet. In fact, you've probably gone negative. So any reasonably intelligent person can see it only makes sense to foster this new relationship so the customer doesn't fly out the revolving door just as fast as he came in.

BIG SECRET NO. 1 REVEALED:

One of the most important phases in the customer romance... and a highly effective secret to building customer loyalty is what you do in the first 90 days of the relationship. I like to call this...

The Honeymoon Phase!

Ignore them during this phase and I can pretty much *guarantee* you'll always have a revolving door business. So what are the most important and effective things we can do in our "reverse customer loyalty" program during the honeymoon phase? My experience has shown one of the most important "touches" is...

The Stick Letter!

And no, sending it via email won't work. It *must* be sent via good old-fashioned snail mail. Or FedEx if your numbers allow the extra expense. Whichever service you use, you need to send it in a creative way that makes it darn near impossible to ignore. (Issue No. 11 of *The Doberman Dan Letter* shows you how I've done this in a couple different niches. More info at MarketingCamelot.com.)

What else can we do during the honeymoon phase to make sure our customers stick around as long as possible? How about...

- Quick order fulfillment...

- Quick resolution of problems or customer service issues...

- Quick and friendly no-hassle refunds...

- Unadvertised after-the-sale bonuses...

- Offer new and useful products and services in creative ways...

- Give away carefully timed ethical "bribes" and bonus gifts. (We'll talk more about this in a sec. It could be the breakthrough you need to *radically* increase your lifetime customer value.)

- Contact them more often with great content and relevant offers. (Everybody *greatly* underestimates how often you should contact your customers.)

In other words, design your customer's experience so he's treated the way you *yourself* would like to be treated.

Interestingly, as I was writing this chapter, one of my trusted vendors, *McMannis Duplication & Fulfillment*, sent me a perfect example to show you. This falls under the categories I mentioned a minute ago:

- *Unadvertised after-the-sale bonuses...* and...

- *Give away carefully timed ethical 'bribes' and bonus gifts.*

Check out this bad boy...

Pretty cool, huh? The gold hammer is to whack away on this massive (9-inch by 12-inch) chunk of chocolate to break it into little pieces. I wanted to pick the whole damn thing up and gorge on this gastronomically gluttonous gratification... but the Colombiana "forbade" it, bless her heart. She made me settle for much smaller pieces than I would have preferred. Me likey me some choc-o-late!

Anyhoo... how do you think McMannis's customers reacted to this big-ass hunk of chocolate arriving completely unexpected? I already LOVE McMannis and wouldn't even *consider* taking my business elsewhere. After getting this unexpected gift, I'm a MORE ardent supporter and promoter of their services. And that has turned out quite profitable for them. When any of my clients or colleagues needs printing, mailing, duplication or fulfillment services, who do you think I'm going to *fanatically* endorse? Because their service and people completely R-O-C-K in the U-S-A, McMannis already had my loyalty. But stuff like this creates raving fans. Even ole DD learned an important "love your customer" lesson.

If you're not doing stuff like this, you oughtta whip it out right this very second (a notepad, dummy) and figure out how to start treating your customers like gold. Like McMannis does. It's not just the right thing to do, it's an absolute *necessity* if you want to stay in business and prosper in our new economy.

Another example: I have an inside joke with friends and family members about a couple words I invented, *kringlebomber* or *kringler*, for short. (Never mind what they mean. Just know if I ever call you that, it's a term of endearment.) I found this bakery at ohdanishbakery.com that ships a pastry called a "kringle." I've sent and received them as gifts from friends who are hip to my little inside joke. My sister sent one that arrived just last night. (She's a "First Class" kringlebomber.)

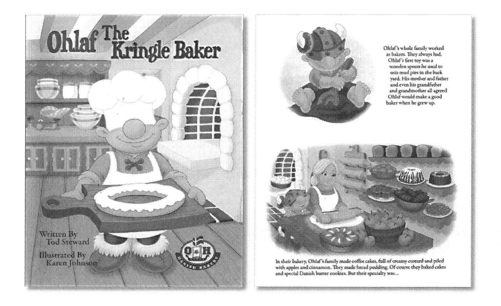

Now usually, they just send the kringle and a catalog. But this time I noticed a little extra surprise.

They included a full-color children's storybook. It elicited a "Cool!" response from me and a "Qué chévere!" response from the Colombiana. I believe that's the exact response the kringle bakers were hoping for. Of course, it doesn't hurt that their origin story is woven into the book... and their website is included on the back cover. I bet people with children will keep this thing around a while. Heck, it may even be on several thousand bookshelves as we speak.

Kind of a cool little unexpected gift to endear the kringlebombers to their customers, isn't it? It probably only adds a buck or two to fulfillment costs but pays off BIG time on the back end.

One last example of unexpected little surprises for your customers: I recently placed an order with www.3dmailresults.com for some $1 million dollar bills. I'm using them as "grabbers" for a sales letter. About three days after the $1 million dollar bills were delivered I got this in the mail:

Inside the card they included one of their $1 million dollar bills:

My mailing is only going out to a small but highly targeted list, so I think I spent $200 or less with www.3dmailresults.com. These guys have a big business, so I'm certainly not a priority customer. Yet the owner still took the time to send me a handwritten thank you. That made a big impact on me... because after more than two decades in the direct response business... and spending millions of dollars with various vendors... I can count on one hand the number of companies who have expressed their gratitude with a gesture like this.

Look, one of the most important and impactful "touches" you can make is a real honest-to-goodness handwritten card or letter. But if you're so slothful that you can't be bothered with sending a REAL hand-signed card, here are a couple options for a reasonable facsimile:

http://www.bluebirdcards.com

https://www.sendoutcards.com

Either of these options are 100 times better than email. But nothing has the same effect as a card or letter really and truly signed in your own hand.

BIG SECRET NO. 2 REVEALED: What are YOU including in your outgoing orders and sending to your customers after the sale to elicit a "Wow!" response and encourage back-end sales? You're leaving TONS of money on the table if you're not doing *something* like these examples.

And if you're not sending bounce-back offers in your outgoing packages, you're *really* missing the boat. (A bounce-back offer is a sales letter or promotion you send in the box with the customer's product.) After all, your customer is paying the mailing costs for you to send them a sales piece. You'd be a drooling, mouth-breathing moron to not take advantage of that, wouldn't-cha?

Alrighty then. Would you like another big secret to keeping your customers with you as long as possible? And spending more money with you month after month?

BIG SECRET NO. 3 REVEALED: Publish and mail...

A Monthly Newsletter!

Yes, it absolutely *must* be a good old-fashioned paper and ink newsletter sent via postal mail. *NOT* email, *NOT a* PDF delivered online, *NOT* a blog, *NOT* a membership site... *NONE* of that online stuff you want to do because you like to cut corners and pinch pennies. Believe me, if those methods worked I'd be doing them... 'cuz it's the lazy way. But I've tested ALL of the online delivery methods and not a single one even comes *close* to the ROI you'll get from a REAL honest-to-goodness, arrive-at-your-home-or-office, hold-it-in-your-grubby-little-hands newsletter.

What does a print newsletter do so well that nothing else can do?

It Builds A *Friendship!*

Customers, clients and patients come and go, easily swayed by competitors offering even the teeniest tiniest of discounts. But friends... people you regularly break bread with and spend time with sharing hopes and dreams... they stick around *much* longer than just a customer. You don't leave your friends, do ya?

Think about this: every month the knights in my Marketing Camelot invite me into their homes as a welcome guest and we have a personal conversation. (TOO personal if they read my newsletter in the bathroom.) They know details about my life even members of my own family don't know. Like...

- I cried on their shoulder after Donner, my Doberman, died.

- Their hearts pounded when they pictured me with a 12-gauge shotgun at the ready, about to smoke a big burly drugged intruder in my bedroom, intent on harming my family.

- They know I suffer daily with chronic pain. And they know that if the pain isn't keeping me from getting a decent night's sleep, the nightmares from the PTSD do a damn good job of it.

- They know I've made millions. And lost millions.

- They know I've been so broke I've actually had to live with my Doberman in a 10-year old piece o' crap Ford Taurus with no air conditioning.

The Colombiana is a very private person and she constantly busts my chops about revealing stuff she thinks should be kept private. But I share it for a reason. I'm trying to create a friendship... and friends share intimate details of their lives.

I'd actually rather *not* share some of this stuff. Much of it is quite embarrassing to me. But experience has shown that sharing this stuff helps people. And very recently, one of the more embarrassing things I didn't really want to reveal helped save a life. Literally.

161

You see, people don't really buy products and services. They buy YOU. And a newsletter (if it's done right) is an intimate form of communication from you. That's one of the biggest secrets of its success. The only thing more intimate is a handwritten letter, phone call or in-person visit.

When subscribers (who I don't know from Adam) meet me in person, they treat me like an old friend they've known for years. *That* is the power of a print newsletter. I've not found anything that even comes *close* to replicating that effect. Pete Lillo, aka Pete The Printer, sums it up quite succinctly...

"If you don't have a newsletter, you don't have a business!"

If you truly value your customers and want to keep them long term, you'll send them a monthly print newsletter. 'Nuff said.

We've been talking about *reverse* customer loyalty. That means you being loyal to your customers, not just expecting customer loyalty because they bought something from you. That means you can't just forget about your customers and let them die on the vine if you haven't heard from them in a while. That's just plain dumb. You don't treat your friends like that, do you? (If you do, I doubt you have any friends.) You check in with them to make sure everything's OK, don't you? So let me reveal one of my most important, most profitable and ridiculously crazy high ROI reverse customer loyalty secrets. (I should have listed this as No. 1 because it's the lowest hanging fruit/most profitable thing you can possibly do in *any* business.)

BIG SECRET NO. 4 REVEALED: **Keep in touch consistently and persistently with your inactive customers.**

I have a client with a (now) rapidly growing business in the health market. Over the past 60 days I helped take them from $400,000/month and quickly dwindling... to $620,000/month. We fully expect to pick up another $30k to $40k before the end of this promotion. How did I do it? Well, we did a LOT of things. (That's another secret) But one of the *biggest* contributors to this rapid growth was simply going after the low-hanging fruit...the inactive customers. And we reactivated a LOT of them. We used "fusion marketing," a combination of multiple "touches," both online and offline. Each offline step was timed very carefully to augment and support the online steps. And vicey versey. It's a system I developed and perfected for my own businesses. Without fail, it always pays off BIG time. Here's a template example of one of the initial letters I use in my "colossal cash crescendo" customer reactivation system:

Dear <insert first name>,

As you can see, I've attached a <whatever grabber you use> to the top of this letter.

Why have I done this? Actually, there are two reasons:

1. What I have to share with you is vitally important for your health and happiness... and with all the junk we get in the mail nowadays, I needed a unique way to get your attention.

2. And... since what I have to share with you can <yadda yadda>, I thought the <grabber> was an appropriate eye-catcher.

Here's what it's all about:

Not very long ago you were a valued customer of mine. But for some reason I haven't heard from you. And that's been bothering me.

I keep wondering... did I do something to offend you? Did I goof something up with your order?

Have you gotten off track with your health and fitness goals? (It's OK. That's normal.) Were there some financial reasons you couldn't keep taking <product name>?

Truth is, I can only *guess* what happened... because I haven't heard from you.

Whatever happened, I want to make it right... IMMEDIATELY.

Here's what I'm going to do just for you:

The letter goes on to make two additional offers:

1. Some kind of no-strings-attached free gift they can get in the mail, email or by digital download...

2. And a "we want you back" offer with a special preferred customer discount and lots of premiums and bonuses.

In the case of my health client, they wanted to make this project difficult for me and reactivate inactive customers into a $100-plus/month continuity program. Kind of a big step to ask an inactive customer to take. But I was up to the challenge.

How did it go? Results are still coming in. And the final few steps in this multi-step system won't go out for another seven days. So I think we've only gotten 60 percent to 70 percent of all the results. But so far, without any sales from the remaining final steps, we've added an additional...

$60,000-Plus A Month In Continuity Income!

And this was money the client had been leaving on the table month after month... for *years*. Although my retainer and royalty initially shocked him, after this campaign, he thinks my fees are a screaming bargain. If I can get him to agree to just one more step (my super-duper secret get-'em-off-the-fence step), we should add at *least* another $20,000 a month in continuity income before the fat lady sings.

I'd be willing to bet that YOU are sitting on a nice windfall like this, too. Thar's gold in that there list of yours. You just gotta go git it.

Chapter 11

How To Boost Your Conversions...
As Quickly And Easily As Possible!

Let's dive right into some low-hanging fruit secrets to transform your sales messages and send your conversions through the roof, shall we?

The first secret I'll share is the one I always start with when I have to breathe new life into a piece of copy. And no, it's not the headline. Although that's not a *bad* place to start, it's not always the biggest "bang for your buck/fastest ROI" one. David Ogilvy said the headline is 80 percent of the ad, and he's right. But when I'm looking to increase the response from a piece of sales copy, I almost never start with the headline. Can you take a guess at where I start?

The Offer!

Nobody spends enough time on their offers. In many cases, it's nothing more than an afterthought hastily dreamed up after all the copy has been written.

Dumb, dumb, dumb.

I like to play a little game when I'm tasked with helping someone take their idea to market. I ask them to explain their offer to me in three minutes or less. Judging by the usual reaction, you'd think I'd just asked them to explain quantum physics. They stutter, look down at their feet and hem and haw. An occasional few are actually able to spit out a couple somewhat coherent sentences.

Look, if you can't explain your offer to me in three minutes or less... or even worse, you don't even understand it yourself... how do you expect anyone else to understand it? But most entrepreneurs and copywriters dive right in and start writing the copy before they've even defined their offer.

So that's step No. 1. Define your offer so you can explain it in three minutes or less.

A few do this. But they never do step No. 2. And that is... probe, presume, ponder, percolate, puzzle over, put-heads-together and powwow with sharp marketing minds to determine...

Does Anybody Actually *Want* What You're Offering?

You'd be surprised at how often the answer to that question is "no." But, in the slim chance the answer is yes, an equally important follow-up question is this: are there *enough* people who want it to actually justify starting a business? Sadly, I've spoken with entrepreneurs who have spent months or years of their life working on a project when the answer to those two questions was a resounding "negatory."

I gotta tell ya, it sucks being the dude who has to tell somebody to ATP (abandon the project.) But that's what I often have to do. I could make a *lot* more money if I just did what LMCs (lesser mortal copywriters) so negligently do... take the money and write the copy. But that's malpractice in my most humble (but accurate) opinion.

Crafting an irresistible offer is crucial. But in this case we're talking about a piece of copy that already exists, has a semi-OK offer and is already in the marketplace pulling in some results. We just need to do something quickly to bump up response. My initial go-to trick for upping conversions is...

Lower The Barrier To Entry!

Especially if the copy is a customer acquisition piece. When somebody who has never done business with me is reading my copy, I want to make it as easy as possible for him to say yes. And I do that by making the cost of entry seem as risk free as possible.

Here's how I did that recently with a supplement offer. The client was doing the typical supplement offer. They offered three options: a one-month supply, a three-month supply with a bit of a discount and a six-month supply with a bigger discount.

A brief but profitable sidetrack: Just about every time I offer three ordering options, a majority of customers take the middle one. So if you're doing the three-option thang, make sure the option you want to sell the most is positioned as the middle one.

Back to our offer. So this three-option deal isn't a *bad* offer. Everybody in the supplement space does it. And that's exactly why I wanted to change it. When a nice, conservative "me too" offer like this is showing signs of life but response is low, a way to greatly increase the response is to turn it into one the prospect will perceive as a no-brainer. And the way to quickly and easily do that is with the...

30-Day Hold!

I've heard that a million times before, dick weed. Tell me something I don't know.

You lovable imbecile. You have eyes, yet you do not see.

Look, I'd probably heard this 1,000 times before, too. But I never actually *did* it. And in spite of what you think, you really haven't "heard" it if you haven't done it. When I finally actually *did* hear it, I heard it loud and clear. That one idea that I ignored for darn near a decade took me from broke, in debt, homeless and living in my car (yeah, I am *not* kidding)... to making...

Six Figures A Month... In Only Four Months!

Do I have your attention now? You got yourself a big ole pair of ears a-flappin' in the wind... but are you finally ready to hear?

You are? Oh, goodie, goodie gumdrops!

Just in case this is new to you, allow me to briefly enlighten you on the 30-day hold. The 30-day hold is easy to implement. There is only one or two extra paragraphs of copy required, which I'll give you in just a minute. You sell the product just like you are currently with your existing copy. The only part that's different is this: when you present the price, you offer the customer the opportunity to get the product for just paying shipping and handling now. They won't be billed for 30 days. Within that 30-day period, if he's unhappy for any reason, he can simply call you and say, "Hey, don't bill me."

Some people make the customer jump through a few more hoops and tell them that they need to return the product prior to the 30 days. Probably not a bad idea. It dissuades the mooches and shysters.

That's it. Simple, huh?

Here's some sample 30-day hold copy:

> A 100 percent risk-free order of *Dump Away* is only $89.95... but you don't have to pay that today. Call now and you can try *Dump Away* by just covering a small shipping and processing fee. We'll immediately ship your order of *Dump Away* and you'll have a full 30 days to try it at absolutely ZERO risk!

At the end of the 30-day trial period, if you like *Dump Away* and want to continue using it, *only* at that time and not a moment sooner will you be billed the remaining balance.

If *Dump Away* isn't EVERYTHING I've promised... if you're not pooping with clock-like regularity... or if you're not satisfied for any reason at all, simply send back the remaining product (or even just the empty bottles) and you won't be billed one red cent. One hundred percent of the risk is on *my* shoulders, not yours.

Based on that generous no-risk, "pay only if you like it" offer, why not give it a try today?

I'm on a bunch of health mailing lists and have been getting a lot of poopalogs. (That's what I call magalogs selling digestive health products. The "log" part of that word amuses me, too. Further proof I've not mentally matured since age 13.) Anyhoo, I just read a bunch of poopalogs yesterday, so poop seems to be on my brain lately. (Not literally. Not that I know of at least.)

And since I'm such a salt-of-the-earth dude, here's some order form copy for ya, too:

Risk Free Trial Certificate

Yes! I want to experience all the feel-great health and energy boosting benefits of healthy regularity! Please rush my 100 percent RISK-FREE trial of *Dump Away*.

I understand I only invest a mere $7.77 today to cover shipping and processing. You will immediately ship my order of *Dump Away* and I have a full 30 days to try it with absolutely ZERO RISK! At the end of my 30-day trial, if I like *Dump Away* and want to continue using it, only at that time and not a moment sooner will I be billed the remaining balance of my order.

> If *Dump Away* isn't EVERYTHING you've promised… or I'm not satisfied for any reason at all, I can simply send back the remaining product (or even just the empty bottles) and I won't be billed one red cent. One hundred percent of the risk is on your shoulders, not mine.

Alrighty then. That one little change can often double or even triple response. But I'm going to add one more little tweak to the formula to make sure this has the best possible chance of success. Let's say, for example, this is the existing headline and deck copy of our poopalog:

"Death begins in the colon. Inadequate and infrequent elimination produce poisons that can kill you."

- Dr. Bernard Jensen

**WARNING: No one – including you – is exempt from the frightening effects of imperfect digestion and elimination.
In fact, 85 percent of all Americans are suffering,
or will soon suffer
<u>dire health consequences</u>…
ESPECIALLY if you're 50 or older!**

INSIDE this special report:

✓ **Put an end to embarrassing digestion troubles... in record time!**

✓ **The key to clockwork-like elimination!**

✓ **Unclog your colon!**

✓ ***This* secret can help you celebrate a healthy 110th birthday!**

✓ **Take a dump every day... no strain, no pain!**

Meh. That's what we in show biz call a "first take." If given the time to obsess and incessantly edit and tweak, I could make this better. But there's a deadline for this chapter and I'm getting so close to it, I can feel that bad boy breathing down my neck. I have to do what drives me insane... squelch my inner perfectionist and move on.

If I were going to use the 30-day hold on this offer, I'd add something like this to the deck copy after all the other stuff:

Try this simple in-home remedy for 30 days... COMPLETELY on our dime. (You only pay shipping today.)

Guaranteed to keep you "moving" every day... or you don't pay one red cent!

I wanted to add something in there like "guaranteed to get you dumping with the force of a fire hose or you don't pay one red cent." But that wouldn't have been an attempt to bump up response. Its only purpose would have been my own amusement. And although that's important, I think it may actually hurt response.

RESPONSE BOOSTER No. 1 SUMMARY: Two simple changes to possibly double or TRIPLE your response...

1. Change the offer to a 30-day hold...

2. Add something in the deck copy to communicate that we're making the offer as risk-free as possible.

Moving on to...

RESPONSE BOOSTER No. 2: I've generated new customers FAST with this one. It's a trial offer into forced continuity. Just another way to lower the barrier to entry and scoop up as many "on the fence" prospects as possible. This works great with nutritional supplements and also many info products like membership sites, newsletters and "thang-of-the-month" programs.

Here's how it works: The customer pays a shipping and handling fee and gets a free supply. Or in the case of info products, the customer gets a free 30-day, 60-day, 90-day (whatever) trial. At the end of the trial period the continuity payments automatically kick in until the customer says "stop." I feel more comfortable doing this when my shipping and handling fee covers product costs and all or most of my fulfillment costs. That's *very* doable with info products. And you can get close to doing it with supplements. But there *is* a downside...

The Mooch Factor!

These are the bottom feeders who just want something free. They have no intention of ever buying from you, now or in the future. They'll cancel before the continuity payments start. Or they'll immediately cancel after the first continuity payment kicks in. And they'll immediately ask for a refund. Or even worse, they'll do a chargeback. These people totally suck out loud and these trial offers seem to bring them out of the woodwork. You always have to deal with these larcenous losers in one way or another with these "lower the barrier to entry" offers. The important question is this: once the smoke clears, how much of a mooch factor can you tolerate? No biggie when you're offering a free trial to an online membership site or some kind of digitally delivered thang. But it *can* be a biggie when it's a hard copy product with hard costs and fulfillment involved.

I hope you try one or both of the conversion boosting secrets I just shared. Because when I finally did, **it transformed my life!** What I shared can very likely be the most successful thing you've ever done for your business. But you're greedy, aren't you? You *still* want to bump up your conversions even higher. OK, I'll be complicit in satisfying your insatiable avarice. Allow me to share another one of my quick and simple "go-to" methods for skyrocketing conversions.

After I look at doing offer tweaks like I just shared, the next thing I focus on is...

The Headline!

I take off my copywriter hat (for me that's the *Heisenberg* by Goorin Bros.) and put on my prospect hat. Then I read the headline and ponder this question:

If I were a prospect in this market, would that headline stop me dead in my tracks and make me so curious that I'd be compelled to continue reading? If the answer is no, and many times it is, it's time to start tweaking the headline.

Would you find it helpful to see how I get my brain to start producing new headline ideas immediately? You would? I think you'll be greatly underwhelmed, but that's a good thing. Because if I can do it, anybody can do it.

My technique is simple really. I just...

Stand On The Shoulders Of The Greats!

Why innovate when you can duplicate? So the first thing I do is whip out my list of classic headlines written by brilliant and successful copywriters. I read through those classic headlines waiting to see what kind of demented synthesis of previously existing ideas pops out of my deranged brain. Sure, in our little direct marketing world, we've all seen these old headlines. So much so that we're sick of them. But prospects in other "normal people" markets *haven't* seen them. And they still work like gangbusters. Just because *us'ns* think they're old hat doesn't mean your prospects do, too.

So...

How To Win Friends And Influence People

Becomes...

How To Build Big Biceps And Get Six-Pack Abs!

And...

Who Else Wants A Whiter Wash?

Becomes...

Who Else Wants To Regain
A "Teenager-Horny" Sex Drive?

And...

Do You Make These Mistakes In English?

Becomes...

Do You Make These Three Sales-Repelling Mistakes
With Your Email Marketing?

Yes, I know I won't win any awards for creativity here. I'm not "creating" anything. I'm just synthesizing. It's doubtful I'll use any of these ideas. That's not the purpose. My reason for doing this is two-fold:

1. It helps me break momentum and get started doing *something*. (It's hard to get started on *anything*. This helps break through the resistance that always tries to keep me from success.)

2. It gets my brain cells and neurons warmed up and firing. Once that's happening I'm much more motivated.

IMPORTANT: I don't self-edit at all. It's almost like a flow of consciousness thang. Whatever pops into my pretty little head gets written down without judgment. So...

Amazing Secret Discovered By One-Legged Golfer Adds 50 Yards To Your Drives, Eliminates Hooks and Slices... And Can Slash Up To 10 Strokes From Your Game Almost Overnight!

Might become...

Amazing Secret Discovered By Struggling Guitarist Embeds Difficult Burning Fast Metal Licks Into Your Brain, Eliminates Slop and Suck... And Can Turn You Into a Frickin' Guitar GOD... Practically Overnight!

Ha! I made myself laugh with that one. Pretty ridiculous headline, I know. But it accomplishes the goal of getting my brain and copywriting muscles warmed up.

Listen, there *is* a method to my madness. You see, self-editing does nothing but kill any potential good ideas. Besides, some of your best and most profitable ideas will come out of giving yourself the freedom to suck. Plus, having fun is always good stimulation for your creativity. And having fun and joking around are how I often come up with some of my best breakthrough ideas.

For example, I was recently brainstorming hook/theme and headline ideas with three of my fellow knights in the Marketing Camelot - Joe Schriefer, Doug Hill and Nate Rifkin, all from Agora Financial. (Discover the secrets of the Marketing Camelot at MarketingCamelot.com.) We started just like I told you. After we had burned through the traditional "how to" and "who else wants" ideas, the best ideas started to happen. Nate and I came up with a bunch of ideas for a product that helps with joint pain and inflammation. Joe and Doug weren't that excited about any of them. They said they were all good classic style headlines and "safe." See, Joe is always instructing us to tell the story nobody else is telling. But all we kept coming up with was stuff our market has seen at least a hundred times or more.

Since I've been suffering with pain and inflammation in my shoulders, I was personally acquainted with the problems prospects in our market are suffering. So after Joe shot down all our headline/theme ideas, I jokingly suggested this as a headline:

"Son of a BITCH that hurts!"

(I had actually said that very thing several times that week.) All I really wanted to do was get a chuckle out of everybody so we could move on to brainstorming *real* headline ideas. But Joe stopped me and said, "That headline is 500 percent better than any of the previous 50 you guys have come up with."

Somewhat surprised, I replied, "I think that headline will definitely grab attention, Joe. But I imagine we'll get a fair amount of complaints."

"Not to worry," he said. "I know exactly how to modify this headline to avert any complaints."

His toned down and "tweaked for compliance" headline?

"Son of a *B!%&H* that hurts!"

I am *not* kidding. That was his tweak. And that's the headline we ran with. We tested it against a much more traditional and safe headline and my "joke" headline won.

I gotta give the entire Agora Financial team props. They've got brass balls. And they're not afraid of shocking people and even offending a few. They understand good marketing is polarizing and you actually *want* to drive away people who aren't your prospects.

Are you getting the idea? I don't really care that my stuff sucks when I start writing. The only important thing is that I'm writing. It breaks the inertia and gets the forward motion started. As long as you keep writing you'll eventually get closer and closer to finding the right headline. Time and time again I've seen miracles emerge from wrong decisions... but...

I've Never Seen *Anything* Good Come From Indecision!

Ya dig? If I start my car and want to go to Cleveland but am heading south toward the Keys... it's just a simple matter of turning the car around and heading north. If I say I want to go to Cleveland but sit behind the wheel parked in my driveway with the car off... well, that probably qualifies as some sort of mental illness. (Wanting to go to Cleveland probably qualifies as some sort of mental illness, too.)

Moving on. What do you do if you still can't get the old gray matter to start pumping out any good headline ideas? Here's a darn near "can't fail" solution I learned from another couple of my knights in the Marketing Camelot, Dr. Glenn Livingston and Terry Dean. It's called the...

Paradoxical Solution!

The first time I did this was in a mastermind group with Glenn, Terry and another brilliant marketer who likes me to keep his name anonymous. We've used it a bunch of times since. It not only works every time, it's fun and always gets us laughing.

The paradoxical solution means we're going to come up with a bunch of headlines so bad that no one will read the copy and conversions will drop to zero. Sometimes we take this idea even further and make the goal to destroy the entire business.

I can't even begin to tell you how emotionally freeing this can be. You see, there are times, when I'm trying to write headlines, the pressure is on to make the promotion a huge success and I'm coming down to the wire on a deadline. When under that kind of pressure things don't always flow. I often feel like I'm forcing it. Sure, if I've had time to let stuff percolate in my batty brain breakthrough ideas often bubble up almost effortlessly. But we live in the *real* world. There are times when you've got to produce something *yesterday*. You don't have the luxury of percolation time. This paradoxical solution process is

177

emotionally freeing because you can do no wrong when your goal is to destroy the company. Or make the headline and hook so bad that you repel all your prospects and nobody responds to the copy.

For example, if I'm selling a nutritional supplement I might write a headline like this:

Attention men over 50...

New Supplement Produced In My Bathtub With Ingredients Found Under My Sink Gives You Uncontrollable Flatulence During Important Social Situations, Pizza-Face Acne, A Unibrow, Instant Tourette's Syndrome...
AND Makes Your Pecker Smaller, Too!

Isn't this fun? It's even more fun in a group with others chiming in.

Let's try another, shall we?

Attention Bodybuilders...

New Toxic Supplement With Potentially Deadly Side Effects Cuts Your Muscle Mass In Half, Increases Your Body Fat By 53.2 Percent And Gives You The Sex Drive Of A Eunuch!

There's something special about this little secret I'm sharing with you. I only started using it recently, but in that time I've never seen it fail. Glenn Livingston has used it for decades and told me his experience has been the same. Glenn used this all the time back when he was hired by Fortune 500 companies to come up with breakthrough marketing ideas. And believe you me, after you've collected a seven-figure fee from gigs like that, the pressure is on BIG time. Just a couple of the ideas produced by Glenn using the paradoxical solution are the company name *Nextel* and the Platinum American Express card. Both of those worked out pretty good, don't-cha think?

After coming up with five to 10 bad headlines, you change gears and come up with five to 10 good headlines. There's something about the paradoxical solution that frees up your internal critic, the little perfectionist self-editor in your head. So when you start writing good headlines, they flow better. I think you might even surprise yourself with the ideas you come up with.

That's the paradoxical solution method of bumping up your conversions with a better headline. Since the headline and lead carry a good 80 percent of the work in your entire promotion, it makes a lot of sense to spend, oh, I don't know... say maybe 80 percent of your time and attention on it. Wouldn't you agree? I thought you would. So let's talk about another way to pump up the power of your headline by hitting more of your prospect's...

Emotional Hot Buttons!

If all we had to do as copywriters was make a list of features and benefits, people would buy based on logical reasons. And this would be one easy gig. And pretty much anybody who can write a grocery list could do it. But people do not make purchasing decisions based on logic. And writing copy is *not* an easy task for a copywriter or business owner. So, if we want maximum conversions from our copy, we have to speak the language and paint the word pictures that evoke and/or intensify the emotions that lead to a sale. And that, my friend, is part science, part art.

Ask a hundred top-level copywriters how they do that and you'll probably get a hundred different answers. Sure, there are commonalities, but we each have our own little secrets, rituals, tactics, tips and techniques.

When I need to create a headline or improve an existing one, I start asking these questions: What is the prospect feeling and thinking? What are his fears, overwhelming lusts and desires? I focus on all the dominant emotions that drive us flawed and fallible human beings. Then I start figuring out how I can make the headline intensify these emotions. The go-to emotion I usually start with is...

Pain!

Why? Because when someone is in pain the overwhelming desire they have is to *not* be in pain. We are more motivated by the avoidance of pain than anything else. Exponentially more than the desire for gain, that's for sure. That's why sticking the proverbial red-hot poker in your prospect's existing pain points can send your conversions through the stratosphere. So I ask... what are my prospect's biggest pain points? What is he freaking out about? What is he deathly afraid of? Worried about? What's keeping him up at night... and how can I intensify and build on that pain and fear in the headline and lead?

SIDETRACK: Did you notice when I ask myself these questions I talk about the prospect, singular? Not prospects, plural. Why? Because I'm not talking to a group. I'm communicating one on one, very personal and down to earth... with one person at a time. Sure, the promotion may go out to millions, but my conversation is with only one person at a time. You see, when I do my research I form a picture of my ideal prospect in my head. I know everything about him or her. And I keep that picture in my mind and write as if I'm writing a personal letter to someone I care about. I connect with that person on an emotional level by thinking of them as a close friend or family member.

Silly? Too woo-woo and touchy-feely for ya? That's OK. I can totally appreciate how you feel. I even felt the same for a while. But I got really sick and tired of mediocre conversions and a half-assed business. You see, there's a reason A-list copywriters get the results they do. And very little of it has anything to do with the mechanics of copywriting. The truly breakthrough results come when you're "all in." When you infuse, embed, imbue, instill, permeate... heck, outright frickin' SATURATE your copy with your emotions and intention. But that's an entire lesson in and of itself. A very *advanced* lesson you might not be ready for. So let's continue with what I was sharing with you about pumping up the power of your headline and leads.

Ummmm... this is starting to sound like a lecture, isn't it? How about an example instead? When financial copywriters were saying things like...

**The Wall Street Insiders Secrets
To 557 Percent Bigger Gains In Your Portfolio**

Mike Palmer wrote...

The End Of America!

Which of those two hooks is more intriguing and hits on stronger emotions? "Wall Street Insiders" hits on greed but "The End Of America" hits on the mac daddy of emotions... fear. People in this niche have seen at least a thousand greed-based themes but fear was obviously a stronger motivator. How do we know that? Because "The End Of America" has been one of the most successful financial newsletter promotions in history, bringing 500,000 subscribers into the Stansberry Research Agora franchise in record time. Last I heard, they now have more subscribers than most (maybe *all*) mainstream financial publications.

Say what? You want another example? Geez, you sure are demanding. But I aim to please. While many financial copywriters were saying things like...

**MIT "Boy Genius" Reveals His Secret Formula To Turn
A $3,150 Investment In Stock Market "Losers"
Into $753,457... In Only Seven Months!**

Copywriting badass Clayton Makepeace said...

The Four Horsemen of The Stock Market Apocalypse!

And if memory serves, the front page of that promo had all kinds of fear-inducing colors, graphics and design elements. Isn't it interesting that I don't remember any specific graphic elements but I remember the emotions I felt when I saw it? That is some damn good copy and design there!

One more? Alrighty then. When LMCs (lesser mortal copywriters) in the health market were saying...

**The Little Known Secret Of The Japanese
That Lets You Live To 100...
But Have The Brain And Body Of A 40-Year-Old!**

Jim Rutz broke all the known "rules" of writing to the geezer crowd and said...

Read this or DIE!

WTF? You're not supposed to talk about death when the average age of your reader is 70-plus. *Everybody* knows that, right? But... which appeal pulled best? The desire for gain... or the fear of loss? In this case, the desire to live a long life... or the fear of dying? Come on... you know this by now. If I had to bet the farm on it, I'd always go with the fear of loss. At a time when health newsletter buyers had seen a million "fix your arthritis/get healthier" promos, "Read this or DIE" was a massively successful landslide winner.

That is the power of hitting on the right emotions in your copy. Remember, you're writing to a flawed, fallible, illogical, scared shitless, wriggling, writhing bundle of emotions... living with cognitive dissonance almost since the day they were born. Logical feature/benefit appeals ain't gonna cut it. You have to paint word pictures that tap into, harness and evoke the emotions that move people to action. To which, with cocked head and puzzled look you reply... "And what, pray tell, are those emotions, oh self-appointed, formerly handsome but still wise King Arthur of the Marketing Camelot?" I'm glad you asked, my dear cherished protégé. The emotions, feelings and desires that all great copywriters use to fan the flames of desire are...

- ✓ Fear
- ✓ Happiness
- ✓ Caring
- ✓ Depression
- ✓ Inadequateness
- ✓ Fear
- ✓ Confusion
- ✓ Hurt
- ✓ Anger
- ✓ Loneliness
- ✓ Remorse
- ✓ Betrayal
- ✓ Revenge
- ✓ Forbidden
- ✓ Frustration
- ✓ Greed

- ✓ Health/longevity
- ✓ Hope
- ✓ Love
- ✓ Passion
- ✓ Lust
- ✓ Powerlessness
- ✓ Relaxation
- ✓ Sadness
- ✓ Security
- ✓ Shame
- ✓ Surprise
- ✓ Urgency
- ✓ Did I mention fear yet?

Yes, I know fear is on the list three times. You see, the other day I spoke with Mike Ward, a super-sharp copywriter, marketer and the big cheese at Money Map Press. (They're growing like a weed on steroids thanks to Mike.) He said something pretty profound. We have a big long list of emotions we want to stir up with our copy, but you can boil them all down to only one...

Fear!

He's right, ya know? Even greed is motivated by fear. So if you write your piece and focus on harnessing the power of just that one dominant emotion, you'll go a long way toward evoking the response you need to get your prospect to respond.

Holy smokes, time flew by in this chapter. Before we wrap up this bad boy and put a bow on it, allow me to pontificate on a few other random but really important things you can do to bump up your conversions. I'll start with...

The L. Ron Hubbard Secret To MILLIONS Of Conversions!

I thought that was an intriguing subhead but it actually applies to *all* cults, sects and religions. See, people want to believe in magic, mysticism and conspiracies. If you can figure out a way to use that in your copy, it's one more way to attract more eyeballs and bump up conversions.

Now let's swipe some marketing secrets from another historical figure who also built himself a worldwide following of mindless obedient drones...

The Master Key
To Napoleon Bonaparte's Success!

Napoleon Bonaparte said that his most life-changing epiphany and the biggest contributor to his success was realizing what he could get men to do for a blue ribbon. Recognition is a HUGEGANTIC motivator. More important than most people realize. More important than money, that's for sure. Wanna know the main motivator most serial killers have disclosed during their confession? *They said I'd never be successful or amount to anything. But I sure showed them. I'm in every news outlet in the country and people all over the world are talking about me.* Gee, if the desire for recognition is so strong that it will drive someone to kill people, skin them and eat their faces, don't you think you can use it to make your copy convert better?

Here's a self-aggrandizing example from one of my pieces:

Imagine how you'll feel when all the dream stealers and negative Nellies who said you'd never make it see you cruising by in your new six-figure luxury car.

That's actually a one-two punch... recognition and revenge. Oh, one last thang. Here's an important tip if you're able to gather some sharp, positive marketing minds around you to brainstorm conversion-increasing ideas. Improv actors and comedians have one very important rule. The ONLY acceptable attitude and response when doing an improv bit is...

"Yes! And..."

It's the big secret to keeping the conversation flowing and the laughs going. You never, ever, EVER respond with "no" or any other negative. That totally kills the creativity and throws a bucket of ice on the whole schmeer.

I was recently in a brainstorming session with three brilliant multimillion-dollar copywriters. This improv comedy secret didn't need to be articulated. Everybody already knew it, either instinctively or from previous experience. And the results were darn near magic. Because of that, this weekly copy meeting is always one of the highlights of my week. I'd love it if YOU had a regular bright spot in your week like that. It not only makes you more money and grows your business, it makes you happier, too. Wouldn't that be nice?

One last thang: Can I let you in on a little secret of the *really* advanced direct marketers? One I'm reminded of quite frequently. One that has been responsible for generating multiple millions in orders for me and the very, *very* few clients I occasionally and reluctantly agree to work with. Once you reach a certain point of competence in this biz, you don't so much need to learn anything "new." Even though everybody lusts after stuff that's allegedly new and shiny, you really just need to be reminded of things you already know. (Or *should* know.) As Vince Lombardi famously said at the beginning of every football season...

"Gentlemen... this is a football."

Complicating things and getting sidetracked on wild BBSO (bullshit bright shiny objects) goose chases is robbing you and your family of time and money. Both now and in the future.

How about *this* instead? Once you've got $10 million in liquid personal assets, I'll allow you the luxury of pissing away your time on BBSOs, OK? Until then, how about we focus on the stuff that actually makes you money, builds equity for the future and has the highest potential ROI for the time and capital invested?

Like the stuff I just shared with you in this chapter.

Sound like a plan?

Chapter 12

The Sales-Boosting Cash Flow Surge System

A few years ago product launches were all the rage in our much maligned (for good reason) and incestuous little Internet Marketing niche. The guys selling $2,000-plus BBSOs (Bullshit Bright Shiny Objects) made it seem like a big fat discomboobulated and complicated process.

You see, it not only helps justify the high price tag when you make a BBSO seem complicated, it also naturally leads to selling the "done for you" service on the back end... for a 10-times to 100-times multiple.

These dudes are smart. You can learn a lot by observing their process of selling these **"Online Magic Riches Button That Spits Out $100 Bills"** products. In fact, you'll learn more by observing than from the product itself.

But a product launch process doesn't need to be complicated. In fact, in this chapter I'm going to show you my simple little product launch system you can quickly and easily implement for BIG sales and cash flow surges. Even more important, once you get my simple product launch process nailed, I'm going to show you how to put it on autopilot. Then you'll have an evergreen moneymaking asset in your business, constantly working for you 24/7 to generate new customers and ongoing back-end sales.

You see, as successful as product launches are for building a list, growing your network of affiliates and creating big paydays and cash flow surges, the way most LMMs (lesser mortal marketers) have taught it has quite a few disadvantages. Don't get me wrong, you can make a lot of money with product launches, but the disadvantages make it darn near impossible to break free from the grunt work. You can have a good business... but you'll be a slave to it.

Why?

- **Launches are dependent on you interacting in "real time" with your customers and affiliate partners.** That's the complete opposite of having what I like to call a "lifestyle business" – a business that allows you a lot of freedom while still producing dependable and reliable income.

- **Every new launch is a brand new "start from scratch" dealybop.** You always have to start from zero. And because each new launch is a brand new deal, you can't really tweak, test and incrementally improve the process like you can with an asset like a successful direct mail promotion or online marketing funnel.

- **Since each launch is a brand new start-from-zero deal, they're not really predictable, accountable and reliable, are they?** Basically you don't know the outcome until the fat lady sings. If your launch doesn't go well, you've invested a lot of time, money and effort for *nut'n honey*. (I love obscure '80s references.)

- **If your launch isn't successful, you probably have a lot of unhappy affiliates.** They've wasted a lot of time and effort with pathetically small commissions. Or zero commissions. Believe you me, it's gonna be a lot harder to get these guys and gals to promote your next launch. If they promote it at all.

- **When it's over, it's over.** And most of your affiliates probably didn't promote it. So you missed out on a lot of new customers and sales. Affiliates have their own schedules. It's arrogant of you to expect them to drop everything else they're doing to promote your launch. This leaves a lot of money on the table that could be yours... *if* you could get all your affiliates to promote it.

- **Many affiliates won't promote due to "list overlap."** In other words, a lot of prospects in the market are on a lot of different lists. For that reason your affiliates might not want to mail when everyone else in your niche is mailing. I can't say I blame them either. That always seemed pretty stupid to me.

- **Many affiliates don't want to participate because you can't give them reliable metrics.** (See the "each launch is a brand new start-from-scratch deal" bullet above.)

- **Customer service overload.** Launches can overload your business infrastructure and your support staff. Unless you're ready for the spikes, your customer service can get overloaded and be unable to respond in a timely fashion. When all your hard work pays off and you start getting more customers than ever before, that's a really bad time for your customer service to go to crap.

- **Launches overload *all* aspects of your business.** Because of all the last minute changes and "improvising" that goes on behind the scenes as you interact with your customers, gather new intelligence based on their feedback... and incorporate what your market is telling you. And you're forced to put out all the fires you never anticipated.

- **Launches can overwhelm YOU.** You have to be the general in charge of the battlefield, giving orders to the troops in response to what's happening in real time. Your troops don't have a set of standard operating procedures for all the stuff that can happen in the heat of battle. Even if they did, they'd probably screw it up.

- **Your business becomes a "one legged table."** See, one of the biggest keys to a successful product launch is all the affiliate partners promoting for you. Not necessarily a *bad* thing... but if you become addicted to the "rush" of launches and wind up too dependent on them, you become too dependent on affiliates, rather than relying on a multitude of marketing channels.

- **You become an "affiliate whore."** To get a decent percentage of affiliates promoting your deal you've got to constantly kiss butt and schmooze them. When they *do* promote for you, you're now in their debt. Which means you have to promote all of *their* offers to *your* list. Imagine having 50 affiliates who promoted your launch and now you have to promote 50 different affiliate offers to your list. You can pretty much kiss your schedule for promoting your own products goodbye. Your calendar will be too full promoting all your affiliates' offers. Talk about overloading your list! But if you don't promote their stuff, they'll never promote for you again.

- **If you ain't in the "good ole boyz club" you won't get a big affiliate push.** Almost every niche has its "good ole boy" network. It consists of the big players with the big lists. These guys are already networked and joint-venturing with each other. Unless you've got some kind of "in" or close personal connection... or you're willing to go to the time and expense of schmoozing them to try to get your foot in the door... it's almost impossible to get the big sales push you need for the huge launch successes you hear about so often. To do the really big numbers, you need the good ole boyz club to promote your launch. And just like the Mafia, you're now indebted to them. (See the "affiliate whore" bullet above.)

- **Launches make you a slave to your business.** For all the reasons I've already mentioned, if you allow your business to become reliant on launches, it becomes more reliant on YOU. There are so many last minute "seat of your pants" decisions you as the entrepreneur/general have to make in the middle of a launch. And it's darn near impossible to delegate it to somebody. Well, somebody competent that is.

Yes, I realize that seems like a lot of negatives, but it ain't *all* bad. I'm just telling you all the possible pitfalls so you can choose to avoid them. Or step right into them with full knowledge of what you're getting yourself into. You can't say I didn't warn you.

I've done really well with product launches. But I've done them on my own terms, using my own techniques to limit the negatives. Yes, it limits the potential pay-off, but I'm OK with that. I'd rather make less money than turn myself into a slave to my business. Or even worse, an affiliate whore.

If it hasn't sunk into your noggin' yet, know this...

Launches Are A Tool In Your Marketing Toolkit... NOT A Business!

Many rookies make the same mistake with the Internet. It's not a business, it's simply a medium. One that should be included with a *mix* of other media if you want a stable, predictable and reliable business. (You wouldn't sit on a one-legged stool, would you?) I just want to make sure after you experience success with your first product launch, you don't become overly dependent on them. They should only be a tool in your toolbox. That's why your Dutch uncle DD is gonna show you a different approach to launches.

A simpler approach.

One that can be implemented quickly. In only a matter of days, instead of weeks or months of preparation needed for the overly complicated launch processes taught to the IM junkies.

Not only do I want to eliminate all the drawbacks of traditional launches, I want you to be able to leverage all your hard work and put everything into an evergreen autopilot system to help free you from the grunt work of your business.

Sound like a plan? Good! Let's get started.

Do you know the No. 1 thing that will determine the success of your product launch?

The Eyeballs Looking At Your Launch Materials!

It all comes down to the list.

And how are you going to make sure the eyeballs looking at your launch process are the ones most interested and most qualified?

List Segmentation!

That's just a fancy way of saying you're going to get the people on your general list to raise their hands and say, *Yeah I'm interested in that topic. Please send me more info.*

I've discovered building sub-lists is a HUGE secret to getting ridiculously high response rates and multiplying your income exponentially. You can do it online and/or offline. For now, let's start with how to do it online. It's really quite simple:

1. Send a fairly blind teaser email to your list to drive them to a squeeze page. The only thing you're "selling" is getting them to the squeeze page. Something like this should work pretty well:

   Hi <firstname>,

   If you want a hard body without the hard work, I've discovered something pretty amazing. The experts said you could never get six-pack abs this easily... but I've proven them 100 percent WRONG.

   Click here to discover all the exciting details.

2. Once they're on your squeeze page the only "sale" you need to make is to get them to opt in to the sub-list. If they have the least little bit of interest in your topic, a squeeze page something like this should accomplish that goal.

I have to give one of the knights in my Marketing Camelot, T.J. Rohleder, credit for that great headline. He showed it to me when I was in Kansas a couple weeks ago. He got the idea while editing copy for a biz-op offer in front of the TV during one of those fitness infomercials. It's brilliant. It's what *everybody* wants, regardless of the niche. But if you're in the fitness niche, I believe you could make a lot of cashola with that headline.

Anyhoo... back to our squeeze page template.

Keep your opt in box "above the fold" if possible. If you can't do that with the style of squeeze page shown, move it to the top right, right beside your video. (Once you get this project going there are several variations you should test. But that's a topic for another time.)

3. Once your prospects have opted in to your sub-list, start the process of "teasing" and building excitement for the launch date. You can do that with a series of videos, audios, PDF reports, emails or a combination of all four.

Now I'd like to share a little known never-before-revealed (to my knowledge) secret you can use to get...

FIVE TIMES More Sales
From Your Launch!

For maximum success of your launch, you should promote both online and offline. Simply adding some offline promotion to your launch process will boost your response. But when you do it like I'm about to show you, it can be a pretty significant boost. It may even eclipse the results from your online stuff.

How much more response can you get from direct mail than the exact same copy sent via email?

A recent article in *Target Marketing* says...

"...mail campaigns draw a better overall response than digital channels. For instance, response rates for direct mail to an existing customer average 3.40 percent, compared with 0.12 percent for email, which is roughly **a 30-fold difference**."

I've consistently gotten 200 percent to 600 percent higher response in direct mail vs. email. *And* a much higher percentage of customers buying the highest-priced options from the direct mail promotion. Which, for the umpteenth time, confirms my copywriting mentor's eloquent statement about the difference between online and offline market conditions...

"People On The Internet Are Cheap Bastards!"

So why don't more people use direct mail as part of their launch process? No idea. Ignorance, apathy, slothfulness, downright bone-headed stupidity. That's my only guess. Because it ain't any harder than sending email, as you'll soon see.

When doing list segmentation offline, I like to call it "lead generation to your own list." It's a little known secret of the big players. And it can generate a lot of money... even from a relatively small house list.

I'm gonna keep this brain-dead simple for you to take away *all* your excuses for not doing it... and at *least* DOUBLING sales from your launch:

1. Take the email copy you used to get people on your sub-list and put it on a canary yellow 4-1/4-inch x 5-1/2-inch postcard. Yeah, just plain black type on a yellow postcard. No fancy graphic designer needed. The subject line from your email will be your headline. And the body copy from the email is the body copy on the postcard.

2. If you want to go to the extra effort and expense of using a PURL (personalized URL) as your response device, go for it. If you were doing lead-gen to a cold list, that's probably not a bad idea. But since this is lead-gen to your house list... people who already know, like and trust you (hopefully)... I don't think a PURL is going to boost your response

enough to warrant the extra hassle and expense. We're keeping this simple, remember?

3. Take a list of your customers who have purchased from you within the last 30 days, 90 days, 180 days... or even within the past 12 months... and send them a simple postcard to drive them to your squeeze page. (Use some kind of tracking so you know which opt-ins came from the postcard promotion and which came from the email promotion.) Your postcard will look something like this:

Your name
106 5th St NE
Barberton, OH 44203

**Turn Over To Discover
How To Get A Hard Body...
Without All The Hard Work!**

Customer Name
123 N Main St
Flunkytown, OH 44203

**How To Get A Hard Body...
Without All The Hard Work!**

If you want a hard body without the hard work, I've discovered something *amazing*.

The experts said you could never get six-pack abs this easy... but I've proven them 100 percent WRONG.

Go here now to get your FREE report and discover all the exciting details:

www.HardBodyWithoutHardWork.com

---

4. Stop worrying. This is all new to you so you're experiencing the wonderful effects of stepping outside your comfort zone. (You should do that more often. Wonderful things happen for the few who regularly do.) **"But I don't know how to send a postcard! This will cost money in postage and printing! Waaaa, waaaa, waaaa!"** Look, sending a simple postcard and even a full multi-component direct mail package is as simple as sending an email. Don't have a cow. And see the next step.

5. All you have to do is send a PDF of your artwork and a .csv or Excel file with your list to a service like click2mail.com, USMailingHouse. com or, my preference, McMannisInc.com. They handle everything for you. (BTW, I've used all three services and can personally vouch for them. Of course, with vendors, things can quickly change, so caveat emptor.)

Don't go getting your panties in a bind about using direct mail, OK? I know you think it's scary because you've never done it before. And email is "free." (Free for those who place no value on their time.) But trust me, you can regularly get two times to 30 times more sales from the same promotion sent in direct mail than email.

If it were up to me, I'd do offline lead-gen to my house list a little differently:

1. I'd still send the postcard, but my response device would be to call a 24-hour recorded message and leave a snail mail address. I'm gonna pitch 'em in direct mail *only* because I get an *infinitely* higher delivery rate, open rate, conversion and ROI in direct mail.

2. We could really start narrowing our offline list down to some hyper-responsive people if we wanted. I would segment out all the known direct mail buyers and only mail my postcard to them. And all the follow-up pieces would go out to them *only* in direct mail. You see, for the most part, people continue buying how they initially bought.

197

(Not always, but it's a good rule of thumb.) So direct mail buyers are direct mail buyers. Online buyers are online buyers. Knowing that little secret, I want to target my known direct mail buyers how they prefer to buy... with direct mail. And drive my online buyers to the opt-in page.

But I'm getting a little off track. I'm supposed to be keeping this simple for you 'cuz you're a direct mail virgin and "you be acting all scared and stuff." So quit stressing about all this direct mail and have yourself a Vesper martini (or two) and relax. Just send an inexpensive and simple postcard like I told you using one of those services to keep it easy on yourself. Don't let me confuse you with all the other cool things I can do to...

QUINTUPLE Your
Return On Investment!

I'm afraid that would make you so much money... and take you so far outside your comfort zone... you couldn't handle it. That's why I'm keeping things simple for you. We certainly don't want you making too much money, do we?

Back to our plan.

We're doing email and postcards to get the people most likely to respond to our launch offer to metaphorically raise their hands and get on our sub-list. Once they're on the sub-list there are endless variations of how you can build excitement for your launch date. And finally "climax" and open this bad boy up for a flood of orders. But I'm trying to keep this simple to minimize the confusion-and-overwhelm, deer-in-the-headlights, frozen-with-fear, taking-no-action reaction so many people experience when they're faced with too many great marketing ideas.

Here's how we're going to build excitement and a "buzz" about our launch. (Building a buzz helps get this thing going viral... your existing customers sharing it with their contacts.)

After they opt-in to the sub-list, take them to a "Congrats, you're in" page with a count-down timer showing the days, hours, minutes and seconds left until your launch. These are easy to install. Any halfway-competent geek on Upwork.com or Fiverr.com can install one for you. But DD's got your back... so I've made one available on a private membership site for the knights in my Marketing Camelot (Details at MarketingCamelot.com.)

1. Have an auto-responder message sent immediately letting your prospect know he's now one of the privileged few on the "inside track." They'll get a jump on all the poor schmucks on the outside who didn't get in and won't find out about this great offer until it's too late... and all the lucky insiders have already picked the carcass clean.

2. Have auto-responder message No. 1 do one of four things:

   A. Direct your prospect to an online video that teases and builds excitement about the launch. (The more "blind" the better. In other words, don't let the cat out of the bag just yet. Just tease about the benefits and hit on the biggest hot buttons.)

   B. Direct your prospect to an online or downloadable audio recording that does the same thing mentioned in "A" above.

   C. Offer a download link to a PDF special report that does the same thing mentioned in "A" above.

   D. Give a link that directs your prospect to an "online special report" (a webpage, dummy!) that does the same thing mentioned in "A" above. All we're doing is priming the pump, getting them excited about the upcoming launch and building a buzz. I've given you four different ways to do that in step one. Pick whichever one you're most comfortable with.

3. A couple days later, auto-responder No. 2 goes out. Same deal as auto-responder No. 1. Tease, build excitement, fan the flame of that buzz that's starting. But don't start lifting your skirt and revealing any leg yet. This is a game of seduction, and if we rip off our clothes and

shout "take me you big stud" at this point, we've ruined the whole deal. Again, choose any of those four options I mentioned above... video, audio, PDF report or online report. They *all* work, so just choose whichever one you prefer. Ideally, it would be nice if you use a variety of those options for each step in this process... but that's not necessary.

4. A couple days later, auto-responder No. 3 goes out. (By the way, as we get closer to the launch date, the frequency of your messages will increase... even to three or four a day – or more – on the day of the launch.) Tease, tease, tease. "Teach" them about your amazing new breakthrough product without revealing any meat. In other words, we still haven't started lifting our skirt. They can still only see our ankles. But they're *imagining* what's north of that. And in many cases, our prospect's imagination is *much* better than the reality. We're still just in the flirting stage, batting our eyes and playing coy. The only thing we want them to do is go to our page on launch day.

Ya dig? We're playing a game of seduction leading up to our highly anticipated event... our launch day.

What's that? You say you want to actually see how I would write a "teasing" email, blog post or direct mail piece as part of this series? Geez, I guess I have to do *everything* for you, huh? OK, I'll do it. On one condition: You take action on what I'm teaching and actually implement your own launch. Deal? Okey dokey. Remember, the theme/hook of our launch is...

How To Get A Hard Body... Without All The Hard Work!

Let's say this is the third or fourth email of our series. The first few were pretty blind. We were only batting our eyelashes and showing ankle. Now we're starting to slowly and coyly lift our skirt a bit.

<u>Subject line</u>: **Contrarian secret for RAPID fat loss (HIGHLY controversial)**

Ya know what one of the biggest obstacles is to the success of your launch?

Getting Your Emails Opened!

Building a sub-list is a big help in overcoming that obstacle. Writing subject lines that arouse curiosity helps quite a bit, too. That's what I'm trying to do here.

Onward.

<u>Body copy</u>:

Hi <Firstname>,

Confused about the BEST way to lose body fat?

You're not alone.

There's so much conflicting information from various "experts"... quite frankly, it's overwhelming.

But today I'm going to reveal a secret almost ALL of the "experts" don't know. One that can GREATLY accelerate your fat loss progress.

Many would consider it fat loss HERESY.

It's probably the exact OPPOSITE of what you've been told to do to lose body fat.

The good news?

It's brain-dead simple to do and you're going to LOVE it.

Even BETTER news?

You get to eat all kinds of DELICIOUS foods you were probably told were taboo.

Ready for the secret?

To lose body fat you need to...

EAT MORE FAT!

That's right. Steaks, butter, eggs, heavy whipping cream in your coffee… all the stuff you've been told will make you GAIN body fat will actually help you LOSE body fat.

BUT…

…ONLY if you eat those foods in the correct combinations… and at the exact times I reveal in my soon-to-be-released "Hard Body Without The Hard Work" fat loss system.

You can get all my best rapid and easy fat loss secrets this Tuesday, January 2, at 12 P.M. Eastern time at…

www.HardBodyWithoutTheHardWork.com

See ya then!

Sincerely,

<Your name>

P.S. Tomorrow I'm going to tell you about the secret exercise I've discovered that helps you burn off body fat 377 percent faster than ANY other exercise you could possibly do.

And even better…

It only take two minutes and 33 seconds to do… and it's actually FUN!

Most people make a game out of it and look forward to doing it every day.

Keep an eye out for my message tomorrow.

Let's talk about this email for a sec and why I wrote what I wrote. It *appears* I'm teaching and giving helpful information. But what I'm really doing is telling them what to do without telling them *how* to do it. The "how" is revealed in the product, which they have to pay for. They can't just eat fatty foods and get ripped. They have to know exactly what to eat… in which combinations… and at what times to eat each different combination, none of which I disclosed in the email.

I reminded them of the launch date, launch time and website, which has a countdown timer. You should remind them of these three things in every email you send.

<u>VERY important</u>: Look at the P.S. again…

> P.S. Tomorrow I'm going to tell you about the secret exercise I've discovered that helps you burn off body fat 377 percent faster than ANY other exercise you could possibly do.
>
> And even better…
>
> It only take two minutes and 33 seconds to do… and it's actually FUN!
>
> Most people make a game out of it and look forward to doing it every day.
>
> Keep an eye out for my message tomorrow.

That's what I call the cliffhanger ending. Just like the old cowboy series. Our hero is riding to his imminent death off the end of a cliff while being pursued by bad guys in black hats. The episode ends at that point with the announcer saying, *Will Cowboy Bob fall off the cliff to a grisly death? Is there any hope to save him from the pursuing heavily-armed band of Black Bart's henchmen? Tune in next week for the exciting conclusion.*

Or something like that.

I'm building anticipation for the next email by teasing with something that is highly desirable or enticing to this particular niche. Now they'll be on the lookout for my next email. That should help with that open rate problem we always struggle with in email marketing.

You should use this "cliffhanger ending" technique in every message during your launch. Heck, you should probably use it in *every* email, period, launch or not. Whether you're selling anything or not. It works like crazy for building anticipation for your next message and getting higher engagement.

Every day during our launch your prospect is going to receive an email like that. On the day of the actual launch you'll send out an email like this in the morning:

Subject: Almost time...

Body copy:

Hey <Firstname>,

The past two weeks I've been telling you all about how you can lose body fat as quickly as possible... and as easily as possible with my new "Hard Body Without The Hard Work" fat loss system.

Well guess what...

TODAY IS THE DAY!

At 12 noon Eastern time today, I'm finally making my groundbreaking "Hard Body Without The Hard Work" fat loss system available to a few lucky people like you.

But I only received 96 sets of the "Hard Body Without The Hard Work" fat loss system from the duplication company.

And to be totally transparent with you... because of cash flow issues in my business... those are the ONLY copies I will have for a while.

Once they're gone, they're gone.

And it may be another eight to 10 weeks until I'm able to order any more copies from the duplicator.

So if you don't want to miss out on getting the fastest, most effective and EASIEST fat loss secrets available today... get yourself to...

www.HardBodyWithoutTheHardWork.com

...at EXACTLY 12 noon Eastern time today.

There are 5,656 people on this special early notification list, and I KNOW all 96 copies will be snapped up quickly.

So don't miss out on the most effective secrets EVER to getting the body you've always dreamed of... without the hard work.

At 12 noon Eastern time today, go here:

www.HardBodyWithoutTheHardWork.com

My brand new "Hard Body Without The Hard Work" fat loss system will be available then.

See ya at noon!

<Your name>

P.S. I'm not joking...

I really only have 96 copies available.

There is so much stuff included with the "Hard Body Without The Hard Work" fat loss system, it was pretty expensive to get everything duplicated.

I just didn't have the cash flow right now to order more than 96 copies.

If you miss out on one of these original 96 copies, you're gonna kick yourself. Because it may be another two months (or longer) until I'm able to order more copies of the "Hard Body Without The Hard Work" fat loss system.

So don't drag your feet and miss out.

At EXACTLY 12 noon Eastern time TODAY go here:

www.HardBodyWithoutTheHardWork.com

I hope it goes without saying you need to find your own reason for fast action. And it better be a good one. The cash flow situation I wrote about above is a common problem for small businesses. Even though it's just an example, it's a *believable* reason for the limited supply, thus encouraging fast action from your prospect.

Or... you can use the same countdown timer we talked about earlier. Then once your product launches, reset the countdown time to only 24 or 48 hours. After that, your prospects can no longer buy the product at the introductory deeply discounted price, and the price goes up by 50 percent.

Or another option: they miss out on some very enticing bonuses. Or a combination of both higher price *and* missed-out-on bonuses. Anything to get all the "fence sitters" (and there are a *lot* of them) to take prompt action or lose out on something valuable.

The day of your launch, take the above message and...

Wash, Rinse, Repeat!

In other words, use that as a swipe, change it up a bit and send out several emails throughout the day reminding them of the countdown. And/or emails updating them on how few sets are left at the special introductory discounted price. Keep sending reminder emails until the very last few minutes of the deadline. Three, four, five or more messages are required if you don't want to leave any money on the table.

Will you get a lot of opt-outs with this frequency?

Maybe. Maybe not. But who gives a flying fart? Do you really want to keep paying to have people on your list who are only mooches and don't want to buy your stuff? Let the mooches opt-out. They're doing you a HUGE favor. Being a successful marketer not only requires you to attract qualified prospects to you... it also requires you to *repel* certain people. That's a key tenet of JSTDT™. Attract the buyers, repel the mooches.

Since this is a sub-list made up of people who are highly interested in this topic, your opt-out rate should be pretty low. Again, don't worry about opt-outs. It's a dumb metric to track anyways. Go back to *Direct Marketing 101* and refresh your memory about the *most* important metric. The one you *should* worry about...

Return On Investment!

Oh yeah. One last thing I almost forgot. After you've announced the launch several times to your sub-list, you should give the people on your main list the opportunity to buy also. You can send two or three messages to skim the cream off the top that didn't opt into your sub-list. Or maybe they came onto your main list after you sent out the messages announcing the sub-list. We're just trying to flush out as many buyers as possible, as many ways as possible.

Before I show you how to put this bad boy on autopilot... so you have an evergreen marketing system instead of a one-shot thang... let me reveal one of my little secrets that could very likely...

Double Or *Triple*
Your Launch Sales!

Ideally, about seven days prior to your launch date, we'd like for a series of direct mail pieces to start arriving in your prospect's mailbox. And arrive with as much "theater" as we can afford. If your product is a Lear jet, you could probably afford to hire Brinks to deliver a locked Halliburton metal briefcase to your prospect's office... containing a video player with a personalized video message and personalized four-color materials. One more thing: instruct the Brinks guard to arrive with the briefcase handcuffed to his wrist, then advise the prospect that for security reasons, the code to open the briefcase will arrive later that morning via FedEx. Can you imagine the buzz that will create at the office? And the curiosity you'll arouse while that guy is waiting for FedEx to arrive with his briefcase code?

Now *that*, my dear reader, is theater.

Obviously you can't afford to do that if you're selling $497 DVD sets. But you *can* do some cool affordable stuff that accomplishes the same thing. And how, pray tell, do I expect you to do that? Oh, come on! You should know how my demented mind works by now. The answer is simple: We're going to use direct mail delivered with an inexpensive form of theater known as...

Grabbers!

For only a few cents per prospect we can get a similar (but admittedly lesser) reaction as the guy who got the briefcase delivered by Brinks. For examples, check out www.3dMailResults.com.

Your prospect will ideally receive a series of at least three direct mail pieces delivered with theater starting approximately seven days before the launch. The purpose? Same as the email series... build curiosity and anticipation for the launch.

Say what? You want *another* example? Geez! I have a better idea: How about you cut me a check for $50,000 plus 5 percent royalties on gross revenues and I create the whole launch process for you? Not in your budget? Not a problem. Instead of writing an example of a launch promotion direct mail piece, how about I give you an example of a direct mail *opener* and let you do the rest. You'll learn a lot more that way than having me do everything for you. (Unless you *do* want to write me that $50,000 check. Although my answer will most likely be "no.")

Anyhoo... how about this for starters: Attach a $1 million dollar bill from 3DMailResults.com to the top of your letter...

...and open like this:

Dear <Firstname>,

(You *do* know personalization is an easy and inexpensive way to bump up your response in direct mail, don't you?)

As you can see, I've attached a $1 million dollar bill to the top of this letter.

Why have I done this?

Two reasons, actually:

1. What I have to share with you is so important I needed a unique way of getting your attention. And with all the junk mail we get, I wanted to make absolutely *sure* my message stood out from the crowd. *And...*

2. Since what you're about to discover is a secret unknown by 98.7 percent of doctors, nutrition experts and fitness trainers, a secret that practically *forces* fat off your body as quickly as possible... making you LOOK and FEEL "like a million bucks"... I thought the $1 million bill was an appropriate attention getter.

Here's what it's about:

Yadda yadda yadda.

Don't forget...

This coming Tuesday, January 2, at 12 P.M. Eastern time you can get all my very best rapid and easy fat loss secrets here:

www.HardBodyWithoutTheHardWork.com

Yadda yadda yadda.

Sincerely,

<Your name>

P.S. Yadda yadda yadda

Yeah, it's what seasoned direct marketers know as the "dollar bill letter." Got news for you, Bubba. It may be old but it sure ain't tired. It's still working like crazy. *Especially* in markets outside the "make money" niche that almost *never* receive unique and creative direct mail pieces like this. (Heck, I'm using it in the "make money" niche and it's working better than ever.)

In addition to the emails your prospects are receiving, imagine the impact of getting a series of three letters sent in lumpy envelopes with attention-getting grabbers announcing your launch. If your prospects have even the teeniest tiniest little bit of interest in your product, your launch is going to be hard to ignore.

Most online marketers I know are pretty lazy so they probably won't invest the tiny bit of time and money required to do this stuff. Their loss. That's why smart guys (like moi'... and very soon *vous*) can pull out a lot more money from promotions like this... with only a little more effort.

Bare with me for a few because I gotta back up for a sec. Everything I revealed in this chapter has been leading up to the launch of your new product. Which entails sending them to your sales page at launch time. But what if you don't want to spend weeks or months writing copy for your launch website. And don't have the money to hire somebody like me to write it for you... which will also take weeks or months?

Wouldn't it be nice to implement your SBCSS without investing the weeks and months required to create a sales page? How about instead of building excitement and sending them to a sales page, we build excitement and anticipation for...

An Online EVENT!

That event can be a teleseminar or webinar. Yes, you still need to write copy in the form of a script or outline... but it doesn't have to be a word-for-word deal like a sales letter.

Is it *better* than a sales letter? At this point, I'm not sure. It *might* convert better than a sales letter. There's only one way to find out. And we'll explore that later when we turn all this into an evergreen marketing funnel on autopilot.

You're getting the idea here, right? This ain't exactly rocket surgery. Basically we're...

- Building excitement and anticipation for our launch date...

- Using the power of the law of reciprocity.

We've provided some cool info, videos, audios, special reports, etc. during this process. We've given some good value to our prospects and now they feel indebted to us. (That's the law of reciprocity in action.) After all, when somebody does you a favor or gives you something, most humans feel a strong and almost immediate need to reciprocate. Based on more than two decades of direct marketing experience... and an almost life-long study of human nature... many actually *will* reciprocate by...

Buying Your Product!

Exactly the reaction we want! (I love it when a plan comes together.) However, that all depends on the quality of your list. If you built your list with the now defunct and outdated "attract freebie seekers and mooches" plan, your response is probably gonna suck.

On the other hand, if you built a list of BUYERS using my JSTDT™ plan, the response to your launch will most likely be, to use the proper direct response marketing term, totally "kick booty!"

Look, I'm not going to dot every "i" and cross every "t" for you. I've given you *plenty* to work with in this chapter. It's now up to you to do a little work and fill in the blanks, OK? Because I want to move on to the part where this all gets *really* exciting:

Putting The Whole Kit And Caboodle On Autopilot...

Now you don't just have a "one-shot and gone" sales boost for a few days. **You have a sustainable new *asset* in your business that gets better and better with time.**

How? Well, you can't tweak and improve your launch when you're in the middle of it, can you? But you sure as h-e-double-hockey-sticks can tweak and improve it *afterwards*. That's one of the many advantages of reusing all the content from your launch and putting the whole system on autopilot. And here's how we're going to do that:

- **Your launch emails:** This one's a piece of cake. Simply copy the broadcast messages from your launch and paste them into an auto-responder in the proper sequence. That's it. You're done with this for now.

- **Repurpose the squeeze page you used to get people from your main list to your launch sub-list.** Put it on an evergreen URL you can drive traffic on an continuing basis. (My best traffic generation secrets were revealed in Chapter 3. There's even more in the next chapter, too.)

- If you used an event like a teleseminar or webinar for your launch, set up an evergreen replay on a service like www.StealthSeminar.com, developed by one of my knights, Sir Geoff of Ronning.

- Contact all your affiliates (especially the ones who didn't promote the launch) and give them the materials they need to add this evergreen promotion to their auto-responder series. Now that everybody and their brother isn't promoting this all at the same time, they might be more open to promoting for you.

This is when things start to get exciting. Instead of a one-shot thang, you now have an ongoing funnel that can be evaluated, measured and continually tweaked for better and better performance. How? That's easy...

- Split test different email subject lines...

- Test different offers...

- Test different price points...

- Offer a three-pay or "30 day hold" option...

- Test a video sales letter against a sales page...

- Ad infinitum...

Since you now have an ongoing stream of prospects opting into this particular funnel, you can constantly test different variations on your control (the messages and copy you used for the original launch) to try to beat its performance.

What If You Have A Brick and Mortar Business?

A smart brick and mortar business owner collects contact info from prospects and customers, just like direct response and online business owners. So, I'm assuming if you own a brick and mortar business, you already have email and snail mail addresses for *all* of your customers. And a good percentage of your prospects. If you have that, you can easily adapt this SBCSS process for your business, too.

You have several unique advantages over direct response/online business owners. You can build toward an actual in-person/in-store event, which can create a lot more theater than an online event. (See Issue No. 1 of *The Doberman Dan Letter* for some ideas on in-store events. Info at MarketingCamelot.com.)

Depending on your market (and budget, of course) this event can be quite the shindig... and could wind up being the talk of the town. One more unique advantage you have over the online business owners is this: you can tell your customers and prospects to invite their friends and family to come with them. Heck, you could even incentivize them with high-value gifts and prizes based on how many people they bring. It's a proven referral technique that cannot only bump up sales from your launch... it could quickly and easily...

Double Or TRIPLE
Your Customer And Prospect Lists!

In addition to the email and direct mail promotions, you could add a phone call to the sequence, personally inviting your prospects and customers to your in-store event. You might be surprised at how many more people that one little addition can bring to your event. It's just one more advantage you have as a brick and mortar business.

There's more we could cover. There are lots of extra little tweaks, tips and secrets to help make your SBCSS even more successful. But I'm out of time in this chapter.

Listen, once you see the stellar and sizeable surge in sales you can experience with this system, you're going to get very excited. And you'll probably want to do several of these each year.

And if you do it like I showed you, it gets even *more* exciting. Because you'll also be creating evergreen marketing assets that continue to bring in sales, month after month... year after year.

And that's better than a slap up the side of the head with a dead fish, right?

Chapter 13

When Should You Hire a Pro Copywriter?

At some point in your business, it's likely you'll have to graduate from president, salesman, chief bottle washer, do-it-all-yourself guy/gal... to the general. The dude who develops the strategy and directs the troops. That will probably also entail graduating from being the sole copywriter to engaging expert freelancers. Or, as I like to call them, "hired gun" copywriters.

Since during moments of weakness – or slight inebriation from too many Vesper martinis – I have been known to occasionally accept a client or two, it might appear that I have selfish motives for writing this chapter. So be it. Really, when you break it down to its core, isn't *everything* motivated by selfishness? Even "selfless" acts? But I digest.

Anyhoo, if you think this is a pitch for you to hire me, you might be disappointed. My "dance card" is presently full for the next twelve months. Actually, it's almost *always* full. Thank you for asking, I'm flattered. And I appreciate you thinking of me. However, unless I can figure out how to clone myself, there's a 99 percent chance my answer will always be "no." Because there's only one lil' ole DD and only 24 hours in a day. (Although I do still occasionally have those moments of weakness... or inebriation. So there *is* a slight hope.)

Even though you're probably not going to be able to hire the original JSTDT™ copywriter (moi!), there are many cases when it makes sense to pay professionals to do your sales copywriting. In order to help you do that, you should have a basic understanding of how hired gun copywriters work.

Small startups rarely hire an A-list copywriter like me. Mostly because our fees are out of reach at that stage. The clients who hire me are what I call "PWMs" (Players With Money.) Those type of clients hire me when they're playing a high stakes game. That's when there's high transaction size and/or customer value. Or the client is going to invest a considerable chunk of change in direct mail or other high-priced media.

Other clients call me when they're in a super competitive market and/or in what we A-listers call a mature market stage. That's a market targeted by the very smart (and very cash-rich) competitors, using the very best copywriters and marketing minds on the planet. That's the space where I usually play. And those are the kind of deals necessary to pique my interest. Those are also the conditions usually needed to afford my fees. As of this writing, my typical project fees run from $30,000 on the low side (plus royalties linked to results) for a sales letter or VSL (video sales letter.) And $100,000 or more plus royalties for more complex, multistep, multi-channel projects.

The local brick and mortar store or single practitioner medical professional doesn't usually have sufficient revenues to justify that kind of investment. In me or other top copywriters in my league. However, I don't always work exclusively with big "800 lb. gorillas." Remember, I got started in this crazy "make money putting words on paper" thang by writing copy for my own "bootstrap" businesses. I had to invest my own sweat equity and my own money, often investing money I didn't have by charging it on my almost maxed out credit cards.

So I still have a soft spot in my heart for "kitchen table" entrepreneurs who make things happen with few resources. That's why a lot of my work has been with small to midsize solo entrepreneur companies. Some with just a few million dollars a year in sales. Others with "begged, borrowed and stolen" capital... but a big dream and lots of grit. Even with a limited budget, they recognize the potentially exponential ROI that can come from working with a world-class entrepreneur/copywriter who can help multiply sales and profits.

If you've never worked with a top copywriter before you might be wondering why anybody would invest $100,000-plus to have sales copy created. The answer is simple. **It's not just sales copy. It's a marketing *asset*.** One that can be leveraged over and over again... for years and years... to create...

MILLIONS In Ongoing Income... And Thousands Of High Value Customers, Clients Or Patients!

That's why my smart clients don't view my fees as an expense. They see it as an investment in an asset. Just like investing in a building or equipment. It's an asset that increases the value of your business while bringing in a steady, predictable and reliable flow of new customers and ongoing revenue.

There's a second reason you should consider outsourcing your copy to a hired gun with a proven track record. It's what I call "windfall paydays." That's when you have a high-ticket product, service or event that has the potential to bring in a huge cash flow surge.

In the case of a recent client, a doctor offering a specialized service with an average lifetime patient value of $4,000-plus hired me to create a multi-step, multimedia campaign. That's a gig I call a "lay down." With just a few new patients he'll get a substantial ROI on my fees. And, like I mentioned a few minutes ago, he'll have a marketing asset he can use for months or even years, often getting an EXPONENTIAL return on his investment.

Another example: I'm often brought in to help a client offering a high-ticket seminar or conference where each attendee is worth $2,000 or more. In those cases, $1 million (or more) may be up for grabs in just a single weekend. Those are the cases when even just a tiny incremental bump in results not only covers my fees, it produces a whopping in-your-pocket windfall for the client. (I *love* being the hero and making that happen.)

There's another reason people hire a proven A-list copywriter. Desperate circumstances. You're either in a war with fierce competitors or it's a last ditch turnaround of a troubled business... and your very survival hangs precariously in the balance. That's why some of the savviest entrepreneurs have me on speed dial. They know they can count on me to ride in on a white horse and save the day just in the nick of time.

Now I realize that a lot of businesses don't have that option due to limited resources. So less pricey copywriters, lacking the experience and skills of an A-lister – or "LMCs" (lesser mortal copywriters), as I affectionately call them – are good enough for less challenging projects.

There are a few other situations that warrant hiring a battle-hardened-in-the-trenches veteran copywriter. Those might include special, one-time campaigns like a grand opening or new product launch. That's when the business needs a meticulously engineered series of strategically-timed communiqués going out to customers, incorporating daily e-mails, direct mail, monthly newsletters, etc. And/or copy for multichannel media like websites, social media, radio and television. In those cases it makes sense to partner with a freelancer with better skills than the business owner is able or willing to develop himself.

So yes, there are hired gun options for every project and every budget. I keep a small stable of "copy cubs" in the bullpen for just these occasions. They're promising, up-and-coming copywriters who, under my iron hand, are more than capable of producing outstanding results. If you have a need for such a copywriter, go to my "Contact Me" page at DobermanDan.com to inquire. One of my assistants, Jackie or Briana, will take it from there.

Another good option is my friends at American Writers & Artists Inc. (AWAI.) They train rookie copywriters and provide ongoing training to advanced copywriters. They also function as the professional association of freelance copywriters. There are several people and organizations that claim to do that, but I rarely see the dedication, devotion and genuine from-the-heart caring as I do with the good folks at AWAI. They truly... sincerely... *passionately* desire your success... and their copywriters' success. And they'll go the extra mile to ensure that. They connect businesses with copywriters via their online job center at http://www.awaionline.com.

If you're thinking about hiring professional freelance copywriters, I have a few suggestions. And these are based on more than two decades experience writing direct response copy... for both my own businesses and those of clients.

When you have the sniffles, a sprained ankle or an ingrown toenail, it's perfectly acceptable to go to your family doctor. However, when you need quadruple bypass surgery or you're gonna die, the general practitioner probably isn't the guy you want. You need a specialist. Even better, a specialist with a proven track record. Preferably one who has apprenticed under a master practitioner and has been performing his specialty for decades.

The same applies to hiring a copywriter. You'll get the best results if you hire a specialist instead of a generalist. In fact, beware the copywriter who claims that he or she can write anything. That's akin to the old West days when you would go to the general store for everything. And I do mean *everything*. The proprietor was also the town barber, dentist, pharmacist, bartender... and also an ordained minister to perform wedding ceremonies. And since he was also the town lawyer, he could annul those marriages when things went south. (As they often do.)

When the stakes are high, it's usually best to find a copywriter with experience specifically relevant to your type of business, products or clientele rather than just a competent generalist copywriter. And really, when we're talking about *THE* most important aspect of your business – generating revenue and customer acquisition – the stakes are *always* high, aren't they?

Lucky for you, there are copywriters for almost all specialties. In fact, the best copywriters usually specialize in fewer than a dozen product/service/market categories. And the best of the best – the A-listers – almost always specialize in just one category, or two at most. And a teeny tiny few of the A-listers are not only copywriters. They're also successful consultants and marketing strategists who can help you plan your entire marketing stratagem. And the infinitesimal crème de la crème of the A-listers is the person who gained his knowledge and skills from putting his money where his mouth is. By birthing, launching and growing his own business(es)...

With Their Own Money
And Their Own Sales Copy!

That's the world I come from. And even though we're as rare as hen's teeth and extremely hard to hire, they do exist.

So it's important you decide on your end goal when you're looking for a copywriter.

Do you want someone just to write an assignment or do you want someone who will view the relationship as a partnership? One in which your success is their success. And even better, there's financial incentive for him or her to invest the blood, sweat and tears necessary to make you successful... whatever it takes.

Now let's chat about what seems to be the number one thing business owners want to know about hiring copywriters...

Fees

Copywriting fees can be all over the board. I bet you can even find people on Fiverr.com offering to write copy for five bucks. When it comes to sales copy, as the saying goes "you get what you pay for." Copywriting fees mostly depend on the experience and track record of the person writing the copy.

You can find copywriters who will do a four-page sales letter for $500, $5,000, $15,000 or $50,000. How much, or how little should you pay? It depends. On many factors.

First of all, you have to assess the potential value of the end product you'll own once the copy has been completed. Can you use it repeatedly or continuously, turning it into a marketing asset that will make you money for months or years? Or can you only use it one time only?

What's the purpose of the copy and what's the value of that purpose? Is it a customer acquisition piece? Or is it back-end copy? (Back-end copy is created to sell products to your existing customers.)

What's the experience level and track record of the copywriter? To use our doctor analogy again, if you need brain surgery you want to find the most experienced, world-class surgeon money can buy. But it would be ridiculous to go to the same guy for a scraped knee. However, since new customers and sales to existing customers are the lifeblood of your business... and underperformance of either of those two could leave you out of business and possibly standing in a soup line... the intelligent entrepreneur would choose the world-class brain surgeon option.

Onward.

Enthusiasm is an admirable trait. And I've seen projects and copy carried quite far on enthusiasm alone. (My very first sales letter, which successfully launched my first mail order business, for example.)

However, be cautious of the copywriter who is "lickety split" quick to agree to the gig. And chompin' at the bit to start tap, tap, tappin' away on the keyboard.

Here's why: successful sales copywriting requires research and preparation. Oftentimes, a *lot* of research and preparation. And the huge, grand slam home run successes require more research and preparation than most LMCs (lesser mortal copywriters) are able and/or willing to do. So it ain't just the writing. Research and preparation are more than half the battle. At the levels I play in, copywriting abilities being equal – as they often are at the "Copywriting Olympics" level – the battle is often won by the better researcher.

That's why you want someone who invests the time necessary for gathering the needed information from you and other sources. You want the copywriter willing to invest the skull sweat required to ferret out everything about you and your product. Even better, you want the dude or dudette willing to dig deep into what even appears to be irrelevant details about you and your product. *That* is the level of commitment required to find any unusual and often overlooked detail that could be the missing piece of the puzzle. The one last "master key" required to crack the code that turns your project into an...

"Outta The Park" Home Run Success!

Again, different levels of mindset and skill set are needed based on your project. (By the way, mindset is often overlooked. By *both* the copywriter and client. Although I've discovered it's *the* most important factor. Especially when comparing A-list copywriters of equal skill set.)

Also, remember this: YOU have a significant impact on the success (or failure) of your copy by how much information you provide to your copywriter.

Here's a way I see many business owners and rookie copywriters sabotage the success of their copy. And/or they cause misunderstandings and dissatisfaction... on both the part of the copywriter and client. And it happens often. That's when there's never complete clarity about the size, scope, deliverables, timelines and other details of the assignment or ongoing relationship. This can almost always be avoided with a contract or letter of agreement. Most experienced copywriters have one. If yours doesn't, you should insist on getting everything in writing. For multiproject or ongoing situations, make sure you have the equivalent of a prenuptial agreement. And most importantly, make sure you both have an "out" clause. So either you or the copywriter can get "divorced" in a way that's fair to both parties should the relationship not meet expectations.

Listen, I totally get the "bootstrap budget" thang. That's how almost all of my entrepreneurial pursuits were started and built. So let's have a tête-à-tête about...

When Should You Hire
A Rookie Copywriter?

Look, we were all beginners at one point, right? And I believe every rookie deserves a shot. Especially one with the right mindset. Because, as I've discovered, mindset can often trump skill set. And even if your copywriter's skill set is lacking initially, with the right mindset, he or she will do whatever it takes to *acquire* the skill set.

There are situations where I've seen even rookie copywriting skills produce good results. Those are small, local businesses with, although significant to the owner, relatively small size opportunities. In many of those cases, copywriting skills acquired mostly from study rather than experience can produce results often exceeding anything the business owner is currently doing with their marketing. Those are also the gigs where you can pay more modest copywriting fees.

If you own a small business with a limited budget, working with a rookie copywriter might be your *only* choice. And it can be a win/win for both of you. You can give a newbie copywriter an opportunity to get his feet wet, gain experience and get a feather in his hat by documenting successful results. And you get a high degree of personal attention and time investment for bargain-basement fees. (In the beginning at least.) In essence, you can grow together.

There's a flip side to this. To whatever degree you can afford it, you should just bite the bullet and pay for experience. Because real world, in-the-trenches experience is almost always less expensive than experimentation.

When someone rents my brain, they get 22 years experience, with millions of dollars of my own money invested in testing and experimentation. Much of that money *lost* during the long, arduous and emotionally painful learning curve of figuring all this stuff out. I've already paid that price... so you don't have to. *If* you can afford me.

Before we close this chapter, let's chat about...

Why I Think You Should Be Able To Write Sales Copy... Even If You Don't

My best clients – the ones I'm able to get the best results for – are so knowledgeable about direct response marketing and sales copywriting, they're perfectly capable of writing it themselves. They just choose to outsource it to hired guns. For several reasons. Those reasons could be faster implementation, time management or the need for outstanding results, compared to "good enough" results if they did it themselves. For others, they often see an exponential increase in results by having two brains working in harmony on the copy. And because they can write copy – even if it's only "good enough" copy – their experience, contribution and critique is a valuable part of the process.

If you just blindly delegate with no understanding of what makes successful sales copy... or how it's created... you're at the mercy of your hired gun. And you don't have any way of evaluating the copy before investing your money to run it up the flagpole. Or... you also could sabotage the success of good copy by meddling with a potential masterpiece with unfounded opinions based on ignorance. (The *numero uno* cause of many copywriting failures is the client attempting to fix the smile on the Mona Lisa.)

That's why I believe, even if you do decide to outsource all your copywriting to professionals, reading this book is a good idea. So thank you for doing that.

Chapter 14

JSTDT™ Case Studies

Imagine...

A wise oracle whispers in your ear.

And he... or she... or it (after all, it's *your* imagination, so make your oracle whatever you want it to be) shares a secret with you.

It's the secret location of an enormous field filled with money.

Enough Money To Bring You Wealth Beyond Your Wildest Dreams!

And, if you choose, there's more than enough money in this field to stack up sufficient wealth to make your next two *generations* rich. (If they don't piss it all away like most people do when given unearned money.)

The oracle assures you that there's an unlimited amount of money in the field. But that money can only become *your* money under two conditions:

1. You have to do some work picking up this money, and...

2. There will be challenges along the way. And how you handle those challenges will directly affect how much money you can get out of this secret money field.

Exciting, huh? You're about to get rich!

With a healthy dose of enthusiasm, you set foot into this big open field. A field where there's practically unlimited amounts of money. Isn't that exciting?

As you're strolling through the field, you start picking up everything you see. In any denomination you see. Pennies, nickels, dimes, quarters... you grab 'em all. One dollar bills... $5 bills... $10 bills. Whatever you see, you start picking it up and stuffing it into the moneybag you've slung over your shoulder. After all, this is...

Fun And Exciting!

Now, in addition to all the various denominations of money, you see that there are IOU notes. A lot of them. As you continue to traverse the field you discover that there are millions of IOU notes. Many more IOU notes than money. No matter. You start picking those up by the thousands and stuffing them into your moneybag. Occasionally, you stumble across pennies (there are a LOT of those), nickels and, with less frequency, dimes. Of course, you stuff those into your moneybag, too.

As you continue to traverse the field, the piles of IOU notes get bigger and bigger. They're like small mountains. And these IOU mountains continue to grow and grow as you make your way through the money field. You're a positive person, always expecting the best. Like most entrepreneurs. You *hope* that those IOUs will eventually turn into money one day. So you do what any optimistic entrepreneur would do. You continue stuffing thousands of IOUs into your moneybag. Because maybe... just *maybe*... one day in the future... if you work hard enough... if God judges you to be a worthy person because of your works... those IOU notes will eventually turn into pennies, nickels or dimes.

Or maybe... if you pray to the ghost of a dead and mediocre science fiction author... those IOUs will turn into quarters. **Or, if all the planets align, whole dollars! *Woo hoo!*** With that hope, you continue cramming IOU notes into your moneybag. Along with the occasional coin. The ratio of IOUs to actual money is about 99 to one. But you're fired up 'cuz your money bag is getting filled up. And filled up FAST. (Could it be that the reason you're picking up so few coins is because you're focused on the IOUs? And that focus is drawing you away from the actual money? *Hmmmm...* I wonder.)

Infrequently, you stumble across a dollar bill. Sometimes even a $10 bill or $20 bill. And much, much less frequently, a $50 bill. Of course, you stuff those into your moneybag, too. But geez... working this money field is harder than you expected. The oracle warned you that there would be challenges. But you thought this would be a walk in the park. You thought you'd have millions by now.

Listen, I've learned something. That which is measured can be improved. With the vicey-versey of that statement also being true. If you don't measure it, you can't improve it. So based on that experience, let's stop for a minute and count up how much money you've picked up so far. After all, you've been working so hard.

Wow! Look at how big and heavy your moneybag has gotten! Never mind the fact that 99 percent of it is filled with worthless IOUs. You're excited! After all, you've got a HUGE moneybag. One you can brag about to all your peers. (Who also have moneybags 99 percent full of worthless IOUs.) Now, if you added up the *real* value of that moneybag weighing you down and making you navigate the money field at a snail's pace, you'd be lucky if you had enough to pay for a dinner for two at a nice restaurant.

But you're getting results, right? Your moneybag is *enormous*. And it's getting bigger and bigger by the day. So you're encouraged. And that motivates you to keep going on your journey through the money field.

Every 1,000 miles or so you find a $100 bill. My *GAWD, man!* It's time to have a bible-thumpin', pew-jumpin', tongue-talkin', snake-shakin' hallelujah breakdown! But you've got a big problem. Your moneybag is so full you barely have room for those very few bills you find. You have to use every ounce of strength to cram them into your almost overflowing moneybag. But it's all worth it. Because every once in a blue moon... after years or DECADES of plowing through that field of money... you get lucky and find a $100 bill.

Praise Jeebus, Yusef and Mariah Carey! Also Moises, Joseph Smythe, Moo-hamud (the cow prophet), Boo-ddah, and L. Rob Hibbard! (Did I cover all the major ones? I don't want to leave anybody out.) But after a while there's a problem. You're exhausted. And no matter what you do, you can't cram even one more single coin or bill into your massive, overflowing, ready-to-burst moneybag. At last... after all that work, THIS is what you've been waiting for...

SUCCESS!

Your moneybag is full. But... are you *really* successful? Let's explore that, shall we? There are two things I want you to do: first, count the ratio of IOU notes to actual money. Still at about 99 IOUs to one unit of money? Now, look a little to your right. There you'll see lil' ole me. Never noticed me before, didja? Well, I've been here the whole time. In fact, I got here decades before you. I'm traipsing through the field, too. Having the time of my life.

How can that be? Because my moneybag doesn't look full at all. In fact, from where you're standing, it looks like it's empty. (Although it IS a little hard to see well with those huge mountains of IOUs blocking your view.) It's true. My moneybag is *not* as full as yours. Mine is easy to carry. But yours... yours is massive, almost bursting at the seams. And it's a backbreaking burden to bear. In fact, you've blown out most of the disks in your lower back. You're constantly in pain. And you've had to hire 10 other guys to help you lug that bulging behemoth around for you.

I'm rich and happy. And you're barely getting by and miserable. What's the difference? We're both working the same money field. My dear, dear reader.

The difference is this: I'm only picking up $100 bills. And $500 bills. And $1,000 bills. That's pretty darn exciting, isn't it? Although it's even better than that. Here's what you *don't* see. Parked on the railroad tracks on the east side of the field sit three cargo cars. And they're filled...

Floor To Ceiling
With One-Kilo Gold Bars!

You also notice something else. I'm completely ignoring all those IOUs. Although every now and then, while I'm picking up a $50 or $100 bill, one of those pesky IOUs get stuffed into my moneybag. But I've installed a special system. As soon as an IOU enters my moneybag, it gets tossed out automatically into the field. That's when I see *you* come by and pick up all the IOUs I've discarded. And I chuckle. You see, I'm doing the exact OPPOSITE of you. That's why my moneybag is light and even appears to be empty.

On the other hand, yours is filled to bursting. And it's backbreaking torture on you and your hired hands to haul that massive monster around. Therefore, since my moneybag looks empty and yours is overstuffed, you're successful and I'm not, right? After all, you're the best IOU-picker-upper in the field. And apparently I suck at that or my moneybag would be so much bigger.

You enjoy bragging about your giant and growing moneybag. I can't do that. In fact, every time you see my small moneybag, you laugh at me. Yet I'm rich. And having the time of my life. And you're broke, exhausted and miserable. From dragging that mammoth monster of a moneybag around.

After a while you simply can't stand it anymore. You invested *years* of backbreaking work, yet you have next to nothing to show for it. Except that gigantic moneybag. Which is now actually causing you to *lose* money. Because you've had to hire so many people to help you lug it around. How could you wind up like this? You've accumulated millions of IOUs. And you've done everything under the sun to turn those IOUs into money. You even sacrificed your cat under the Festivus pole in accordance with the prosperity rules of the dead sci-fi author you worship. And you've faithfully recited the alien prayer of prosperity every day. According to the rules...

You Should Be Rich By Now!

But you're not. So what do you do? You go grab another moneybag and start cramming it full of more and more IOUs. THAT'S the secret. If you just have enough bags full of IOUs, they'll eventually turn into money, right? That's what all the ex-spurts told you. Hell, it's even written in the book of Moo-hamud the cow prophet. If you're a good person... with enough bagfuls of IOUs... you'll eventually be successful.

[Pregnant pause.]

Didja get a chuckle outta any of that? Or a revelation? A revelation that YOU, dear friend, have been that person running through the field picking up a bunch of worthless IOUs.

Don't feel bad. A lot of marketers have wasted years and millions of dollars picking up worthless IOUs. It's what they were taught by the ex-spurts. After all, that model *did* work for a while. (More than 10 years ago.) But it sure as hell ain't working now. My knights at Agora Financial stopped picking up IOUs all the way back in 2007. Those folks are a sharp bunch. Ahead of the curve on so many things related to marketing and copywriting. You should watch what THEY are doing instead of listening to the ex-spurts.

Say what? You *still* don't get my analogy? I realize my warped but genius mind is always seven steps ahead of most LMMs (lesser mortal marketers.) But I was sure you would make the connection. Just to be safe, let me spell it out for ya...

The "give stuff away free to get an opt-in" model is the guy in the money field picking up IOUs. Back in the day you could turn a small percentage of those opt-ins into money. But things have changed. Nowadays, going for opt-ins builds a list that's 99 percent freebie-seeking, "the world owes me a living" mooches. These entitlement attitude folks have no intention of *ever* spending a dime with you. These are the people who think everything online should be free. Because dammit, the world owes it to them. For all intents and purposes it builds a list of IOU notes that are virtually worthless. In fact, a list of people who have only spent a mere *penny* with you would be EXPONENTIALLY more valuable than a free opt-in list.

Sure, occasionally you get a sale out of a freebie-seeker list. Just like in our money field analogy, it's rarely a "$100 bill" sale. It's usually just picking up a penny, nickel or dime and cramming it into your bulging (with worthless IOUs) moneybag. So isn't that worth *something?* **It's only worth something if you place no value on your time. 'Cuz you're gonna waste an awful lot of it building a freebie-seeker list.** And you're gonna piss away a lot of money, too. Money and time you *could* be investing building a list with exponentially more value. I'm talking about...

A Buyers List!

I *could* beat a dead horse here. And I guess I have done that a lot in this book. But if you haven't gotten the message by now, then I guess you'll just have to learn it the hard way. Like I did. TWICE. So if you refuse to learn from my experiences... and the experiences of every other smart marketer I know... you'll have to learn it by frittering away years of your life and losing untold amounts of money building a big huge moneybag full of IOU notes. Sure, you can brag about the size of it. (Your moneybag, you perv. Get your mind outta the gutter.) But you'll still be broke. Because all you did was cram thousands of worthless IOUs (kinda like the U.S. dollar at this late stage of the Keynesian game) into your moneybag. And unlike 10 years ago, almost NONE of those will *ever* turn into real money.

Geez, even though I didn't intend to, I did wind up beating a dead horse. OK, how about this? I'll stop beating the poor old nag when you start DOING what I tell ya. Fair enough?

Onward. With more proof to show you that I'm right about this. (Actually, I'm right about *everything*. And how do we know that? Because it says so every month in *The Doberman Dan Letter*.)

I'd like to share another cardinal sin I see frequently committed by many LMMs (lesser mortal marketers), LMCs (lesser mortal copywriters) and the non-enlightened folks not yet exposed to my JSTDT™ (Just Sell The Damn Thing™) system. And I shall (as I often do) impart this wisdom through an analogy. Because it's more fun for me. AND it creates a deeper, more emotional, longer-lasting neural imprint for you. (Every religion on the planet backs me up. On *that* point, at least.)

Picture this:

You go to a car dealer. You're not just browsing. You're ready to buy. The salesman spends 90 minutes with you showing all the details about the different models and options. After a test-drive, you're ready to whip it out (your checkbook) and buy. The salesman tells you he'll be happy to help you acquire your new car. You simply have to do this: go home and wait 10 to 14 days while you read through his daily "build-a-relationship-by-giving-away-free-content" email series. *Then...* in message 14, you'll be provided a link you can click. At that URL you can fill out all the paperwork yourself and, barring any technical difficulties, you can finally buy your car.

Rrriiiiiight. (Spoken in my best Dr. Evil voice.)

Wanna know why that's so ridiculous? Simple.

Delay Is The Death Of A Sale!

You laugh at the car salesman analogy, but this is exactly what most online marketers do with their email marketing. In fact, just a couple weeks ago a young copywriter paid me to evaluate his email follow-up series because it wasn't converting. It took me less than two minutes to figure out the problem. He was more than two weeks into daily "give away free content" emails before he ever asked those freebie seekers to plunk down some money.

Any amount of money.

So problem number one: attracting freebie seekers. That entire business model just sucks, plain and simple. 'Nuff said.

Problem number two: Don't waste precious minutes of your life "building a relationship" with looting mooches, 99 percent of whom will NEVER buy from you. Find the 1 percent as fast as possible by making them...

An Irresistible Offer Immediately!

Then, go right ahead and invest the time building a relationship. Because you're doing it with the people who matter. **The BUYERS.**

Now... take a little peek-a-boo at this:

1	The #1 secret to getting clients... from a... Send a test | Delete | Copy to Drafts | Settings		Send immediately	0 spam score	24.5% opened
2	My TERRIFYING encounter with a black... Send a test | Delete | Copy to Drafts | Settings	M-F starting at 5...	Send 1 day after the previous message	0 spam score	25.2% opened
3	Quick thought... Send a test | Delete | Copy to Drafts | Settings	M-F starting at 5...	Send 1 day after the previous message	0 spam score	21.5% opened
4	THIS sucks (understatement of the dec... Send a test | Delete | Copy to Drafts | Settings	M-F starting at 5...	Send 1 day after the previous message	0 spam score	21.2% opened
5	The 1 percenters. Are YOU one? Send a test | Delete | Copy to Drafts | Settings	M-F starting at 5...	Send 1 day after the previous message	0 spam score	21.6% opened
6	What the hell happened to... Send a test | Delete | Copy to Drafts | Settings	M-F starting at 5...	Send 1 day after the previous message	0 spam score	21.6% opened
7	Why I will never cancel THIS subscriptio... Send a test | Delete | Copy to Drafts | Settings	M-F starting at 5...	Send 1 day after the previous message	0 spam score	22.4% opened

You're looking at open rates from the first seven messages in my auto responder series. Not great but not bad either. These are average open rates to a freebie list. Now squint really hard (I had to make it small to fit on the page) and look at this:

64	Jigsaw puzzle (Confusing!) Send a test Delete Copy to Drafts Settings	M-F starting at 5...	⏰ Send 1 day after the previous message	0 spam score	12.8% opened
65	Overwhelmed? Confused? AFRAID? Send a test Delete Copy to Drafts Settings	M-F starting at 5...	⏰ Send 1 day after the previous message	0 spam score	13.9% opened
66	THIS is what I'd do if I needed money FA.. Send a test Delete Copy to Drafts Settings	M-F starting at 5...	⏰ Send 1 day after the previous message	0 spam score	14.2% opened
67	What if you DON'T change something? Send a test Delete Copy to Drafts Settings	M-F starting at 5...	⏰ Send 1 day after the previous message	0 spam score	14.1% opened

This shows the steady decline in open rates (therefore lowering conversions) you'll have the further your mooches get into your auto responder sequence.

Just so you know, I do take my own medicine. I'm not telling you to "just sell the damn thing" while I continue to do the freebie-seeking moocher thang. Nope. This auto responder series is for people who find DobermanDan.com from either referral or pure dumb luck SEO, which is what I get from the 300-plus blog posts I've written. (What a waste of time *that* was. Gawd, I'd LOVE to have that time back right now.) I don't even invest one second of my time (anymore at least) driving traffic to this or creating any new emails for it.

So yes, I do practice what I preach.

I just wanted to explain why I still have freebie opt-ins occasionally flowing onto this damn near worthless list. And why I still have emails going out to these mooches. Because it requires ZERO minutes of my time and not a penny of monetary investment. And very, very, *VERY* infrequently, through pure dumb and unpredictable luck... wonder of wonders, miracle of miracles... I actually find a buyer on that list. 'Cuz they're pitched something every single day in the auto responder messages. So I'm just letting that all run on autopilot for now. **But if I were dependent on that model to support my two bad habits... sleeping indoors and eating somewhat regular-like, well... I *wouldn't* be sleeping indoors and eating regularly.** Unless I wanted to eat out of dumpsters. And it would be *exceptionally* stupid to run paid traffic to build this list of looting, entitlement-attitude mooches. I know. I tried.

Shall we proceed with something else? Something that will stack a superabundance of shekels and silver onto your soon-to-be scaturient stockpile of savings? Good! I thought you'd like that.

I did something recently that I haven't done in a long time. I released a new product. It was for a product called **How To Make Big Money From Small Lists.**

The price point for "civilians" (people who are not knights in my Marketing Camelot) was $497. But I let my knights buy it for $397. (My knights always get preferential treatment and discounts on any new products I release.) If you missed out on this launch, I forgive you. But the offer is no longer for sale online.

Yes, there *is* method to my madness... and a reason why I pulled this new offer off the Internet. Because I'm going to use what I reveal in *How To Make Big Money From Small Lists* to create an ADDITIONAL six figures from this new list of buyers. (But that, my treasured troubadour, is a lesson for another time.) For now, let me share the titillating technicalities that turned up while tracking this topical trial.

If you've bought into my JSTDT™ philosophy, what I'm about to reveal should elicit a "Duh!" reaction from you. More than 70 percent of the good, salt-of-the-earth folks who bought my new *How To Make Big Money From Small Lists* product were my knights in the Marketing Camelot. In other words, almost all of the sales were generated from...

My *Buyers* List!

Big surprise, huh? Anyhoo, let's take a look at how this bad boy performed. **First of all, my sales page converted at 4.7 percent.** Is that good? Bad? Mediocre? I have no idea. I stopped labeling things as "good" or "bad." For me everything is simply this: it is. Whether it's good, bad or any variation thereof is determined by one thing and one thing only. My mind.

Cut the Zen crap, DD. Is this a good conversion rate or what? Geez, no matter how hard I resist, they always try to pull me outta my preferred delusional reality and back into the real world.

OK, let me just say this: I have a couple 800 lb. gorilla clients who, if they got a 4.7 percent conversion on one of their back-end offers, would be having a good ole fashioned, bible thumpin', pew jumpin', tongue talkin', snake shakin' hallelujah breakdown, praise Jeebus! And they're *atheists*, for cryin' out loud! (Well, agnostics at least.)

Listen, a 4.7 percent conversion for these dudes on just *one* of their back-end offers would mean an elephantine escalation in earnings. And before it fatigues, a promotion of this magnitude could earn the copywriter a healthy seven-figure royalty. Or, if it has a crazy long life, like the renowned *International Living* copy, it could make *both* the business owner and the copywriter wealthy for life. So *you* decide. Based on your values and mindset, is that "good?"

Now, my numbers aren't as impressive as my 800 lb. gorilla clients. They have massive customer lists. In comparison, mine is infinitesimal. But hey, if I had a massive database of customers then I'd kinda be a hypocrite selling a product called *How To Make Big Money From Small Lists*, wouldn't I? You see, I practice what I preach. I really *do* pull surprising amounts of money from teeny tiny lists.

Now, would I prefer a massive list of customers to the pleasantly petite one I currently have? Of course I'd prefer a bigger one. (And no, that's *not* a euphemism for something else.) However, while I'm in the process of growing my buyers list – keyword there "BUYERS," not opt-ins – I can still create enough income to live an insanely good lifestyle.

Think about it: I work from home, doing the things I want to do. Which, much more importantly, means I no longer have to do the things I *don't* want to do. Yet I make more cash-money-in-my-pocket (not gross) than most neurosurgeons. Not bad for a broke Barberton boy, huh?

Listen, I don't say that to brag. My humble Midwest upbringing *still* causes me guilt feelings about that. So I ain't braggin'. I say all that with just one intention...

To Inspire!

But really, inspiration is *your* job. I can try, but when the rubber meets the road, you are the dude or dudette who has to inspire yourself to action. However, if you *do* happen to get yourself inspired enough to start making things happen in your life, I think I can speed your process along much more quick-like with a few titillating tips, tools and techniques I'm gonna share. Right here. Right now.

I did my own little email launch process to kick off my *How To Make Big Money From Small Lists* product. Yes, I totally get the typical online marketing launch process used by a lot of well-known marketers. It works. However, one of my highest superpowers is my ability to string words together on the page to convey messages. Powerful, emotional "word picture" messages. Messages that cause the reader to take action. That's my forte. AND my comfort zone.

You see, although my notoriety regularly forces me into situations where I have to play the role of an extrovert, the truth is, I'm an *extreme* introvert. (With a strong emphasis on the word "extreme.") I'm highly uncomfortable doing videos. And the official online launch model requires a series of videos doled out during the launch period. I think I suck on video. It ain't my core competency and I don't want to do it. So I do my own launch thang using my core competency. And that, my cherished cavalier is this:

Scrawling a *scrupulously* synthesized series of syllables and sentences... shaped and smoothed through superfluous stages of scrutiny... to squeeze scads of specie from the insatiable souls scanning my sales scribble.

Whew! Gasp, gasp gasp! I need to catch my breath after *that* verbose verbalization. Even for me, that was alliteration O.D. But I had fun writing it... and I hope you had fun reading it.

Let's move on and I'll show you how I used email in my *Big Money From Small Lists* product launch. I used a combination of JSTDT™ emails interspersed with more "blind" emails, designed to elicit curiosity. Here's the email that launched the weeklong series:

<u>Email No. 1</u>

SUBJECT: How to make BIG money from small lists...

Listen... in spite of all the stuff you've been led to believe...

...you do NOT need to build a big list to make a lot of money.

And I can prove it.

I made an extra $205,000 last year... working part-time from home...

...with a list of only 130 people.

Yeah... only 130 people.

A puny list most marketers would laugh at.

But I know better.

'Cuz I know a few secrets that all the LMMs (lesser mortal marketers) are completely clueless about.

<u>And I'm finally spilling the beans here</u>...

Listen... if you want to make an extra $100,000 (or more) this year...

...only working a few hours a month from the comfort of your own home...

...what you'll discover here will be one of the most exciting messages you've ever read.

Best,

Doberman Dan

As you can see, it's pretty JSTDT. There ain't no sneakin' up on 'em. It's obvious I'm gonna pitch 'em something.

What were the results? Exactly what I expected.

Let's take a look, shall we? As long as you promise to not be underwhelmed by my humble results from my miniscule list. It ain't the "million dollars a minute" results everybody brags about online. However, when combined with my other pursuits, it allows me to do my thang. Which is live like J.D. Salinger, banging out words on a keyboard while hidden in my underground bunker. And generating enough cashola to live what many would describe as a life of wealth and luxury.

Anyhoo, take a look-see. Since the entire screenshot was too wide to fit onto this page, I broke it up into two images.

Name ▲	Clicks	Leads
4-3-17 civilians Big Money Small List email	123 [138]	1 [1%]
4-3-17 knights Big Money Small List email	73 [97]	0

Sales	Amount	Value
1 [1%]	$497.00	$4.04 per click
5 [7%]	$1,985.00	$27.19 per click

As you can see with your prodigious peepers, I had two different series of emails going out. One to my civilians list (non-knight freebie opt-ins) and another series for my treasured Knights of the Round Table. What you're looking at here are the results of email No. 1 out of a series of 18 total emails. (The last day I hammered 'em with 10... yes, **10** emails.)

Look at the difference in response from this first email in the series. The civilians list converted at 1 percent and brought in $497, with a $4.04 per click value. The knights list converted at 7 percent and brought in $1,985, with a $27.19 per click value. *Hmmmm*... math ain't exactly my strong suit, but if I'm not mistaken, that means with this first email...

My Buyers List Outperformed
My Freebie Opt-In List Four To One!

I ain't exactly the sharpest knife in the drawer, but in my manic yet marvelous mind, that means that maybe... just *maybe*... I should invest the bulk of my time and effort marketing to my buyers list, right? Crazy thought, I know. But dagnabbit, that seems to produce a lot of profit. In most cases, ALL the profit.

Depending on whom you listen to, I did a lot of things "wrong" with this email series. Because I used some really long emails. The longest was 967 words. Some ex-spurts say that's a no-no and people will never read emails that long. So I guess I suck at email marketing and I did it all wrong. However... some of my longest emails produced the most sales. Could it be that maybe people actually *do* read long emails? It appears so. But just in case, I also interspersed shorter emails throughout the series. And I alternated between blind, curiosity-based emails and JSTDT™ emails, ones where it was obvious I was selling something.

Something else interesting happened during this launch. It's something you need to be aware of should you decide to copy my simple little launch process. AND it's a great lesson in human behavior that will make you a LOT of money.

There was a deadline for this offer. Why? First and most important, delay is the death of a sale. So I needed something to get the apathetic, slow moving,

"I need to think about it" folks off the fence. The second reason is that I plan to put this offer in rotation as new people get knighted. And even though my opt-in list is darn near worthless, I'll still pitch it to the civilians, too. Because, just like our money field example, very, very rarely a REAL person stumbles onto that list and winds up buying something. Although that's so rare and unpredictable, I'd starve if I were dependent on that opt-in list.

So in my most humble (but accurate) opinion, you gotta have some kind of deadline or scarcity on these launch offers. Like mine. My scarcity was that the offer was gonna come down at the deadline. But you could offer a discount in price and have the price go up after the deadline. Or offer some super compelling bonuses that expire after the deadline. You get the idea. Something that will make your prospect think that if they miss out they're gonna feel terrible.

Anyhoo, here's why I don't want you to get disappointed if the first few days of your launch only produce a teeny tiny trickle of sales. Because, if you do it like I did it, as you get closer to the deadline you're gonna be...

FLOODED With Sales!

Here's what I mean. Look at the results from the first half of the "it's ending soon" emails sent on the last day. Oh, one thing I should explain. Antiquated old 1shoppingcart tracks "leads" and sales. They call it a "lead" when a new customer purchases. The emails that show sales but no leads mean it was a sale to an existing customer. Make sense? OK, *now* take a look:

Name ▲	Clicks	Leads	Sales	Amount	Value
4-9-17 civilians Sunday email 1	102 [107]	1 [1%]	2 [2%]	$994.00	$9.75 per click
4-9-17 civilians Sunday email 2	94 [101]	2 [2%]	4 [4%]	$1,589.00	$16.90 per click
4-9-17 civilians Sunday email 3	68 [70]	1 [1%]	1 [1%]	$497.00	$7.31 per click
4-9-17 civilians Sunday email 4	75 [78]	1 [1%]	3 [4%]	$1,491.00	$19.88 per click
4-9-17 civilians Sunday email 5	32 [37]	0	0	$0.00	$0.00 per click
4-9-17 civilians Sunday email 6	45 [48]	0	0	$0.00	$0.00 per click
4-9-17 knights Sunday email 1	14 [14]	0	0	$0.00	$0.00 per click
4-9-17 knights Sunday email 2	30 [31]	0	1 [3%]	$497.00	$16.57 per click

See how they all finally started getting off the fence the day of the deadline. That proves that hardly any of us have changed since high school. You had an entire six weeks to write your report but you waited until the night before to start it. And that, my respected reader, is why you need something to get 'em off the fence and buy.

Also, look at the difference in response from the civilians and the knights. Although the civilians *did* surprise me on this launch. There actually were some people who bought stuff. Wonder of wonders. Will miracles never cease? Like I said, I've already got the list and it's only a mouse click to add them to the email send. So why not, right? However, the results still prove that building a freebie-seeker opt-in list is a piss poor, highly inefficient business model.

Let's take a look at another one of my emails in this weeklong series:

SUBJECT: RE: My previous message...

Just following up on my message from earlier.

Did you get it?

I wanted to give you a last minute "heads up" that what I told you about in my earlier email is about to expire.

Go here for all the details...

But you gotta do it quick if you don't want to be left out.

Best,

Doberman Dan

As you can see, this was a blind email. It's designed to elicit curiosity. And I have to say, it accomplished its goal. It got an 18.9 percent open rate and a 3.2 percent click-through to the civilians. But here's the only metric that matters: it got a 3 percent conversion and generated $1,102 in sales at $11.36 per click.

Now... the same message to the knights did this: 48.6 percent open rate, 14.8 percent click-through, 11 percent conversion, $46.89 per click and $1,688 in sales. (Knights got $100 off. It would be $1,988 generated at the civilian's price. DOUBLE what the same email brought in from civilians.)

What can we learn from this? Well, I've learned some super valuable lessons. But here are a few lessons for you:

1. My launch process is simple. After the two-month-long disaster of getting the membership site working right, it really only took me one day to write the email copy and get this thang launched. Total "ready, fire, aim." So there's nothing from keeping you from doing one of these every month.

2. The email copy drives the whole deal. I alternated JSTDT™ emails, curiosity emails and emails written to make a deeper emotional foot print in the heart and brain of my reader. And it worked like gangbusters. Which ties in nicely with your third lesson...

3. There's no need to innovate when you can duplicate. And since this dealy-bop was successful, why not duplicate lil' ole me?

To clarify point No. 3 above, I'm not talking about swiping my email copy. That would be stupid. It's total Doberman Dan. It's *my* unique voice. And it ain't gonna work for anybody else. What you *can* do is use it as a model and write the emails in *your* voice, dig?

Want another JSTDT™ case study? Instead of running my big mouth, how about I let you hear from one of your very own. Here's a letter from one of my knights in the Marketing Camelot:

Thursday December 8, 2016 9:10am

Greetings from Brooklyn...

Hello Sir Dan of Doberman…

Hope all is well and fruitful in horse country.

Here in The Big Apple, it feels like we're getting ready for war...

...from 34th Street to 42nd Street (Times Square) the cops are all decked in military gear and we have a ton of Army here as well.

So,

Why am I writing this to you?...

Well I gotta tell you sir that everytime I see my monthly bank statement and see the ~$98 bucks to Arrango, I say to myself...

What a rip off!!!!

Honestly, I feel that what you're offering is worth way more than $98 bucks a month sir. Of all the money that I ever invested in personal education, college included, this is by far thee best investment EVER!

From the Marketing Camelot…

...to the monthly newsletters, your shit is sick!!! And now with your JSTDT funnel, you sir are single handedly empowering us mere mortals to greater heights.

By the way…

I took a break from **all** podcasts and learning material to focus on developing my "Kitchen Table Business" and…

The timing sucked!!!!

My fasting on podcasts started on June 30th and ended on November 30th. My 5 month fast produced a ton of awesome benefits but when I heard episode #80 just a few days ago "I getz mail" which aired on July 21st, I looked like...

A crazy man just escaped the nut house.

Can you imagine… I started pacing back and forth and in a circular motion and fast too. Then I started to do little hops and skips while listening until a cop approached me and asked "hey buddy you ok?"

It gets better…

I ran home and replayed it for the fam and now we were all looking like nuts (in the safety of our apartment)

So…   *"Thank you".*

I'm taking your stuff and implementing it. It may not be perfect but at least I got it going.

This is what happened...

I took your JSTDT funnel + your copywriting template and applied it to my bidness, selling eyeglasses and contact lenses.

-Page 3-

In order for me to quit my JOB, a.k.a Just Over Broke position, I needed to produce a minimum of $50,000 per year.

Me, my wife and kids severely downsized so $50,000 was the bare minimum.

Starting out on a severe shoe-string budget... and I mean

severe shoe string budget...

I couldn't spend no more that $50 bucks a week on mailing letters out.

So..
...with no leads, contact list and no direct marketing experience I was off and running.

Say hello to my lillo fren...

Property Shark. It's a database used by real estate agents. Most of these guys and gals use it to mail out intro letters, you know, "Hi my name is so and so and I'm your local agent." This is real B pile crap that never gets read.

Enter You And The Marketing Camelot

For $40 bucks, I got a list of 2,000 names of homeowners from a specific zip code. I then proceeded to go deeper and slice off the zip code into a 3 block radius.

Since I wasn't able to mail all of the people on the list I mailed out $50 worth per week. I did this...

RAINMAN STYLE!

-Page 4-

The results...

600 Letters In 90 Days...

Sept	200 letters
Oct	200 letters
Nov	200 letters

Something is always better than nothing.

Check this out...

I got a 25% response out of 600 letters.

25% equals 150 people. Out of 150... 67 people made a purchase and the rest opted to stay in the loop.

The real numbers...

New Biz	Average Sale	Total
67	$250	$16,750

Total 90 day Investment	$600
Total Gross Profit	$16,750
Gross ROI	2792%

So if this continues, my annual gross income will be $67,000. Not bad considering that I only worked about 15 hours per week.

EXTREME SIGNIFICANCE...

A 2,792 percent ROI. If you did that in the stock market, your picture would be on the cover of the Wall Street Journal and they'd be calling you a gosh-dern jeenyus!

So a quick $16,750 in the bank... and a potential yearly income of $67,000. All generated from a simple little JSTDT™ letter written on the kitchen table.

Not bad, huh?

The story gets better. And it backs up what I was talking about earlier. Because this success didn't come easy. Not at all. Sir Dan of Maldonado has been through the fire. And he came out the other side with singed and smoldering clothes smelling of smoke. But he proved his mettle... and the universe rewarded it. He continues...

```
                        -Page 5-


        When you consider that the most that I
   was able to earn annually, in 2015 and 2016
   was $21,000 (most employers thought that I was
   overqualified and only hired me for a few
   hours per week) this was tremendous.

   More Takeaways...

        • I did all this from my kitchen table.
        • No need to invest in a brick-and-mortar
          biz.
        • Massive time freedom.
        • Non-reliant on current economic
          conditions.
        • Totally self-confident with regards to
          generating leads and making sales with
          copy.



        Honestly Dan, I can go on and on.
   Once again, thank you for all that you do.







   Sincerely...
   -Dan of Maldonado.
```

Listen, there's nothing from preventing YOU from experiencing the same tantalizing titillation of a winning promotion just like Sir Dan. You simply need to know how to create the elements of a successful JSTDT™ funnel. I'm talkin' 'bout the whole enchilada of a JSTDT™ funnel. Traffic, offer, copy, post-sale reassurance/stick letters (almost NOBODY gets this one right)... ALL the components necessary to ensure you extract every possible penny outta all your efforts.

I LOVE "KTBs"... kitchen table businesses. That's how *all* of my own businesses got started. So I have a special place in my heart for "kitchen table commandos." I'm also fortunate to have the opportunity to work with a few "800 lb. gorillas." So for this next case study let's take a peek at how even some of the biggest of the big PWMs (players with money) are using my JSTDT™ system.

A couple years ago I was presented the opportunity to work with one of Agora's most successful and fastest growing franchises...

Agora Financial!

A "YOOGE" debt of gratitude to Sir Caleb of Osborne for introducing me to Joe Schriefer there at Agora Financial. I've learned a ton from all the spectacular people on the Agora Financial team. If I start naming names, we'll be here forever. And this chapter will be 99 pages. So let me just say that I gotz *mucho amor* for everybody on the Agora Financial team.

I lied. I *will* mention one person. Well, actually... I already did. Joe Schriefer, one of the head honchos. He helped me with my research for this case study and helped fact-check my content. Thank you, Joe! (That dude does the work of four people. No exaggeration. I have no idea how he does it.)

In this case study, I'd like to share some of the lessons I've learned from working with Agora Financial. So you can swipe them for your own personal gain... and cram copious quantities of coin in the cache where you keep your cash. (Isn't alliteration fun? It would have been *sooooo* boring to just say "make a lot of money," wouldn't it?)

Let's start with...

The Agora "30,000 Feet From Above" View...

Let me tell you a little bit about how Agora Inc. is set up. Then I'll get into the specifics about how Agora Financial works. And more importantly, how you can swipe what they're doing to make mucho moolah for your greedy little self.

As far as we know, Bill Bonner is still the majority owner of Agora Inc. Since it's a private company, who owns how many shares is never made public. The next time we're munching on croissants and sipping café au lait in his massive chateau in France, I'll ask Bill. But for now there's no reason to believe that he's no longer the majority owner.

Agora Inc. is a large holding company that holds all of the independently operating LLCs under the Agora umbrella. They provide centralized resources that are shared amongst each one of the independently operated affiliates. So Agora Inc. provides human resources services, IT services, database management services, etc.

Everything else is managed by the different franchises. They control their own ideas, editorial, copy, traffic, analysts... and all the rest of the marketing and logistical stuff. So each different Agora franchise operates as its own independent business. Because of that, there can be wildly different ideas and ways to run the business amongst the various Agora franchises.

If you look at Agora Financial specifically, those smart dudes have structured themselves like Agora Inc. Each franchise or publication under the Agora Financial banner operates like its own independent business. And Agora Financial is a centralized resource supporting them. Agora Financial (which I'll abbreviate as AF from now on) provides centralized services like website design, promo production, customer service... things that don't require ideas. All of the idea stuff comes from within each separate franchise.

For example, the technology franchise: They come up with their own editorial and sales copy ideas, write their own copy, drive their own traffic... all the stuff an independent business owner would do to build the business. The macroeconomic franchise built around Jim Rickards works the same way. The income franchise built around Zach Scheidt and Matt Insley works the same way. The Laissez Faire franchise run by Doug Hill works the same way. AF also has its own health franchise and nutritional supplement business, which yours truly had a hand in creating and launching.

So AF is the Agora Inc. of Agora Financial's entire business. And each of the independent franchises is like the Agora Financial of Agora Inc. That setup is radically different than all the other Agora affiliates. The other Agora affiliates are structured like regular businesses. In other words, they don't have leaders heading up each one of their franchises/divisions/publications. They have one thought leader – their executive publisher. But they don't have independently operating businesses under their umbrella like AF.

To give credit where credit's due, the vision to operate AF this way was conceived and created by Addison Wiggin, AF's executive publisher. And one kick-ass copywriter, by the way. Addison has worked at Agora for more than two decades. He was there when Agora Inc. used to be one big business. Then he saw when Agora Inc. split off and became just the provider of centralized functions for all the different independently operating LLCs. He witnessed how quickly the Agora machine grew after that happened. And that was what he always wanted AF to be – more of a centralized resource for all these independently operating franchises that are part of the AF family.

Obviously that arrangement has worked out pretty darn well for Agora Inc., based on their $1 BILLION a year in sales. But how's it working out for AF?

Well, check this out: When I first started working with AF in 2014, they did $51 million in sales that year. Not bad. Not bad at all. In 2015 they did $78 million in sales. In 2016 they finished up a tad more than $120 million.

That means since I started working with them, AF has...

More Than DOUBLED Their Business... From $51 Million To Over $120 Million!

And yes, I *do* take all the credit.

But seriously... how often do you hear of a $51 million/year business *doubling* in only two years? It ain't that difficult to do if you're a $100k business... or $500k business... or maybe a $1 million business. But a $51 million business? *That* is a HUGE accomplishment few businesses can pull off. Which is a credit to the brilliance of their leadership, their copywriters and everybody else on the team. (Of course, it doesn't hurt that they treat their people like gold. And compensate their copywriters EXTREMELY generously. Thanks, guys!)

Now... let's talk about AF's marketing model. More specifically, how people come into the AF funnel. And then what happens after they acquire a new customer. 'Cuz *this* is the part you can swipe for yourself and make MILLIONS, if you so desire. Which I highly encourage you to do. So you can afford to hire me and pay me the obscenely high fees I rightfully deserve. (If you can't presently afford my fees, then you need to hire me even *more*.)

From about 2002 through 2011, the first step of the AF business model was to get people to subscribe to a free e-letter. Traffic was driven primarily with Google AdWords. (Boy, I sure do miss the good ole days when AdWords was a viable medium for us kitchen table commandos.) Over the course of that almost-a-decade, they spent a ton of money attracting people by offering some type of freebie. Usually a free report like *Three Best Stocks to Buy For 2009*. Or *Terrible Event Coming. Learn How To Protect Yourself Here.*

Stuff like that.

After clicking on one of the Google AdWords, the "suspect" (because a freebie seeker doesn't even qualify as a prospect, in my most humble – but accurate – opinion) was taken to a "prisoner" landing page – an opt-in page with no external links. The landing page said something like, "Sign up to get this free report... and oh, by the way, you're also going to get *The Daily Reckoning*."

Or whichever free e-letter they were funneling their suspects into. (Yes, Mr. Fleming. I know I'm never supposed to end a sentence with a preposition. But ritin gud inglesh ain't never made me no munny. And obsessing over stupid rules they taught in high school is the sort of pedantry up with which I will not put!)

They *used* to make that model work. But after Google changed all their policies – like no more prisoner pages – it drove conversion rates down so low... and cost per lead up so high... that the old business model crashed and burned. (I revealed all the details about the build-a-list-of-freebie-seekers vs. the JSTDT model in Chapter 1.)

From 2012 to today, the model is radically different. The ONLY way to get into the AF funnel is with a paid front-end subscription. In other words, like all smart direct response marketers, they're following my famous "JSTDT™ funnel." Why did they trash the business model of attracting freebie seekers? Several reasons actually. The most important being...

EXPONENTIALLY Higher
Lifetime Customer Value!

Which translates into a metric TON more profits... and a stable, steadfast and secure long-term business. One that grows month after month, year after year. As opposed to the "attract-cheap-bastards-who-think-they're-entitled-to-free-stuff" model – which builds a "revolving door" business that leaves you broke, frustrated and hating life.

Back in the days of their freebie opt-in model, they used to pay eight, 10 or 12 bucks for a lead. Then, if everything was tweaked to absolute perfection...

Working together in seamless synchronicity...

With world-class copy, created by some of the best copywriters in the world... who practically sweated *blood* to birth it...

And with a MASSIVE budget to spend on advertising... and the ability to go negative for as long as twelve *months* to acquire a lead...

Even after all *that*... (Damn! I feel tired just *thinking* about it!)... they considered themselves lucky to get 5 percent of those leads to ever buy a low-cost, front-end product. However, back in the day, they could still make that model work. But those days are over, my scrupulous sidekick.

So these days, those sharp-as-a-tack AF boys and girls only use JSTDT™ and go right for the initial $49 front-end sale. In most cases, that's a newsletter subscription. This way they can afford to advertise anywhere and everywhere... online *and* offline... in as many places as possible.

Now to back up my JSTDT™ argument (and also remind you that I'm always right), AF has completely dropped the free e-letter model. *'Cuz it don't work no mo'.* (Yes, English *is* my first language.)

They now ONLY go after an initial "whip it out right now" (a credit card, silly!) front-end sale. Most of the other Agora divisions have given up on free-lead generation, too. There might be one or two of their small and struggling siblings out there still trying to make it work. But all of the smart Agora players have abandoned it.

Listen: We're talking about the best direct marketing businesses in the entire world, my dear reader. An aggregate of $1 BILLION a year in sales. Which is why I wonder how "kitchen table commando" business operators think they can pull off the free opt-in model these days with their limited budgets and experience. Even the mighty Agora can't make it work. Not just because of rising competition and CPA (cost per acquisition). But for all the psychological reasons and positioning problems we talked about in Chapter 1.

Onward.

Now here's where it gets interesting. And if you're paying attention, this little lesson can make you a multimillionaire like Bill Bonner.

My adored and admired AF peeps are willing to pay anywhere from $100 to $175 to acquire that $49 customer. This boggles the minds of LMMs (lesser mortal marketers.) 'Cuz most don't understand LCV (lifetime customer value) and how you *actually* make all your profits with direct response marketing. The back end.

Yes, the CPA (cost per acquisition) is a lot higher than the old outdated opt-in model. But when you do the numbers, they're getting about the same number of new names on their list as they used to with the freebie model. The difference is that now they're building a list of...

Buyers!

A list worth about 100 million times more than a list of freebie-seeking mooches.

And that, my precious and periodically precocious protégé, is how you build a rock-of-Gibraltar business. And THAT is how you double – yes, I said DOUBLE – a $50 million business in only two short years.

'Nuff said.

After the initial sale the new customer is directed to a series of one-click upsells. The goal is to turn a $49 customer into a $100 customer on day one. After that, the new customer is added to the publication they bought and to two free e-letters that are complementary to their paid publication.

For example:

If the customer buys a macroeconomic newsletter, they get swept into *The Daily Reckoning* and *The Five Minute Forecast*, both free e-letters. From there they send a dedicated email to the free e-letter files every day.

The customer gets 100 percent content delivered through the publication they bought. No sales offers. But through *The Daily Reckoning* and *The Five Minute Forecast* they get daily editorial with two or three space ads for AF's other products or affiliate products.

Advertising media is a constantly changing parade. What works best now might not be the best media tomorrow. However, this JSTDT™ model allows AF to constantly test different media, adding and dropping sources as needed.

Another one of AF's keys to success is that they're a...

Multi-Channel Marketer!

Their business model allows them to use almost any media. And they'll use anything and everything that's working for them... like...

✓ Newspapers

✓ TV

✓ Radio

✓ Print display ads

✓ Email drops

✓ Pay-per-click

✓ Online display ads

✓ Facebook ads

✓ Direct mail

✓ And more.

If they could make matchbook cover ads work for them they'd use that, too. Or even yogurt lid ads. (That one's for you, Sir Brian of Kurtz.)

Up 'til now I've been showing you how AF acquires customers. But that's only half the formula. As you've seen, intelligent direct response marketers don't try to make money on customer acquisition. That just limits you and slows your growth. The *real* key to making money in this biz is in the back end.

Let me tell ya... AF has this down *cold*. They have an established stable of back-end products that bring in tens of millions in profits every year. They also launch at least two to three new back ends each year.

And *that*, my dear, cherished student is...

THE Secret Of Their Recent Unprecedented Growth!

For example: Recently they launched a product called *Rickards Gold Speculator*. It's already up to $10 million in net sales. (For tracking purposes and also for calculating copywriter royalties, AF defines "net" as gross sales minus refunds.)

Last year they launched a new product called *Currency Wars Alert* that brought in $26 million in net sales. They also released *Rickards Intelligence Triggers* that did another $8 million in net sales.

The year before that they launched a new product called *FDA Trader* that did a little over $9 million in net sales.

See how those multimillion-dollar launches with new back-end products can bring in voluminous and velocious venditions? (OK, even *I* have to admit that's too over-the-top with the fiddy cent words and alliteration.)

Even better... those products and funnels are now evergreen assets. They continue to bring in millions month after month... year after year.

Now... finally... at last... *for the love of all things good and holy*... like your grandma, apple pie and puppies...

Do You *FINALLY* See Why I'm A Broken Record On This Subject?

'Cuz doing this like I teach you can give you the life of your DREAMS! That's why I'll never, ever in a million years understand why most entrepreneurs suck at doing everything they could to maximize their back end. Because the intelligent few listening to me are getting richer than Midas, for cryin' out loud.

Rant over.

Let's talk about price points.

Because the AF folks have tested prices every way to Sunday. And they've discovered some interesting marketing intel that just about any savvy marketer could use to make massive mounds of moolah. AF doesn't offer a back-end product for less than $1,500 dollars. Because years of testing has revealed some interesting discoveries.

First, their back-end product price used to be $1,000. Sure, they tested all different price points. Anywhere from $200 to $1,000. Yet they never saw a difference between a customer willing to spend $200 and one willing to spend $1,000. Pretty interesting, huh?

After the $1,000 baseline price for back ends was established, they exhaustively tested $1,000 versus $1,500. That price change made no difference whatsoever in conversions and refunds. The only difference was they made five hundred bucks more. More surprising, in some cases they'd see refunds go down. Probably for all the psychological reasons I shared with you in Chapter 1. That's why most of their back-end products are in the $1,500 range. And they're constantly price testing, by the way.

Joe was kind enough to sketch out a "bar napkin" diagram of the whole process:

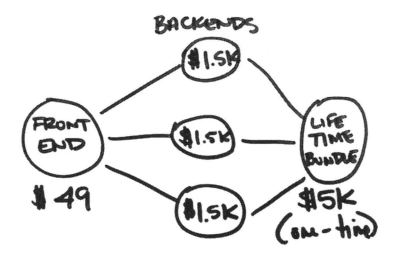

You're getting a peek behind the curtain of a JSTDT™ funnel that built a $120 million/year (and growing) business. And it doesn't involve...

- **Playing *Jeopardy* with your customers** – asking them a hundred survey questions before you try to sell them something... months later.

- **Content marketing**... investing hours, days, weeks and MONTHS creating info that's not valued and rarely read. And worse, almost *never* generates sales.

- **Complicated, 569-step, "if/then" auto-responder sequences**... with 95 percent (or more!) of your messages never getting opened or delivered.

- **Social media**... pissing away HOURS of your precious life trying to get the attention of people looking at pictures of cats in tutus. (These ne'er-do-well ninnies don't even qualify as *suspects*, let alone prospects!)

- **Blogging** – *Please*, don't get me started on THIS one. I'd give all the guitars in my cherished collection just to have back a teeny tiny *fraction* of all the time, tears and torture I invested writing blog posts for people who will never, ever, *EVER* in a million years cross my palm with even the tiniest sliver of silver.

- **Tweeting** (You're kidding, right?)

- **Podcasting**...

- **YouTube videos**...

- **Pinterest** (Come on, now it's just getting ridiculous!)

- Or ANY of the other "grunt work" taught by clueless marketing gurus that rarely, if EVER, result in you making money.

Nope. AF and the handful of other intelligent marketers I work with don't waste their time on any of that "activity without results" stuff. Instead, they focus on the *numero uno*, most important, most CRUCIAL activity in their business...

JSTDT™!

There's one small thing missing on the diagram. It's one more back-end product offered in between the $49 front-end and $1,500 back-end offers. It's an offer to get a lifetime subscription to the front-end product the customer just bought. It's sold for $250 and offered as part of the upsell process... then offered on the back end to the customers who didn't take the upsell.

The value proposition on AF's lifetime subscription offer is this: if you're going to be a subscriber for longer than five years, the lifetime subscription will pay for itself after five years.

Smart. For two reasons:

1. Their publications are so good that they regularly keep subscribers for more than five years. So this is a good value for their customers. And...

2. A very pragmatic reason. Isn't it better to get all the money now than wait five years for it? And/or risk not possibly getting the whole five years worth of subscription income?

The only other part of the diagram we haven't talked about is that lifetime bundle on the back end. After selling one of the $1,500 back ends, they offer a lifetime subscription to that service for $3,000. They also offer franchise-specific bundles for a one-time $5,000 fee. Then, for the "playas" they have what I call...

The Mother Of All Offers!

My name, not theirs. They call it the *Agora Financial Reserve*. Probably a more appropriate name considering their audience is investors, not uncouth heathen like me. The Agora Financial Reserve is a one-time investment of $10,000 that gets you access to everything they offer. For life. This is what we direct response people call a "slack adjuster." Because you don't have to sell many to take up the slack. Just a handful of sales each month... or even every several months... is a whopping windfall to what it's all about: the bottom line.

For smaller businesses, a slack adjuster just might make the difference between barely squeaking by or getting out of the red and into the black.

I could stop right now and you would have already gotten more than enough secrets to create a multimillion-dollar business. But I'm not done. I'm about to give you...

The Master Key To Growing Your Business... And Personal Wealth... As FAST As Possible!

Listen, what I'm about to share can create a continuous cornucopia of cashola... and make you preposterously prosperous and ridiculously rich. In RECORD time. Ironically, it's probably the number one thang most business owners screw up.

Here's what I'm talkin' about: Many people are shocked by how much the AF crew is willing to pay and how much they're willing to go in the hole to acquire a subscriber. Yeah, they *lose* money to get a new customer. In fact, a fairly *significant* amount of money. Why? Because they know their numbers. And they understand another metric that most business owners don't get: lifetime customer value (LCV). That allows a totally different mindset. You see, they don't get a customer to make a sale... they make a sale to get a customer. **And *that* mindset is one that gives you the best possible chance of success in business.**

Remember when I told you earlier that AF's cost per acquisition is between $100 and $175? That's what they pay in advertising costs to make a $50 sale. Those aren't just arbitrary numbers. It's based on a proven formula. They look at their six-month life-to-date subscriber value and are totally cool with paying that to acquire a customer.

For example: If they know a Jim Rickards subscriber is worth $175 "net cancels" to Agora Financial at their six-month mark, that's where they set the cost per acquisition. How can they afford to do that? *Judas H. Priest!* I can't believe I have to say this *AGAIN!*

The Back End!

They make all their profits selling their back-end products. That's the ONLY reason to get a new customer. (I'm gonna keep saying it until you get it. And more importantly, DO IT!)

Let me preface the final JSTDT™ case study and lesson with a little levity:

A priest, a Pentecostal preacher and a rabbi want to see who's best at his job.

So each one goes into the woods, finds a bear and attempts to convert it.

Later, they all get together to share their results.

The priest begins:

"When I found the bear, I read to him from the catechism and sprinkled him with holy water. Next week is his First Communion."

"I found a bear by the stream," says the Pentecostal minister, "and preached God's holy Word. The bear was so mesmerized that he let me baptize him."

They both look down at the rabbi, who is lying on a gurney in a body cast. "Looking back," he says, "maybe I shouldn't have started with the circumcision."

Speaking of conversions, let's chat about that for a minute, shall we?

More specifically, how you can...

Up Yours!
(That subhead was written for the skimmers.)

In fact, how would you like to "up yours" to... *hmmm*, let's say 91.11 percent? From COLD traffic.

Impossible!, you say. *Ever since he has been getting into Quantum Physics... and ranting about it on his highly entertaining, informative and world-renowned "Off The Chain" podcast – available on iTunes and at OffTheChainShow.com – that Doberman Dan has gone completely batshit crazy.*

First of all, thanks for listening. But world-renowned? Wow! Thank you! Remember, YOU said it, not me.

Second of all, I don't believe I've ever claimed to be sane. And insanity has worked out quite well for me, thank you very much. After all, as a great philosopher (Star Trek's Mr. Spock) once said, "In an insane society, the sane man must appear insane."

However, in numerous cases, these insanely high response rates are a reality. For several of my knights smart enough to use my JSTDT™ (Just Sell The Damn Thing™) system. I have copies of their marketing reports that prove it.

Speaking of that, here's what Sir Kevin of Wichtendahl wrote me just one week ago:

"Depending on the campaign, I went from a 30 percent to 40 percent conversion to 55 percent to 80 percent conversion. It also cut my costs in half."

Do you have any idea how much of an enormous deal this is? And what a MONSTROUS impact this makes on your bottom line "take it off the table and pack it into your personal pullulating pockets" NET profits? Of course, it helps a great deal that the direct mail piece yours truly wrote for Kevin was already producing a five-to-one return on investment from cold, rented lists. (He said, while practically dislocating his shoulder to pat himself on the back.) Now, combine this preposterously successful direct mail piece with these breakthrough new psychopathically insane high conversion rates... and Kevin will have his "private jet money" – the original goal he shared with me when I helped him get started – in no time at all.

NOTE TO SELF: I didn't charge him enough. And my fees have just DOUBLED. **NOTE TO KEVIN:** You promised me a standing invitation to jet around with you on your private plane any time I want, remember?

In this last lesson/case study... I shall reveal every single solitary secret about how YOU too can use these JSTDT™ secrets to experience a...

Transformational Boost
In Your Conversions!

Although I have a couple hurdles to overcome to do that. The biggest being that I have to get you to consider implementing a different conversion step than you're probably already using. Unlike your current conversion process, one that's both efficient *and* effective. Because most likely, if you've just been following the crowd, your current conversion step is efficient... but a lot less effective than it could be. And probably not producing the results you want. (Like the rabbi's conversion step.)

So you need to consider a *new* conversion process. More specifically, you should consider adding this new conversion process to what you're already doing as an alternative. And you just might discover two things:

1. Your conversions DOUBLE... practically overnight. And...

2. As many as 40 percent of your prospects and customers prefer this new conversion process.

OK, I'll stop teasing and close the loop now. I'm talking about offering your prospects and customers the opportunity to...

Place Their Order By Talking To
A Real Living, Breathing Human Being!

Too "ole skool" for ya? I think not. Depending on the market, many of your prospects and customers prefer the ole skool way. Especially if you're in health or financial. Or really, if you're selling *anything* to Boomers and seniors. And since they control 70 percent of the discretionary income in the U.S. (and possibly the world), you *should* be selling to them, shouldn't ya?

If you're smart enough to be using multichannel marketing... especially space ads and direct mail... based on my experience, this new conversion process should be the *only* one you use.

Here's why: the only purpose of your space ad... and the only "sale" it needs to make... is selling the reader on calling your 800 number to inquire about the product.

Now, I can predict (with relative accuracy) the very first question about to come out of your purty lil' mouth. Especially if you have an online business...

Can't I just drive to a website?

Good question. Here's the answer: Macromark Media is the biggest buyer of newspaper space ads in the country. They've seen it all and have tested *everything*. Dave Klein, the President of Macromark, told me about a test he did recently. Contrary to his advice, one of Dave's clients insisted on including his website in his CTA (call to action) in the newspaper ad. In every test he has run, Dave has seen the inclusion of websites *suppress* response. But nothing Dave said could convince this bone-headed client otherwise. So he finally got him to agree to a split test. They tested two versions of the ad. The only difference was one had the website as the CTA and the other had an 800 number as the CTA.

The results?

The ad with the 800 number pulled a respectable 1.8 MER (media efficiency ratio, aka return on ad spend.) The ad with the website CTA pulled a .8 MER. What's that tell ya, my beautiful and beguiling banneret? Well, it tells *me*...

Don't Send A Website To Do A Human's Job!

Why does a URL kill conversions in space ads... and in direct mail, too? I can't say I know for sure. But I have a theory. And I believe it definitely holds water. First and foremost, **delay is the death of a sale.** And it seems to be easier to delay response when the CTA is a website. Picking up the phone just seems more immediate to us ole skool folks. (And really, those are the ONLY people you should be selling to. Remember that 70 percent of the discretionary income thang.) And based on my research and obsessive observation, many Boomers and seniors seem to have a paradigm firmly embedded in their melons that websites are to be viewed on a computer. And a phone is for making phone calls.

Yes, they know they can view websites with their smart phone... but that tiny little screen. When your eyes start to go, viewing webpages on that little thang is hard. Secondly, a lot of people in the Boomer and senior demographics just prefer to order by phone. Sure, they'll order online. That's obvious. But only because that's the only option offered. If given the choice, as many as 40 percent prefer to order by phone. I guess they want to talk to a real human being. And talking to a real living, breathing human being is where the magic happens. The "magic" being, much higher conversions, higher average order value (AOV) and, ultimately, higher lifetime customer value (LCV).

Here's the consistent reaction I always get when someone calls my 800 number and speaks with Jackie or Briana: **"It's so nice to know you guys are a REAL business. And it's nice to be able to actually speak to someone."**

With emphasis on the "real business" part. Because that phrase comes up a lot. Now what does that tell me? It's something I find quite interesting because most of my knights are Internet savvy. But that phrase tells me this: even among Internet savvy people, **most still don't view an online business as a "real" business.**

That's why I prefer my CTA to drive to a device that I know everybody has access to, knows how to use and allows me to have almost total control over their experience once they arrive in my world. Or, at the very least, offer it as an option. Because driving your prospects online sends them to a portal connected to a million distractions. And you have an extremely high chance of losing the sale due to the "online rabbit hole" effect. After all, it's doubtful that your offer is more exciting than looking at pictures of cats in costumes on Facebook. Or the titillating temptation of free online porn. (For some reason, "titillating" seemed like the perfect adjective.)

So why not add this tried and true method as an ordering option? (If you're a knight in my Marketing Camelot, see Issue No. 51 of *The Doberman Dan Letter* for all the details about working with a call center... and my personally vetted vendor recommendations.)

I'm sure you've figured it out by now. The JSTDT™ process that's getting as high as 90 percent conversion is driving your prospects and customers to a phone call. However, *how* that call is answered is the secret to getting these astronomical conversions. And the secret is a...

JSTDT™ Phone Script!

Which, even though it has personally set me back MILLIONS to figure it out, in this chapter I'm going to *give* you this script. (Ain't I a gem of a guy?) But first, I'm going to show you a typical non-JSTDT phone script that has been pulling 25 percent to 50 percent conversions. Which ain't bad at all, is it? Compared to online conversions, even the non-JSTDT is a HUGE improvement. What follows is the phone script I used a couple years ago when I launched a new supplement business exclusively with newspaper ads.

Enzoplex

Company: Healthy Victory

Type of Product: Joint Pain Relief

Type of Offer: Print- Unpriced

Guarantee: 60 days

CS Number:

Benefits: Anti-Inflammatory, Joint and Muscle Pain Relief

Cross Sells: Energy Boost

Dosage: Two Vegetable Capsules daily (60 capsules per bottle)

Notes/Comments:

Greeting:

Thank you for calling Enzoplex! My name is _____, may I have your first name please?

Needs Questions:

-What made you decide to call us today?

-Are you calling for yourself or yourself and a loved one?

-On a scale of one to 10 (10 being the worst), how would you rate the pain you're experiencing?

-Where do you experience the most pain?

-Tell me about your joint pain and how it is affects your everyday life.

-What are some things you have a hard time doing due to your joint discomfort and lack of mobility?

Features and Benefits:

||CALLER||, I'm glad you called us today! Whether you suffer from joint pain, muscle pain or both, we can help with a safe, all natural product called Enzoplex! While many other products on the market only mask your pain, Enzoplex offers potent ingredients, available in a vegetarian DRcaps capsule, an innovative capsule that helps protect ingredients from stomach acid helping to ensure that the benefits of the product are not compromised. Not only do we make sure that the capsule we use will deliver the maximum results, but the ingredients that we use are astounding!

Enzoplex provides you with an astonishing enzyme derived from the Silkworm, which is safe a highly effective way to control chronic inflammation. Enzoplex re-ignites every cell in your body with a potent supply of synergistic enzymes and powerful herbal compounds. Basically, EnzoPlex is the answer you've been looking for, we guarantee it! Imagine having the ability to live a pain free and active life, the type of life you deserve! I don't even expect you to take my word for it! Get our product and use it as directed. See and feel the benefits for yourself! We are fully confident that you will love the results. If for some reason you aren't 100 percent satisfied, we offer you a 60-day unconditional money back guarantee!

Let's go ahead and get you started with one of our great packages today!

More Information (If Needed)

One of the main ingredients in Enzoplex is Serrapeptase {Sarah-pap-tace}. Serrapeptase is used for painful conditions including back pain, osteoarthritis, rheumatoid arthritis, osteoporosis, fibromyalgia, carpel tunnel syndrome, migraine headache, and tension headache. Sounds great doesn't it?

Remember the energy you had when you were a kid? That's because you had an abundance of metabolic enzymes to help create that 24-hour, non-stop youthful ENERGY. But as you get older, enzyme production slows down. Research shows your production of enzymes decreases at least 13 percent with each passing decade after age 21. Enzymes are the catalyst that makes EVERYTHING work in your body. You can't digest your food without enzymes. You can't heal from injuries. You can't fight off a cold or illness. You can't build new heart, brain, skin, bone or tissue cells – or replace dying ones without enzymes. Many symptoms are caused by having an enzyme deficiency, which is exactly why you need Enzoplex!

Additional Benefits

Dozens of studies show the formula in Enzoplex can help:

* Reduce inflammation, the root cause of most serious health issues…

* Lower cholesterol…

* Break up blood clots that cause heart and brain disasters…

* Thin your blood without the side effects of prescription blood thinners…

* And much more!

Main Offer: Buy Four Get Two Free @ $199.95 + $TBD S&H

Typically, Enzoplex sells for $59.95 per bottle. Today, when you buy four bottles we will send you three bottles absolutely FREE! That's six bottles for only $199.95 with $TBD S&H. We don't expect you to fall in love with EnzoPlex today. We know that once you try it and experience the results for yourself that you will agree it's worth its weight in gold. I'll go ahead and get your started with the buy four get two free promotion today, OK?

Upsell: Biggest Savings- Buy Five Get Seven Free @ $299.95 + $TBD S&H

||CALLER||, since many of our callers are ordering multiple packages due to the promotional prices we just released our Biggest Savings promotion. Today, when you buy five bottles I will send you another seven bottles for free! This promotion offers you a full year supply of Enzoplex for only $299.95! That breaks down to just under $25 per month and is our best price promotion and you receive free shipping! Let's go ahead and get you started with our Biggest Savings offer right away, O.K?

Downsell No. 1: Buy Two Get One Free @ $119.95 + $TBD S&H

||CALLER||, obviously your health is very important to you, right? I understand that you would like to start getting relief right away, so here's what I can do for you. I can offer you our Buy Two Get One Free special for only $119.95 + $TBD S&H. This will allow you to evaluate our system and make an educated decision based on your results. Honestly, it really just makes sense! Let's get you started with our three-month supply right away, OK?

Last Resort: Single Trial Bottle- One Bottle $59.95 + $TBD S&H

I would suggest that you at least try a one-month supply. A one-month supply is just 59.95 plus $TBD shipping. That way you can see for yourself the amazing benefits and I know that you feel a difference. You can always switch to a larger package after you see that you get the results you want. Our Single Trial Bottle will do just that for the rate of only $59.95 plus $TBD S&H. I'll get you started with the one bottle offer today, OK? Great!

Pain Relief Program- Auto Delivery @ $39.99 + Free S&H (Not available on one-year supply)

As a FREE bonus, you can get an instant upgrade to our Pain Relief auto shipment program. As a Pain Relief member, all future supplies of Enzoplex are greatly discounted and shipped with FREE S&H! Here's how it works:

After your current supply runs out, we'll automatically send you a fresh one-month supply every 30 days charged monthly for the low price of just $39.99 per month with FREE S&H. For your convenience, we will charge the same MOP you used today, and the charge will appear as Health Victory. You can cancel or change your Pain Relief shipments at any time by calling our customer service number at: ||CS NUMBER||, Okay? (Must get a clear "YES" or OK)

Cross Sell: Energy Boost @ $39.99 + Free S&H

||CALLER||, in order to give you a full spectrum of total body health I'd like to offer you our Energy Boost supplement! As I'm sure you already know, having a lack of energy throughout the day negatively affects just about every aspect of our lives! Our product Energy Boost is a drink you take when needed to help boost your energy levels, mental clarity and concentration! I'm sure you can think of a lot of things you would love to do once your joint pain decreases and you have a lot more energy!? Right? Well today we can provide you with Energy Boost that can give you these benefits without flooding your body with calories and sugar like most energy products. I can go ahead and add as many bottles of Energy Boost for only $39.99 today, how many would you like to add to your order today?

Shipping and Delivery:

It generally takes TBD business days to receive your order.

CONFIRMATIONS: MUST READ!

I want to go ahead and confirm your order, OK? (Wait for answer) OK great M/M____. I'd just like to confirm that you've ordered (list anything the customer is being charged for)

Your name, as it appears on your MOP is (spell it back to them). Your address is (read address, city, state, zip and phone). Your MOP will be charged (SEE TOTAL) under the company Health Victory. Is all your information correct? (Wait for affirmation) Your order number is _____ and the customer service number is ||CSNUMBER||.

Pain Relief- Auto Delivery Program Confirmations:

Now, after your current supply runs out, we'll automatically send you a one-month supply of Enzoplex at the discounted rate every 30 days until you call our customer service department to cancel or alter your shipments, which you can do at any time. We will charge your MOP just $39.99 per month, OK? (Must get a YES or OK)

Final Sale authorization:

For security purposes and to confirm I have your approval for this order and you agree to the terms, please read back the last four digits of the account you have provided today.

*THE LAST FOUR NUMBERS MUST BE THE SAME AS THE NUMBERS OF THE ACCOUNT PREVIOUSLY PROVIDED

Wrap Up Info

Customer Service hours:

Customer Service Number:

Customer Service Location:

Available Method of Payments:

Shipped to PO BOX:

Auto ship available: Yes, not available on one-year supply

Auto ship available on checks:

Ship to Canada (Additional cost for shipping if applicable):

Ship to Alaska/Hawaii (Additional cost for shipping if applicable):

Ship anywhere else (Additional cost for shipping if applicable):

Ship via (FED EX, UPS or USPS):

Shipping time:

Rush available:

Shipped from (City/State/ Country):

Company name: Health Victory

Charges will appear as: Health Victory

Sales tax:

Here was my thought process at that time. This ain't how I would write this, but these call center guys are the best at this stuff. They're constantly testing new scripts, price points and offers. So I deferred to their expertise. Although it appeared to me that this was way more foreplay than necessary.

And listen, 25 percent to 50 percent conversion ain't nuttin' to sneeze at. But my gut was right. That was too much chatter. After all, they're calling in from an ad offering a product. Shouldn't we just assume the sale until the prospect says otherwise? Or brings up some questions and objections?

Sir Kevin of Wichtendahl brought up another point I hadn't considered. In his own words...

> I think there is another reason your JSTDT works that you may not have discussed. When someone calls into a health supplement line and the rep starts asking about their health issue, the person calling actually starts to think that the person asking the questions actually KNOWS something about that health issue. Little do they know that this is some part time mom reading from a script. With the JSTDT method you immediately frame the conversation with the caller as "this is an order line just place your order."
>
> So I changed my script to: "Thank you for calling XYZ. You are calling to order the XYZ product, correct?"

The rep got their name and credit card info and pitched the packages.

So, as Sir Kevin has proven, we can do better. In some cases, *much* better.

Something else to keep in mind: in certain media like newspaper ads, direct mail tear sheets or any kind of advertorial, the only "sale" we have to make is selling the prospect on calling the 800 number. That's it. Sure, the advertorial does some selling. But the close (the conversion) is done by the human being answering the phone. That's why you need a kick-ass JSTDT™ phone script. And we'll get into that in just a minute. First, let me show you an example of the advertorial copy that drives this whole moneymaking engine. Here's a piece that was a big success. This brought in a 3.0 (or better) MER (media efficiency ratio) every time it ran. Until it eventually tired out, as all ads do. By the way, MER is simply the return on ad spend. So a 3.0 MER brings in $3 for every $1 invested in advertising. An ad like that can be scaled up quickly in the newspapers, often bringing in seven figures per month. Take a looky-loo at the headline complex:

It continues...

Writing advertorials, especially for newspapers, seems to be a dying art. The CEO of Macromark, the biggest media buyer of newspaper space, told me there were only two hired gun copywriters who could write newspaper ads that convert well. Yours truly and a really smart dude named Steve Wexler. Neither of us are writing newspaper ads anymore. So this is an art I would like to pass along to you. (Actually, it would take an entire frickin' *seminar* to do that.) But not in this book. In this case study we're talking about the JSTDT™ conversion system. I just wanted to show you an example of how your prospect gets directed to the JSTDT™ conversion step.

We continue...

Hmmmm... breaking this into parts makes it a little difficult to see the flow of this thang. That's why I've included a PDF of this ad in our exclusive knights-only membership site at MarketingCamelot.com.

Let's move on to the CTA (call to action) in this puppy:

And because you take phytoceramides orally

Real Stories, Real Results

"My husband left me for a younger woman last year and he took my self-esteem with him," says 50 year old **Lydia S. of Tampa, Fl.** "When I read an article about Dermex-P and how its main ingredient was clinically proven to restore a youthful appearance, I thought, "Why not?". Lydia goes on to say with a smile, "What they say is true, living well is the best revenge. I have my confidence back and am dating men half my age. My friends and family cannot believe the difference!"

54 year old **Joan from Phoenix, Arizona** says "After using Dermex-P for four weeks, I looked in the mirror and felt like a 30 year old with 24 years of experience!"

"When Kanye's mother died of 'complications due to plastic surgery', I think a lot of us decided beauty was not worth our life and accepted the fact that wrinkles and dry patchy skin were a way of life." **Anita from Little Rock, Arkansas** explained. "But when I ran into an old high school friend from 25 years ago and she looked like she hadn't aged at all, I assumed she had had a face lift. Boy was I wrong! I can't thank her enough! Thank you, Sheila!" laughed Anita.

comparison. And it gives you shockingly similar results," says one successful Beverly Hill's surgeon. "The medical community is up in arms because the average cost of a facelift is about ten thousand dollars; and the recovery time is painful and can take as much as 2-3 weeks! We will soon start to see the trend steering away from medical procedures to a safer, more inexpensive solution like Dermex-P."

The distributor of Dermex-P is offering a 100% Risk-FREE 30-day trial supply to anyone who asks. They say, it's the best way for people to see for themselves how well it works. Try it for 30 days – if your wrinkles don't disappear from your entire face and neck, return the bottle, even if totally empty. You'll be completely refunded – no questions asked. But no one's promising this offer will stay open forever. Considering the demand for Dermex-P, the FREE trial supply could prove too costly for the company to keep up with. That's why it's important to call now before the FREE trial is no longer available.

We will also send you a FREE GIFT just for trying Dermex-P and of course you are backed by our unconditional 30 Day Money Back Guarantee on all of our products. It's that easy! Call **1-800-940-1562** now before this offer is closed forever.

THESE STATEMENTS HAVE NOT BEEN EVALUATED BY THE US FOOD AND DRUG ADMINISTRATION. THESE PRODUCTS ARE NOT INTENDED TO DIAGNOSE, TREAT, CURE OR PREVENT ANY DISEASE. RESULTS BASED UPON AVERAGES.

After reading that, isn't it obvious that the prospect is going to be offered to buy this product when they call the 800 number? Exactly! So why screw around playing 50 questions? Just sell the damn thing. Or, more accurately, just assume the sale until the prospect says otherwise.

The stereotype of this demographic... that they'll talk your ear off... is true in many cases. Many seniors are lonely. And if given the chance, they'll chatter away for hours. Especially about their health problems. My grandmother's bowel movements seemed to be her favorite dinner table conversation. Especially during holidays when the whole family was present.

That's why I believe my original Enzoplex script didn't convert like the JSTDT script. Because delay is the death of a sale. The prospect called to find out about the offer advertised in the paper, yet the call center person got them off the rails talking about their health problems. And God knows where it went from there. Even though this is a pain/inflammation product, I can imagine the prospect blabbering on about how her favorite son married a gentile 20 years ago... and that's when all these health problems started. OK, I'm exaggerating a little bit. It didn't go off the rails *that* bad. I know because I listened to all the calls. (That's "deep dive" research LMCs – lesser mortal copywriters – simply NEVER do. But that's what causes the big "home run" breakthroughs.) But still, according to *my* quirky cranium, all the health questions are unnecessary. Why not just sell the damn thing?

So that's what a few crafty caballeros and I have done. And *now*, when a prospect calls that 800 number, magic happens.

The script is basically like Sir Kevin said:

"Thank you for calling Flunky The Late Nite Clown Nutritionals." (I really enjoy obscure '80s TV references.) "You're calling to order our blown out prostate supplement *Prost-ease*, correct?"

OK, so that's a bit of an oversimplification. It's actually like this:

> **Product Name: Heart Drano**
> **Company:** Flunky The Late Nite Clown Nutritionals
> **Type of Product:** Heart health
> **Type of Offer:** Print- Unpriced
> **Guarantee:** 60 days
> **CS Number:**
> **Benefits:** Heart health, healthy blood pressure, healthy blood flow
> **Cross Sells:** Energy Boost
> **Dosage:** Two Vegetable Capsules daily (60 capsules per bottle)
> **Notes/Comments:**

Greeting:

Thank you for calling Flunky The Late Nite Clown Nutritionals, this is (agent name).

Are you calling about our Heart Drano offer in the newspaper?

Great!

Main Offer: Buy Four Get Two Free @ $199.95 + $TBD S&H

Normally Heart Drano sells for $59.95 per bottle. Today only we have a special new customer introductory offer. When you buy four bottles we'll send you two bottles absolutely FREE! That's six bottles for only $199.95 with $TBD S&H. We know that once you try it... and see and FEEL the results for yourself... you'll agree it's worth its weight in gold. I'll go ahead and get you started with the buy four get two free promotion today, OK?

As you see, there's no foreplay here. After all, the prospect initiated the contact. So in my marvelous but marginally manic mind this is a "wham, bam, thank you ma'am" deal. We ain't got time for foreplay. After all, the foreplay was our ad. Now it's time to close the deal.

You'll also notice that I did a few little tweaks to make this more conversational. In other words, it's written in a way that sounds like most people talk. For example, I used contractions. It just sounds better. Reading the original script as written makes the call center agent sound like she's reading a script. One written by an LMC (lesser mortal copywriter.)

We continue...

Upsell: Biggest Savings- Buy Five Get Seven Free @ $299.95 + $TBD S&H

||CALLER||, because of the big discounts with our new customer introductory offer today, many of our callers are ordering multiple packages so they can save a lot more money. Today, when you buy five bottles I'll send you another seven bottles for free! This promotion offers you a full year supply of Heart Drano for only $299.95! That breaks down to just under $25 per month and it's

our best price promotion. AND you get free shipping, too! Let's go ahead and get you started with our Biggest Savings offer, OK?

You might as well start skimming the cream off the top (the 20 percenters) as soon as possible. And you do that by offering your biggest "Mac Daddy" offer as the first upsell. By the way, make a mental note: you probably want to pitch these big package buyers bigger back-end offers... and more frequent back-end offers... than the rest of the people on your list. Listen, my valiant victor... with that one little tip – whether you realize it or not – you have just been handed...

The Keys To The Kingdom For Making As Much Net Profit As Possible From Your Business!

And that isn't even our topic. Just an afterthought. Let us proceed:

Upsell Rebuttal Script

I appreciate what you're saying. One thing to keep in mind is you're getting an entire YEAR'S supply of Heart Drano.

You're saving $## right off the bat. This is a great time to take advantage of this special today and get free shipping, too.

Let me update your order.

(Wait for response, if they don't take the upsell, move on to Downsell No. 1.)

Downsell No. 1: Buy Two Get One Free @ $119.95 + $TBD S&H

||CALLER||, obviously your health is very important to you, right? I understand that you'd like to start getting relief right away, so here's what I can do for you. I can offer you our Buy Two Get One Free special for only $119.95 + $TBD S&H. That way you can give it a try and then make a decision based on your results. It just makes sense! Let's get you started with our three-month supply today, O.K?

(Wait for response, if they don't take the upsell, move on to Downsell No. 2.)

Last Resort: Single Trial Bottle- One Bottle $59.95 + $TBD S&H

Here's what I suggest: try a one-month supply. A one-month supply is only 59.95 plus $TBD shipping. That way you can see all the amazing benefits for yourself and I know you'll feel a difference. You can always switch to a larger package after you get the results you want. Our Single Trial Bottle will do just that for only $59.95 plus $TBD S&H. Let's get you started with the one bottle trial offer today, OK? Great!

Pain Relief Program- Auto Delivery @ $39.99 + Free S&H (Not available on one-year supply)

As a FREE bonus, you can get an instant upgrade to our preferred customer auto-ship program. As a preferred member, you'll get all your future supplies of Heart Drano at a big discount and FREE S&H, too!

Here's how it works:

After your current supply runs out, we'll automatically send you a fresh one-month supply every 30 days for the low price of just $39.99 per month with FREE S&H. For your convenience, we'll charge the same credit card you used today, and the charge will appear as Flunky The Late Nite Clown Nutritionals. You can cancel or change your Heart Drano shipments at any time by calling our customer service number at: ||CS NUMBER||, Okay? (Must get a clear "YES" or OK)

Cross Sell: Energy Boost @ $39.99 + Free S&H

||CALLER||, lots of our customers are complaining of low energy. As I'm sure you already know, feeling low on energy throughout the day negatively affects just about every aspect of our lives. Our product Energy Boost is a supplement you take when you need to help boost your energy levels, mental clarity and concentration. I'm sure you can think of a lot of things you'd love to do once you have a lot more energy, right? Well today you can get Energy Boost at a special low price. It can give you an energy boost without all the calories and sugar like most energy products. I can go ahead and add as many bottles of Energy Boost for only $39.99 today. How many would you like to add to your order today?

One of the reasons why I love writing JSTDT scripts is because speed matters. If a call center is getting bombarded with calls, you want to determine if the caller is going to buy or not. The more time that elapses where they don't, you run the risk of losing someone else who's on hold who will buy.

Adding an ordering option like this with a 50 percent to 80 percent-plus conversion rate sounds like a smart thing to do, huh? But how can we use this insanely high converting JSTDT™ process with an online business using online media? *That* nut, my treasured troubadour, has already been cracked for you. Thanks to yours truly. And a couple of my knights who were smart enough to listen to me, Allen and Erin Baler.

Here's the story in a nutshell:

The Balers were part of my first ever Gold Mastermind. I guess the Balers finally got tired of my relentless rhetoric, ranting and raving about the superiority of my JSTDT methods. So they decided to put ole DD to the test.

Allen buried a POTS (plain old telephone service) number in tiny eight-point font at the bottom of their website. Overnight (literally) they started getting more than a hundred calls a day. Now keep in mind, this was a phone number intended for customer service calls. But many of those calls were from prospects who watched the VSL and had questions. And a hefty percentage of those calls turned into sales. So many, in fact, that this turned into a substantial source of shekels. Found money. Cashola they were leaving on the table every month until they discovered this little money-spinning secret. That, and many other smart things the Balers did, was the key to them growing their business from a "kitchen table" venture... to becoming the 800 lb. gorilla in their niche with high eight-figure sales... in record time. *And* getting recognized as one of the 500 fastest-growing private businesses by Inc. Magazine. In less than two years, if memory serves.

Yes, the Balers are smart. (Well, Erin's smart. Allen... he was smart enough to marry Erin.) But they ain't any smarter than you. So that begs the question...

why don't YOU do the same? So YOU can pick up some found money, too. And stuff scads of shekels into your soon-to-be superabundant strongbox.

Now go forth boldly and just sell the damn thing.

COMPLIMENTARY BONUS – A $4,196 Value

JSTDT™ Cheat Sheets And Templates

I'm offering a few special complimentary bonuses for readers of my book. Go to www.JustSellTheDamnThing.com/bonuses and you can download the following:

✓ **My JSTDT™ sales copy template.** This was originally created for nutritional supplements but with just a few little tweaks you can use it for *any* product or service. It's hard to assign a value to this, because if you use it, you could make MILLIONS... literally. Since it took a couple hours for me to put it together, I'll assign it a $4,000 value. (My current hourly rate x 2.)

✓ **The DIQ Sales Copy Formula Report.** DIQ (pronounced "dick"... because I haven't mentally matured since age 14) stands for "Dilemma, Inflame, Quick fix." This report shows how to use a simple three-step formula to create effective JSTDT™ sales messages... FAST. This isn't available for sale *anywhere*. In fact, I highly doubt it ever will be. Use this in combination with the JSTDT™ sales copy template and you've got what I call a *creatio ex nihilo* system. A system that lets you practically create money from thin air. At *least* a $98 value.

✓ **JSTDT™ online seminar replay.** This is a replay of a webinar for the knights in my Marketing Camelot. A true $98 value because my knights invest $98 a month for the privilege of getting on a live online seminar like this every month.

You might be thinking, *Isn't Doberman Dan violating his JSTDT rules by giving his book buyers all these valuable tools FREE?*

Not at all. Because of one key word in the sentence you just uttered... BUYERS. You see, you sidled up to the DD cash register, whipped it out (your wallet that is) and invested money in this book. Yes, I know it wasn't a *lot* of money. That's irrelevant. The fact that you spent *any* amount of money makes you an infinitely more valuable customer than the cheap bastard freebie-seeking mooches infesting the Internet. (Valuable in terms of potential customer value. As a human being you're already valuable. Just so you know.)

Plus, it's a way of showing my appreciation by going the extra mile.

Use these and prosper.

And above all else... just sell the damn thing.

How to Get More Information from the Author

Wanna hear more from me after reading this book? Go to www.DobermanDan. com. You'll find hundreds of articles on entrepreneurship, direct response marketing and copywriting. You'll also be presented the opportunity to enjoy a steady stream of "Doberman Dan-ism" emails. All designed to help you build your business, put more money in your pockets... and make your experience on this planet the best it can possibly be.